THE GOOD BREAKUP

Take a Deep Breath and Remember Who the F*** You Really Are

Alexandra Filia

This book would not have been possible without the help and support of all the men in my life. You know who you are – I will not mention your names for your own safety.

CONTENTS

GOING, GOING, GONE

"Pain is inevitable. Suffering is optional."
– M. Kathleen Casey

You may be in the midst of a breakup, just getting over one or wondering whether clouds are gathering over your relationship. Whatever your situation, this guide will help you deal intelligently with your current or potential breakup.

Getting dumped is a challenging time no matter how you dress it. It is never mutual, there is always one party hurting a lot more than the other and it can happen suddenly and with little warning. I know because this is what happened to me when my husband of 22 years decided to bolt and leave me nursing a broken heart and a broken home. As I struggled through unchartered territory, I learned a great deal and also regretted quite a bit. I had to pick up the pieces quickly and move on for the sake of my sanity and also for my two lovely daughters.

I hope that those of you out there bawling your eyes out over some guy (who more than likely does not deserve it) find my experience useful and your breakup easier to cope with. This is a guide to prepare you, so that you know what to say and do to create the best possible outcome for yourself.

Here is how to navigate this book: If your relationship has already ended, you may want to skip straight to **The 28-Day Plan.** If you suspect that you are about to enter heartbreak territory, but are still in a relationship, read on.

My Bad Breakup

I would not be playing fair, if I did not tell you the story of my worst breakup, so here it is:

After a relatively uneventful making up and breaking up love life at age 30, I met the guy who was going to be my second husband. This was not love at first sight; It took a full year before I warmed up to him enough to end my previous on/off passionate affair. What he had going for him was that he was the most predictable and dependable guy on Earth and he said he loved me and he seemed the right guy at the right time to settle down and raise a family. We had amazing adventures together, including sailing for seven years, which kept the relationship sailing smoothly as well. Twenty-two years later we had two daughters and a home together, and I had started up and sold a very successful business.

A few months after my 51st birthday, he started acting up. Mood swings, playing the piano loudly, dramatically and badly, coming home drunk at 3am; I knew something was up. He denied everything claiming: "It's not you, it's me. I am depressed and I don't know why. Nothing makes me happy".

In his search for happiness, he subscribed to a website: "Dating for the Divorced" and left an open pack of condoms in his nightstand for me to discover. A couple of months later, he must have found his path to happiness, so he asked me for a divorce via WhatsApp while I was on a skiing holiday with the kids. Despite his well-paid job, on his way out he also demanded 50% of the proceeds from the business that I founded and grew. There was a lot of nastiness, during which his hair fell out in clumps (to my great amusement) and then a year later, the divorce came through and it was over.

I won't lie, I did a shed a lot of tears (mostly about the 38% of the assets I had to give him) and the astounding level of betrayal on his part. At the same time I started thinking about ways to get over the breakup and get used to life as a single person. This book is the result of that period of introspection which helped me get over a relationship of 22 years and move on with my life. I am now with a wonderful new partner and we have been together for almost four years. My "ex" is just a nightmare from the past and I am very excited and hopeful about the future.

A BREAKUP FEELS LIKE AN EMOTIONAL DEATH

"Every night you're in my dreams, and it is gotten to the point where I don't want to wake up."
– Anonymous

So, back to your situation… the door closed behind him and, through your tears, you are trying to understand how it all went wrong. Darkness has descended around you and you feel isolated from the rest of the world. You feel hopeless and paralysed. This relationship that you two created together has vanished into thin air. Your life stretches ahead of you without him and all the plans and dreams you made together are just a mirage in the desert.

The pain of a breakup is real. You feel it deep in the middle of your chest or, as in my case, like a metal band slowly crushing your skull. I remember collapsing on the sofa and thinking to myself: "I am having a brain aneurysm, I am going to die like my sister and my daughters will be orphans." That's how intense the physical aspect can be.

The pain is magnified, with the knowledge that he is somewhere out there living without you. Maybe he is updating his dating profile at this very moment. You will not wake up next to him again or trust him with your inner thoughts. You are floored by the feeling of him not existing in your life anymore.

As much as it feels like it, however, a breakup isn't death. You are still breathing, living and walking in this world. There will be a day when this pain will fade away and you will feel hopeful about the future again. Keep this firmly in your mind as you read through this book. The withdrawal pain with its obsessive thoughts will subside and you will be able to breathe freely.

Mourning the end of your relationship is natural, expected and helpful to your mental health. Give in to it and don't beat yourself up. Something important has ended and you need time to process the pain and the consequences. Sooner rather than later, you will meet someone new – everyone does – and what you are feeling today will be nothing but an entry in your journal.

Chin up, sister, let's get you out of this mess!

WHY DO RELATIONSHIPS BREAK DOWN?

"It is not a lack of love, but a lack of friendship that makes unhappy marriages." – **Friedrich Nietzsche**

A thousand different reasons can bring about the death of a love affair, and I have set aside a whole chapter for guys to discuss what made them decide to end a relationship. In my view, the most common reason is that couples stop being on their best behaviour as the relationship becomes established. The standards slip and the magic goes walkies.

The days when he picked up his own underwear off the floor and put it in the laundry basket become a dream from the past and the inner slob is revealed. Or, you may feel that you are secure enough in your relationship to wear your greying, soft and comfy underwear and spend your evenings watching soap operas. Many women in a stable long-term relationship slowly transform from alluring mermaids to shrieking wenches – *not* something that guys relish.

We women are also quite bad at voicing our displeasure openly, afraid that our man will walk away. What we tend to do instead is explode for seemingly unrelated and trivial reasons. This is interpreted by our partner as general female craziness or being that time of the month. They don't get it, so we get angrier and angrier and give them the silent treatment. The more this happens, the more cracks appear in the relationship.

Control is also a biggie, when it comes to breakups. Silent resentment builds when you or your partner feel justified to control most aspects of the other's life. From a woman's point of view, we like to domesticate our men, controlling what they wear or drink, or even when they are allowed to see their friends. Men can get bossy about what you wear, when you cut your hair, what you watch on TV or how you keep house. You are not alone, many couples are guilty of trying to control each other, but if you allow your partner full control, your relationship becomes toxic.

Jealousy rears its ugly head. One bad behaviour often stems from another. The imbalance of power creates control issues which go hand in hand with jealousy, the poison in a relationship. Neediness, unreasonable behaviour and attachment issues bring the whole thing crashing down.

Here are some of the "baddies" that manifest as things go downhill.

- Bad behaviours: smoking, drinking, gambling
- Cheating
- Misdirected anger
- Being unsupportive
- Withholding affection and attention
- Lying
- Stealing (in 30% of divorces)
- Not communicating
- Becoming a slob, both at home and in your personal hygiene
- Gaining weight
- Death of sex

Finally, there is the problem with commitment. Most women want to get married and many men don't. This makes the relationship feel forced and the elusive marriage proposal becomes the elephant in the room. Suddenly, you want something from him quite badly and he is withholding it. You don't feel that it is right for you to keep asking about it, so you get angry about unrelated things instead. He does not know why you are so furious all the time, but he does not like the tension in his life. If you are nodding your head yes, you totally get what I am talking about.

And you know the most disturbing aspect of it? The more you act crazy, the less you qualify as wife material and the more likely you are to become an ex-girlfriend.

In my case, I believe that my marriage died because my startup business flourished. It takes a very secure man to be able to stand next to a successful woman and maintain a healthy relationship and a viable sex life. Men need to be the provider and the top dog. A man needs to be a man. In today's competitive work world, women often surpass their male counterparts. If this woman is you, well done – but keep it to yourself.

Most high-powered women end up in trouble when it comes to relationships. No man wants to be surpassed by his female and, if he is, he does not want his face rubbed in it. Men cannot stand the competition and don't want to be the "losers". Relationships like this almost always fail, and quite predictably. Firstly, the sex dies. Men find it hard to perform when they are the second fiddle. They become dispirited, a bit depressed and passive-aggressive.

Years may go by and then, quite suddenly, he is off with a new partner, someone you may even consider a vacant bimbo. Guess what? He is superior to her and this has brought back his libido from the dead. You cannot compete, and you are left holding the bag. Professionally, tick; personally, flop. How do I know? It happened to me in *exactly* this way after 22 years of marriage. My guy could not handle my success and it spelled the end of an otherwise successful relationship.

I have not discussed cheating in this chapter, as I class infidelity (probably the most painful aspect of some breakups) as a symptom of the broken-down relationship rather than the reason for the breakup. It is a rare man who will poop on a good relationship by cheating on his partner. For him to risk it, something crucial is usually amiss on the home front; she becomes too needy and suffocates her partner with her demands for attention.

WHEN DO RELATIONSHIPS BREAK DOWN?

Someone once described relationships that don't work out as miniature lives that burnout like stars. I love this analogy, it is so romantic. The truth, however, is a bit *less* romantic. The end of the relationship is less like a burning star and more like a seething sewer. It is a trip into the worst of human behaviour, full of tears, accusations and shameful begging. It is the dashing of hopes and expectations, and the end of love.

So, when do relationships break down?

Here is the story as statistics like to tell it: 60% of couples break up in the first two months of a relationship and 70% in the first year. If you make it to one year, however, the statistics start working in your favour with the probability dropping by 10% per year over the first five years.

The one-year mark is when things get serious. Once you have been together for a year, some sort of breakthrough in the relationship is expected. Perhaps an engagement or offer to move in together is not an unreasonable next step. At the same time, it signals the time when couples feel comfortable with each other; the masks drop and they revert to their usual behaviour and simultaneously they become less tolerant of behaviours they tolerated during the early stages. This is a tinderbox ready to blow and here is what can happen:

- Projection, disillusionment and power struggles between you.

- Certain times are breakup-prone (breakups happen more often on Valentine's Day, two weeks before Christmas, Christmas Day itself and April Fool's Day).

- The façade fades.

- Coming up to a year, things get real. What you tolerated before, or simply did not see, suddenly becomes a central irritation in the relationship.

- Your brain deactivates at first, especially the part that judges the other person. You can't see what the other person is really like because you have gone googly-eyed and you think they are absolutely wonderful.

- Couples, especially women don't want to give up too soon. They want to get a return on their emotional investment.

- You realise that people don't change.

The average relationship lasts two years and nine months.

THE FIRST SIGNS

Here is the funny thing about a breakup. It is such a catastrophic event that the injured party cannot even imagine it happening. So, even though all the signs are there, it almost always comes as a surprise. The longer you have been together, the more incredulous you may be that he is ready to leave you.

Here are some of the signs that things are about to go pear-shaped:

- You argue all the time. It may be about trivial things or there may be an underlying serious issue that you don't seem able to resolve.

- He does not argue with you anymore. All the important disagreements seem to have disappeared. You may be hearing a lot of "whatever"s.

- He seems to have given up on solving any problems you two have. Even though you set aside time to talk about your relationship, he is unresponsive and negative.

- He says he is depressed, but he does not know why. Nothing makes him happy. He is distracted and distant.

- The sex has changed and not for the better. It may be rougher, aggressive or gone all together.

- He gets annoyed by everything you do or say. It is like you are walking on eggshells around him. He is perpetually in a bad mood.

- He criticises you: your clothes, your makeup, everything.

- He prefers spending time with other people and he seems happier around them than with you.

- He agrees to attend any event you propose, no matter how boring; or, he doesn't agree to any future events you propose in either case because he knows he will not be around for it.

- He is always busy with other things and does not seem to find any "together" time.

- He does not agree to any future expenditure that includes you such as holidays, things for the house, etc.

- Anything that involves the future he glosses over and shows no interest in.

- He accumulates a whole new wardrobe without asking your opinion and takes extra good care of his appearance.

- He starts returning things that you left at his house.

- He says the dreaded "you deserve better".

- He does not respond to texts.

- He does not post any photos of you together and he has removed such photos from his social media.

- His friends are ducking your calls and don't seem to want to hang out with you.

- He does not seem to care about your feelings or thoughts and is acting belligerent.

- He cuts you out of events you would normally be invited to, especially family events, events with his friends or work functions.

These signs are universal and you will see some – or all – of them whenever a relationship is about to go bust. If you think about it, it is human nature and he is probably not trying to hurt you intentionally. He may not even know that his behaviour is causing you pain and sleepless nights. What he is doing is becoming unattached. In his mind you are already broken up and he is going through the practicalities.

I recently read in a 2016 analysis of all US divorces 75% of men contemplate divorce a full *three years* before bringing it up. This may be surprising, as most breakups seem to come out of the blue. This research reveals that they are actually processed internally for several years. What does happen suddenly is an affair or some other event that breaks the camel's back and paves the way to the final curtain.

Here is what I heard from a recently separated friend: "Had it not been for the affair, I may have gone on miserable for a few more years. The new love in my life, gave me the courage to break it off. Secretly, I had been hoping that she would find out about it and leave me, but even though the signs were there, she seemed to be turning a blind eye. I had to finally tell her."

What a great insight for us ladies – ignore it at your peril. When my own marriage was breaking up the suddenness of the final act took my breath away. Looking back however there is no getting away from the fact that I ignored the warnings which in retrospect were painfully obvious. The little things he said, the new hobbies he had which did not include me, changes in his appearance, not asking my opinion on the new additions to his wardrobe, the endless hours on his phone and computer, paying special attention to his social media profile, nothing significant on its own, but taken all together…

I really wish that breakups were easier, and when a guy was about to leave he would just say so in a civilised and rational way. But leaving a relationship, especially a long-term one is complicated and difficult even when the love is gone. His behaviour is his way of preparing you. So, grind your teeth and get ready. In fact, this may even be a good time, for you to end it. Take the hint and leave with your pride intact. It is always better to be the dumper than the dumpee.

"THE TALK"

You have probably been having problems for some time. You disagree a lot, maybe fight, he seems distracted and takes ages to return your calls. Recently, things between you have deteriorated rapidly and none of it is instigated by you. Chances are, he is preparing for "the talk".

"The talk" can take many forms. He may be man enough to sit down with you and give you the real reasons why he is breaking up with you. Don't hold much hope for this happening, however. More than likely, he will say things like: "it's not you, it's me", "I don't know what's wrong with me", "I am depressed, nothing makes me happy". Empty, cowardly statements that leave you none the wiser.

Then, there are the ones with truly unacceptable behaviour such as ending a relationship via text, email or WhatsApp, or even simply doing a runner and ghosting you.

Whichever way "the talk" is delivered, you will be left sad, upset and nursing a broken heart. Your hopes have been dashed, a hole has opened up in your life and nothing will be the same again.

Yet, almost immediately after the surprise of the door closing behind him, comes hope that it is *not* final, only a bump in your road to a forever relationship.

Having said that, "the talk" is your best opportunity to fully understand what happened with your relationship. Most women, however, are in a state of shock and here is what they do:

- Try to change his mind. The natural response to this will be for him to stick to his guns and defend his decision.

- In between sobs ask him why, oh why does he want to break up. In defence, he is now furiously thinking of even *more* reasons to break up with you.

- Pretend that this came out of the blue and they are totally surprised

- Promise that they will change, and all will be well again. This, of course, confirms to your partner that he is right to break up with you because you are indeed the problem in the relationship.

- Break out into accusations and hysterics. Men hate both of these reactions and again you will be confirming his decision as correct.

Instead, you should do the following:

- Take a deep breath and gather your wits. Maybe walk to the kitchen and get a glass of water to steady yourself, or find another way to buy some time to think about what you want to say.

- Through discussion, while remaining calm at all times, let the problems surface one by one. Are you on the same page? Are you surprised by any issues he is raising? Take your time during this step. You want to walk away crystal clear as to why he is breaking up with you. It is a terrible feeling, post breakup, to be left wondering about what happened and to be speculating about this and that and "if only".

- Are these issues insurmountable? Be honest. If you think that there are realistic fixes to the situation, make sure that you discuss them at this stage. Let him tell you why he believes otherwise. Again, if you do not go over this step at this stage, the opportunity to clarify will be lost and you will find yourself in the middle of the night looking at the ceiling, sobbing and wondering.

- Tell him that you understand his points and would like to think about what he said. Ideally, you want to win some time to process the conversation and for him to rethink his decision based on your calm, rational reaction. He may, however, be unwilling to drag this out, and if this is the case, do not argue. You will not win this one. If he agrees, there is a chance that at the root of the breakup was a misunderstanding or something that can be changed. If this is the case, give him the time he needs and cut your fingers off before you start calling, texting and otherwise badgering him about what he is going to do. The minute you do that, it is well and truly over.

I WILL WIN HIM BACK

"Sometimes God sends an ex back into your life to see if you are still stupid." – **God Meme**

Once "the talk" is over, and the initial shock has worn off, assuming that he stuck to his guns in terms of breaking up with you, I suspect that you will immediately start plotting how to get him back. This is especially true if his pathetic speech gave you reason to believe that he still loves you and that the rift was caused by unspecified things beyond his control.

As long as you are hopeful that you might eventually get back together, there is little chance of you ever completely getting over him. Hope is a wonderful thing, and it is something that can often carry you through a difficult situation, or even keep you alive in certain circumstances. However, it is also a form of denial, and in this case it can do more harm than good. The best way to keep hope from interfering with the need to get over him is to keep your wits and ask all the questions you need during "the talk". This will allow you to be 100% certain that the relationship is indeed over, leaving no reason for hope. If you let him walk away without clarifying every aspect of what he said, you will keep wondering and hoping for months or years.

Thus begins the usually fruitless and painful "how to get him back" game.

You may try one or all of the following:

- Crank up the heat with his friends to get more information on his frame of mind

- Send your friends to get more details
- Try to make him jealous
- Have a makeover
- Pretend to have changed your ways that led to the breakup
- Send him drunken texts, emails or voicemails in the middle of the night
- Invite him over for "breakup sex"
- Stalk him in person and on social media
- Create a fake Facebook profile and send him a friend request

Unlike death, which is final, respite from your feelings of despair can come with a text or a phone call. You can't resist and thus begins the cycle of shame.

I would like to recommend to you ladies, to not debase yourselves, have breakup sex or beg him to come back. In the not too distant future, you will feel a lot better to have kept your wits and your dignity.

CAN IT BE SAVED? BEWARE OF THE DOOM CYCLE

"'Elaine, breaking up is like knocking over a Coke machine. You can't do it in one push; you've got to rock it back and forth a few times, and then it goes over."
– Jerry Seinfeld, Seinfeld Season 9: The Voice

When a guy delivers "the talk" the only sane thing to do is to start preparing for the inevitable. It takes a lot for a guy to reach this stage, especially after a long-term relationship and he has probably been mulling it over for a while before gathering the courage to say something. Once the words are out of his mouth, the chances of your relationship working out in the long run hit bottom. Most women react to "the talk" by doubling up their efforts to win him back.

At this stage, in your heart of hearts, you probably know what went wrong as well as the reasons. Unless those reasons can be easily rectified and do not involve either one of you fundamentally changing your ways, I would suggest that it is probably over.

Do not work at it, don't hold much hope and don't stay up at night wondering what you can do to keep him. You will be working yourself into a frenzy of drama that will make the breakup even more painful.

Hire slow, fire fast; this adage applies to relationships as nicely as it applies to business. In both cases, it costs money and time to languish in a situation that is hopeless. If your heart is aching, you want to start healing it, not scratching the wound.

Guys usually demonstrate their dissatisfaction for quite some time before saying anything. What they do not make clear are the real reasons for the dissatisfaction, as they are often embarrassed to talk about what *really* bothers them.

Take this real example of a breakup. Jake and Steph were together for a year. During that year, they had a wonderful time, going out to dinner and on some wonderful vacations. Steph gradually gained a bit of weight. Jake did not want to say anything, but he did not like it. Soon, that was all he was thinking about, imagining a future where the weight would get out of control and he would have a fat girlfriend. This fear made him decide to break up with Steph. The reason she got was a vague, "It's not you, it's me…I don't know what's wrong with me." He was too embarrassed to tell her the truth. Steph agonised for months over the breakup. She tried everything to get him back, except the one thing that really bothered him.

This story is real (names have been changed to protect the not so innocent) and similar stories are very often at the root of breakups. The girl ascribes some lofty (usually emotional) reason for the guy walking away, while the guy hangs his head in shame about the real reason but does not divulge it.

In 40% of breakups, there is an attempt to reconcile. Obviously, for the relationship to work the second time around, something has to change. Like Einstein said: "It is madness to expect a different outcome if you keep doing the same thing." Look at your relationship critically. Is there a practical reason why it did not work? Something besides yourself that, if changed, would save the relationship? For example, you may be working night shifts and you never see each other. You can choose to change this sort of thing. Was your breakup due to life goals which are now better aligned? Then you may have a chance.

However, if your breakup was due to personality differences, chances of the relationship working out in the long run are nil. Thus lies the reason for these ever-recycling relationships that can take months or even years to reach their inevitable conclusion. People don't change and can't change, despite making a valiant effort to be on their best behaviour when they get back together. Soon enough, the same conflicts re-emerge and the cycle closes. For every attempt at reconciliation, the time together gets shorter and the breakup easier and quicker to come about.

Paul McCartney said (about the Beatles getting back together): "You can't reheat a soufflé." This holds true for the majority of relationships. Once the dreaded words have been uttered, it is easier and easier to repeat them at the first sign of conflict.

Relationship coaches will have you believe that, under their expert guidance, differences can be resolved. Good luck with that. Dragging a guy to a "relationship coach" to be told that he should be more open will remind him of being told off by his primary school teacher, assuming you can succeed in getting him to such a meeting in the first place.

I will talk about this later in this book, but for now just take my word for it. There is a small chance that a relationship can work after a breakup, but for the majority it is a matter of time before the reunion falls apart. Time filled with heartache; wasted time that many women simply cannot afford.

BREAKUP MISTAKES

Here are some of those things that you should avoid doing at all costs. Each one has been tried and they all result in adding insult to injury in what is already a difficult situation.

- **Convincing him to come over one more time**

  I cannot emphasise enough what a terrible idea this is. Nothing makes a breakup worse than getting dumped several times rather than just once. Guys are weak that way. If you call them and beg them to meet up with you one last time, they often will, and you will probably end up having breakup sex. Sex full of tears and drama, and possibly the best sex of the relationship. You know the one I am talking about. "One last time, for old times' sake." Never, *never* a good idea.

  Like the song says: If you are under him, you ain't getting over him. Unfortunately, many women mistake drunken middle-of-the-night phone calls for the guy missing them and wanting to get back together. It is never that. In the morning, he will get dressed and walk out the door thinking that he did you a favour.

- **Trying to be friends five minutes after you break up**

  So, you think you can be friends five minutes after he dumped you? Who are you fooling? I see the pigs warming up to fly…

  He can see right through the pretence that you are already over the breakup and you want to be friends. If you are honest with yourself, you will of course realise that your desire to be friends is fuelled by your hope that by maintaining contact you may get back together, not to mention keeping an eye on him and any future potential girlfriends that may surface.

- **Dating the first guy that comes along to make him jealous and to repair your self-esteem**

So, this follows the "friends" ploy. You are thinking: "If I show him that I am still attractive and I can quickly find a new mate, he will get jealous and want to get back together. Also, it will make him more likely to agree to be 'friends' because *clearly* I am over him." This is so damaging and such juvenile thinking, that I hope you will think it over carefully before you fall into this trap.

One of two things can happen; neither will be what you want. He will either be delighted that you are with someone new and he has no need to feel guilty, or he was right to leave as you did not have real feelings for each other. Even worse, he may briefly come back to exert his power over you and make sure that he is still top dog and then leave again, as none of the problems are solved, leaving you in much worse shape than after the first breakup. I am not even discussing the sacrificial lamb in this whole manoeuvre, being the poor guy that you used and abused to make this ploy work.

- **Immediately creating a Tinder account**

Getting rejected is a very painful experience and a giant blow to the ego. He can live without you, while you are losing the plot, bawling your eyes out and contemplating all sorts of self-destructive behaviour. One such behaviour is going on Tinder to look for validation from other guys. As we all know, online dating with all its pitfalls including ghosting, meat market mentality and minimisation of individuality, is the last thing you need in your delicate state. Online dating requires a strong disposition, even in the best of times. You need to be able to shrug off rejection as easily as you swat a fly. Repeated whacks are totally wrong for you at this stage.

- **Keeping hope alive by reading horoscopes, visiting fortune tellers or believing the stories that you weave with your friends**

As humans, we are attracted to patterns and try to make them fit to our situation, especially when we really want a prediction that corroborates what we want to happen. Even though horoscopes and other such future predictions are always vague and quite general, we shoehorn them to fit our facts. If you don't believe me, randomly read any horoscope without knowing which one is yours. When scientists did that, they found that people identified perfectly with every one, regardless of their zodiac sign.

Even though every horoscope comes with the warning that it is for entertainment purposes only, women in a vulnerable state can believe that salvation is written in the stars and their man will return.

Platitudes of the variety, "it's not you it's me," or "we have not been getting along," or "we are not right for each other," etc., unfortunately leave room for interpretation and generate endless discussions with friends and confidantes as to exactly what he really meant. A simple "I don't love you anymore" would have been a lot more effective in setting a girl on the road to recovery. True and succinct, and would have cut off all misplaced hope coming from a horoscope or other future-predicting methods.

- **Crying on the shoulder of strangers and baring your soul to people who do not have your best interests at heart**

Your friends will be there for you during a breakup. They always are and this is why they are your friends. They are there to listen, dry your tears, get you blind drunk and take you on a trip to see the pyramids and forget about the creep who broke your heart. Trust them and let them do their friend magic. Unfortunately, drama of any kind attracts the drama vultures as well. People you barely know will jump on the bandwagon of advice because they feed off your pain. You need to recognise and avoid these guys. They are untrustworthy and you must never confide in them.

Also, you must steer clear of his friends. Many of you will seek out his friends, looking for "inside" information, or in the hopes that they will kindly relay your messages. Some of you may be so naïve as to think that his friends, after hearing you pained story, will try to convince him to return to you and give it another go. Normally, when women are thinking rationally, they can clearly see the craziness of this sort of thinking. Unfortunately, in the depths of despair, all rational thought goes out the window, and these scenarios arise to the detriment of all involved.

- **Facebook stalking**

  Why do this to yourself? All social media stalking is self-harm. BLOCK, BLOCK, BLOCK, UNFOLLOW AND UNFRIEND! There is absolutely no reason to be the teary and silent witness of his blossoming new romance. Did you know that guys hook up with a new person almost right away? It is the male way to recover and get over a relationship. And you, my friend, want to be there watching it all? You want to see the parties and events that you are no longer invited to attend? Your shared friends having fun without you? Here are two common excuses for not unfriending:

  - **I am not ready yet.** Not ready for what? He is ready. He left. Are you not ready to stop beating yourself up and taking the scab off the wound?

  - **I am just curious as to what he is doing.** Curiosity killed the cat! Plus, you are not innocently curious – you are really checking up on him.

  The truth is a bit more sinister than any of these reasons. Stalking is a form of addiction. And the more you stalk him, the more likely you are to develop really negative feelings that eat you up: jealousy, betrayal, loss, hatred and – worst of all – it causes your feelings for your ex to strengthen, rather than lessen. It is a heart-breaking habit, staying on top of his new life. To heal, you must erase him.

A quick note on fake Facebook profiles. I know the thought of creating one crossed your mind. Don't do it. It serves no purpose and he will know it is you anyway. Don't humiliate yourself. Who cares what he is up to, anyway?

- **Minimising what happened**

  Breakups are never easy, even ones that follow short relationships. It is the cruellest form of rejection, because it is a rejection of our core. Our innermost feelings, our personality, our looks, and our very best behaviour. Someone we like looked at us in the bright sunshine and said, "No thanks. I don't like you enough to be with you." It is a painful event that cannot be swept under the rug. I am not advocating that you should go around weeping and tearing your hair out, making a fool of yourself. By all means, keep your dignity. But take some time to grieve and heal before you declare yourself over him. It will be therapeutic and will help you move on and form a new, healthy relationship.

- **Having an affair before the breakup**

  This is common, particularly when there is a lot of insecurity involved. I have heard it often, where a girl says: "If it wasn't for so-and-so, I would have never gathered the courage to leave." Of course, overlapping relationships is the most hurtful of ways to end a relationship. Betrayal is a very painful emotion and it takes a long time to get over it and forget it. I hope it never happens to you and I also advise you to not inflict this kind of pain on anyone else. You will be building a new relationship on the tears of the old one. Not a brilliant start. Furthermore, what does this say about you to your new partner? He may not say anything, but in the back of his mind he is thinking of you as untrustworthy and heartless. Not a good look, ladies.

- **Comparing the new relationship with the old**

  And here is the mother of all errors and the most common obstacle to future happiness. In fact, it is so bad that I know of women who ruined their entire lives comparing every new relationship to these mythical creatures that they once dated.

- **Using the breakup as an excuse to eat too much pizza and ice cream**

"Bad days call for foods that are bad for your butt." – **H.M Ward**

You should avoid the trap of getting fat during a breakup. Some women are very lucky and extreme sadness makes them beautiful. They lose their appetite and acquire the look of ethereal distressed maidens. Most of us unfortunately camp on the sofa, remain unwashed for days and get Domino's pizza on our speed dial. This coping technique is OK for the first day or two, any longer and…

If you cannot see this for yourself, let me assure you that this is a very bad strategy. Becoming fat and stinky will make you feel much, much worse than you would have felt otherwise. It will also do nothing in terms of your hopes to win him back, but more on all this later.

IN THEIR OWN WORDS

"I like my relationships like I like my eggs: over easy."
– Jarod Kintz, It Occurred To Me

At this point I would like to interject a bit of reality. I asked several guys (aged 29-40) to give me some perspective on their breakups and the aftermath. What they said and the similarity of their views is quite revealing. Read on and make up your own mind if they are worth crying over.

1. What is the main reason you actually decided that it was time to break up?

- Met someone else.

- Moment of anger.

- She was about to make a big investment in the relationship. I was going to breakup with her soon anyway, so I did not want her to do it. For example, I had a long-distance relationship and she said she wanted to move near me.

- Most of my breakups have been because I felt that the spark was gone. Any excitement in the relationship mostly originated from my part and there was an imbalance between what I gave up (freedom), what I gave (support, time, attention) and what I received (needy attention and support I didn't need).

- Reasons for the breakup vary, here are some: We were very different and wanted different things. Partner gained weight and I just didn't fancy her. Realised she was a fruitloop, I got involved too fast and idealised her. She was selfish and never did things for me, this was her nature. Wanted kids and this was her next big goal in life. This last reason is very common in my case.

- I felt suffocated, asphyxiated.

- Usually it is a combination of factors, but by the time I reach the breakup point I have already decided that this person is not someone with whom I want to spend my future or have children.

- The sex is getting bad/they are gaining weight/becoming unattractive

- I feel restricted/can't do the things I want to do without being guilt-tripped.

- We're not connecting emotionally/arguing/disagreeing over core values.

2. What is the one thing that broke the camel's back?

- Hygiene/sloppiness. She smells, poops without closing the door, no makeup, baggy clothes, and kitchen is a mess.

- She says something terrible like "I would never be with a guy like that, he is the type you just meet and fuck in the bathroom" or "I like rap music".

- The "aha" moment is quite often that I've been away from the girl for 3-7 days and I am happier on my own than with her. Jealous outbursts, general craziness and excessive demands on my time and attention are the usual culprits. I have some other pet peeves: I can't stay with someone who is complaining about a problem and does not attempt to address it. I dislike anyone shouting at me with a passion - and I lose respect. In general, if I lose respect for her, she's out of the race as a long-term partner. Boring sex is also a straight back breaker… But that's usually screened for before I start dating someone.

- I give up quite easily, so it won't take a collection of reasons, it is usually the first one.

- Demanding to be more present, to talk through problems, to spend more time with me when I feel like less (cheating is not as crucial).

- Most often it's the arguing. When you know you're reaching the end in a relationship…everything always tends to end in lots and lots of arguing, to the point where you just can't take it anymore.

- Sex (although restricted freedom by guilt-tripping is really just as bad).

3. Do you show any outward signs that a girl should look out for?

- I talk less, ask less, rearrange/cancel dates more and suggest fewer and fewer activities.

- I want to see her less, I seem uninterested, I want to do more things without her, I stop making plans.

- I show a lot less interest in sex

- Signs I would show would be: being irritable, having a lack of interest in her, lack of attention, lack of affection, being critical of her and the things she does, choosing to spend time with my friends over her, never being around, etc. And finally, the main one – I no longer want to have sex with her.

- Not wanting to have sex.

- Getting frustrated and angry at her on a regular basis.

4. Is there anything she could do at this stage to stop you from going through with "the talk"?

- A positive surprise where you suddenly see/re-see her in a new light (e.g., wow, I completely forgot she could look that good, was that smart, had the same interests as me, was that kind, or something else positive) .

- She could take a trip or some time off the relationship. She could relax and give me space, see me less.

- Spark the relationship with exciting activities to do together. Focus on the fun. Articulate what she enjoys, what she'd like more of, etc.

- It is probably best if she brings this up and asks me diplomatically during a chat. I think women often know the reason why a guy is losing interest but are scared to chat about it. I'm personally happy to discuss these things but many men are not and don't like this sort of discussion. As for me, by the time I've plucked up the courage to have the chat, that's it. It is much like leaving a job really.

- Honestly, once I've reached this point...no, there isn't. However, when in a previous relationship the girl I'd split up with quickly started seeing somebody else, it made me jealous and I regretted my decision. I went ahead and won her back and gave the relationship another shot. Unfortunately, the same problems re-occurred and it ended the same way as before.

- Become very attractive (lose weight, dress better, be sexy in any way possible).

- Become very caring (take a genuine interest in making me feel happy and supported emotionally).

5. What do you normally say?

- I don't think we're right for each other.

- It's not working, in the beginning it was good because of A, B or C, but now I'm not interested in this.

- I've loved these years, but I don't want this to continue.

- That I'm not in love and you deserve someone who is – OR – we are at different stages of our lives and we don't match right now.

- I find it very hard. I usually let things deteriorate in the relationship to such a point that I think if I didn't bring up the chat, she would soon leave me anyway. I always do it in person. I usually just say it's not working out and we'd both be better off with other people and then highlight some of the differences.

- I need some time off from the relationship…it is not your fault, but…

- These days it's along the lines of, "I've realised you're not the person I want to spend the rest of my life with, I'm mid-30s now and don't want to waste time in relationships which I don't see going anywhere," etc.

- I'm not happy in this relationship.

- We're too different/not right for each other.

- If the message is not getting across, I will simply explain that I don't love them anymore.

6. How long does "the talk" last?

- A half day, unfortunately often including make-up sex.

- 30 minutes to several hours. It depends on quite a few other factors: How long have we known each other? How emotional is she? How close are we emotionally?

- From maybe an hour to two, I find it very hard to do

- Used to be days…now it is short. 1-2 hours. I do them outside at a café or restaurant.

- Between 15 and 30 minutes, I'd say.

- 1-2 hours.

7. What do they normally say and do?

- Cry, say it can be better, that they will change, explain how I haven't been perfect either, ask questions like, "Is it because of this, or that?"

- Some women are too proud and maintain some kind of composure; enough to feign agreement and acceptance. Some ask for more time/chances or try to paint an alternative future where we are a great couple.

- Some agree, some cry and can't accept it, I've never had anyone hate me or be abusive and only one ex still emails me regularly after the chat.

- They become aggressive, some say they will commit suicide, or they call me and sound deeply depressed and I worry if they will do something stupid. Only one woman, where I initiated the break, was honest and straight (she said you never lied to me so I cannot say anything against you).

- This really varies, I've had more than one become very angry but most get very sad. Some try to change my mind and some just accept it. Some try to stay friends while a few firmly don't.

- Cry and protest.

8. What do they do in the week following the breakup?

- What they usually do is send a friend over to try and find out what I am up to and more details on why I broke up with them. They also try to setup a face-to-face meeting to talk things over and find out what made me break up with them. They say things like: we had something special, this a mistake, if that one thing changes would I give it another go, etc. They can stay in touch for years by sending me messages on my birthday to see if anything has changed.

- Sometimes they try to make me jealous by posting a picture with another guy, when it is obviously a ploy.

- Some don't write at all. Some write after a few days (3-10 days). A lot of them suggest that we remain friends (almost never happens).

- I don't hear from them.

- They message and they call. They are always very upset.

- This again varies quite a lot. One I'm told locked herself away from the world for weeks crying. Another hit the town, partied hard and got herself laid. One quickly got into another relationship. Some I never heard from again.

Others tried to stay in touch. Others tried repeatedly to get back together.

- Drunk dial.
- Make their social media accounts look great.
- Connect with my friends.

9. Do they stay as Facebook friends?

- Mostly yes, but not always.
- Some… If they were there before.
- Depends, but usually not.
- Yes, usually.
- Some yes, some no.
- Sometimes yes, sometimes no.

10. Do they text or contact you?

- Yes, sometimes for years.
- Most, yes.
- Usually not, I don't tend to hear from them again.
- I usually stay friends with most of them and have contact but much, much, later
- At first yes…but I'm not currently in touch with anybody I've previously been in a relationship with, interestingly.
- Usually.

11. Is there anything they could do for you to take them back?

- They can be better. After a few months of being single, at some point I will contemplate, "Wasn't that past girlfriend maybe good enough? Would going back and just settling with her be the right move?" Then I remember why it didn't work and forget about it.

- Eh…. Hard to know. I haven't done it yet. I've hooked up with an ex, but never started dating again.

- Most of my "get togethers" with an ex are not to build a new relationship…

- If you ever get back together with an ex, make sure you've fixed the issue. 9/10 times that isn't done and the old bad patterns re-emerge, and both involved waste their time and energy.

- I'm unusual - I've never split with someone and then gotten back together again. I like moving on and don't want to be going backwards. Probably a part of this is the excitement of being single after a relationship and meeting other people, I tend to get over them very quickly.

- They can give me space.

- Making me jealous by getting with other people is quite effective for a hook-up in the short run. That is the only thing I can think of. Honestly with me, when I've made my mind up – that's it!

- I doubt it. The only possible thing would be extreme sexual allure so as to overpower any logic.

I always marvel at the simplicity of the men's responses compared to the complicated and convoluted stories that we invent and torture ourselves with during a breakup. All the men, more or less, say what one man summarised below:

"I've noticed when I'm in a relationship, that in the back of my mind and even subconsciously, I am always thinking and assessing: "Is this person the one?" Meaning, is this the person who I want to have children with and subsequently spend the rest of my life with? I'm not really fussed about marriage to be honest, but I am always looking at this person thinking, "Do I want to have children with you, and do I really want to spend the rest of my life with you?"

It's also worth mentioning that getting the wrong woman pregnant is one of my greatest fears in life. So, when I decide internally "No, this person is not the one," my behaviour towards them changes. Without realising, I begin to criticise her, stop doing things with her, become irritable and make myself scarce, which then leads me to not wanting the physical part…and when this happens, I have to break up with her!"

Here are some of the key takeaways:

1. Often a man will decide to break up with you over what seem like trivial reasons.

2. The outward signs are pretty much universal, and they involve a period of behaving badly and making you miserable.

3. Once they give you "the talk", there is really no way back.

4. They tend to be quite honest but vague during "the talk".

5. The length of "the talk" varies, but they hate doing it.

6. The girls cry a lot, sometimes threaten and occasionally keep their composure (well done to those of you who manage!)

7. After the breakup most women call or write, try to make the guy jealous, send a friend to find out more information and say that they want to stay friends.

8. In most cases, ladies, there is really no way back. There may be a brief reconciliation or breakup sex, but the old patterns re-emerge and the inevitable happens again. A real recipe for prolonging your pain and suffering. Yes, the royals Kate and William did get back together and eventually married, but they are the exception rather than the rule.

Please, *please* ladies, believe me when I tell you there is no backstory to a breakup. No great mystery that you need to unravel. There is nothing special that goes on in his mind for you to find out. Men are quite simple creatures. Once they decide that you are not the one or you are too much trouble, first they act badly, then they breakup with you and they don't really care what you do afterwards. Crying, begging and threatening does not work at all, so you may as well walk away with your dignity intact.

NOW WHAT? YOUR 28-DAY PLAN

To sum up, he dumped you, he left and you decided to not pursue a reconciliation. Now what? How do you live the rest of your life without him?

What follows is a day-by-day survival guide that I developed to help me get over my breakup. All the strategies are tried and tested, and I have provided alternatives to suit different tastes. The idea is to get you moving and living; the rest will take care of itself, I promise you. Doing a little positive thing every day can be enough to gradually get you out of the deepest, darkest pit.

In the next 28 days, you will pamper yourself, sweat at the gym, write angry letters, keep a journal and lean on your friends for support. When the month is over, you will be ready to face life again and maybe – why not? – date again.

DAY 1 (AFTER "THE TALK")

Today, you are in shock and you are allowed to tell the world about it, starting with your best friend. I suggest you go really easy on yourself. You will feel better if you manage to get out of bed and have a shower or a bubble bath. If you are a runner, a nice, long run will for sure shake off some of the worst feelings. If you are not the sporty type, indulge yourself without guilt and do some of those things that you normally ration. Drinks? Go for it, girl! Ice cream, cake, crisps – whatever rocks your boat. Getting one of your good friends to come over for an all-nighter of alternate talking and sobbing is an oft-employed strategy for the first 24 hours post-breakup.

Talk as much as you can about what happened. This makes the breakup real and gets you out of the nightmare state that he put you in. Research has shown that putting feelings into words lowers the intensity of sadness and anger. If you don't feel like talking and want to be alone with your black mood, I suggest you go all-out black. Make a playlist of the saddest songs you know, peppered with some of your favourite couple songs, a bottle of wine and a journal. Spend hours writing, drinking, listening to sad music and wallowing in self-pity. Belt out "Someone Like You" on a loop while sobbing his name. Put down on paper all those things you wish you had told him, all the misunderstandings, the slights, the horrible things that he did to you and every fair (and unfair) criticism you want to pile on.

If you are a doer, you may want to do a few practical things to solidify his exit. Remove everything from the fridge that only he would eat or drink. Chuck out his toothpaste, shampoo, shaving cream, anything around your house that you will be running into during your daily life.

Before temptation to contact him one more time to see if he's changed his mind creeps in, block him on Facebook and other social media and delete his number from your contact list. Go one step further and tell your friends that you decided to cut off all contact. They can then support your decision and bring you back to the straight and narrow if you look like you are thinking of straying.

I Am Homeless!

I hope for your sake that the breakup does not make you homeless and a lot of the advice that follows assumes that you have your own place and either he moved out or he had never moved in. However, if it is his flat and you end up without a home post-breakup, here is what you should do.

If possible, and when he is feeling the guiltiest, try to negotiate keeping the flat to yourself, at least for the first two weeks. He will need to move out and stay with a friend, as it is a very bad idea to be in the same space post breakup. If you play your cards right, he may agree to that. You will need to bring forth your full vulnerability, remind him of the good times, bring his attention to your predicament, demonstrate that you will definitely and proactively find a home quickly and above all, don't act crazy. Acting crazy or completely helpless is a bad strategy. No man will leave a crazy, jilted chick alone in his flat with all his prized possessions. Remember this when you are about to start smashing the coffee table and before throwing his granny's porcelain figurines at him. Acting dazed and completely helpless is just as bad as he will envision a future where you are moping around the house, unable to even turn on your computer and look at flats for rent.

Even though you are in a very delicate and precarious state, possibly deeply traumatised and in shock, for your own sake, you need to gather your wits and negotiate this in a business-like way.

I have good reason to believe that this will work, but if it doesn't you will have to call in favours from your best friend, or the friend who has a spare room/bed/car to give you shelter and a hand when moving your things. Speaking of things – in your shocked state, remember to not leave behind anything that is yours, even if you think you do not want it. When you are feeling better, you may change your mind and beat yourself up for being so weak and gullible. You can always give any unwanted items to charity when your sanity returns.

"I never hated a man enough to give his diamonds back." – **Zsa Zsa Gabor**

You are probably not feeling up to what I am about to say, but you must also raise the subject of things you bought together, gifts that were given to the both of you, your pet, and possibly bigger possessions like a shared car, property, etc. Say something along the lines of sending for your stuff once you have your new address, and you will discuss how to divide common property via email or through a trusted friend. Anything especially prized or valuable, take with you when you go, or you may never see it again. When he stops feeling guilty he may decide to keep everything, so try to get as much as you can on the day and very shortly after "the talk".

If your property is shared, he will have to move out, no question about it. *Under no circumstances should you agree to move out.* Hold your ground on this one. Depending on how long you lived there, you probably have some rights regardless of ownership, so again, refuse to move until you get legal advice. You may also have put up half of the deposit on a rental flat. You will need this for your new place, so do not leave until you have this in cash. If, however, it is his flat and you moved in recently then you probably have no grounds to negotiate staying for more than a couple weeks (if he is nice about it).

If you share a car, make sure you take it when you go as insurance that you will get the rest of your stuff when the fog clears. Same with any pets. Take Fluffy in the car with you. You will be glad to have a loving companion who fully understands your pain and is squarely on your side. Fluffy will also be a reason for you to get out of the house during those first few dark days, unless Fluffy is a cat, hamster, snake or goldfish.

In a way, being thrown into homelessness can be a good way to energise yourself and spring into action. Finding a place to live is a major undertaking and it will certainly take your mind off him and the drama of the breakup. In fact, it may help you get over him quicker as you negotiate viewing, couch surfing and other practicalities that nobody likes. He put you in the predicament, so you can unleash your anger more quickly.

In any case, most of what follows applies to you as well, with the addition of finding a place to live. And this may be a good thing, don't knock it. A new environment is energising and will help you get over him a lot easier and quicker.

A problematic complication would be if he says that you can continue living with him and sharing the flat as roommates. He may do this because he cannot afford the rent on his own or he is clueless or dismissive about your feelings. Either way, you cannot accept this situation. If you are on the lease, you may need to talk your way out of it or find someone to take your place. It may be tempting to stay put, avoid the hassle of moving and keep him nearby (even in this unsatisfactory way), but I am telling you now that it will be an unmitigated disaster and the suffering will be primarily yours. Either he moves or you move, *period*. Try to negotiate the best deal with this in mind.

DAY 2

"Even on my weakest days, I get a little bit stronger." –
Sara Evans

Reality kicks in today when you wake up and realise
that you only need to worry about yourself – and
possibly your pet, if you have one. This will, of course,
bring a fresh wave of tears and self-pity. Things may
also feel slightly unreal, especially if you left his stuff
untouched in your bathroom and you come across it
first thing in the morning sans coffee.

Here is what you do today. If you did have the foresight
to crash on your best friend's sofa or your friend is
sleeping on your sofa, well done you. You can continue
from where you left off the night before. If, on the other
hand, you wake up on your own today, go ahead and
take the shower you did not have yesterday. Put on a
trace of tasteful makeup (not too much, in case you
start sobbing during the day), grab a handful of tissues,
and march out the door as soon as possible.

If you happen to be a runner, I would strongly suggest
a quick 5K to set your head straight before you go out
to face the day. Don't call in sick today, go to work and
muddle through as best you can. If it is the weekend or
you work from home, you must still try to stay busy,
busy, busy…

Here are some suggestions:

- Go to the gym for an exercise class, then a
  leisurely swim and 20 minutes in the sauna

while you condition your locks with a lovely coconut hair mask

- Arrange to meet friends for lunch
- Have a deep tissue massage, Indian head massage or reflexology session
- Go for a mani/pedi

According to research the brain cannot distinguish between physical and emotional pain, so pampering the body is guaranteed to improve your mood, too.

No matter what you do, I also suggest that you turn your phone off or leave it behind completely. I am assuming here that you blocked him and deleted his contact details. Either way, you must extinguish all hopes or expectations that he will get in touch because this is the best and most important step towards regaining your confidence and happiness.

When evening comes, the best strategy is to stay at a friend's house or have a friend over. Make popcorn, sit on the sofa and watch anything that is not a romcom or love story. War movies, fantasy, Harry Potter, or documentaries about wildlife are perfect for tonight. Don't drink too much, as you will get too weepy and may be tempted to reach out to him. In fact, tell your friend that he or she is supposed to stop you from becoming your own worst enemy and take your phone/devices away when you become too drunk to handle weapons of mass communication.

DAY 3

If you are at all sporty, wake up today and do something physical. Run, do a body combat class, anything that makes you feel powerful and centred. If you are not feeling as energetic, how about relaxing yoga, a leisurely swim or even a brisk walk? Next, a shower to make you feel refreshed and wonderful.

In general, sticking to a regular workout will make you physically tired and help you sleep through the night. Nothing is as frustrating as staring at the ceiling at 2am, wondering what went wrong and alternating between thoughts of how to get him back and how to bring him down. So, don't sweat him; hit the gym and just sweat. You will be glad for it on multiple levels and you may even end up with a new healthy habit.

Now, to recap: your hair is done, your nails look fab, you had a workout and you have jumped into your second favourite outfit. Life is not so bad, after all...

The key in these early days is to keep the positive actions happening every day and to keep taking good care of yourself until the worst of the storm blows over. Staying busy is the best way to work through a breakup. I am not saying that you cannot think about what happened. This would be quite impossible. What I am suggesting is that you think about it while doing something positive for yourself. An excellent strategy is to make a list of things you enjoy doing and schedule one for every day over the next 28 days. Visits with friends and family, socialising and being outdoors should take priority.

DAY 4

This is a good time to start contemplating and exercising your new-found freedoms. How about staying up until 4am or sitting on the sofa and watching chick flicks all day? You can do anything you want, and you don't need to get his approval or agreement. How does this feel? Doing something that is "not him" is an easy way to remember who YOU are, so do something he hated (and you like). How about that fringe you always wanted, or the bright orange nail polish he pooh-poohed?

Play the little game of finishing the sentence: "I am better off without him, because..." Document all answers on a piece of paper and stick it on your fridge so that you can refer to it several times a day.

This week is also an excellent time to remember and possibly document the bad times in great detail. Amplify the experience by recollecting HIS bad habits. Did he chew loudly, pick his nose or snore? Now is the time to picture him belching on the sofa with bits of food stuck IN his beard, while picking at his toenail sticking out of a ripe sock. Whatever you can remember, let it surface freely.

Stop acting like he was God's gift to women and give a good kick to that pedestal you put him on. Encourage your friends to bad-mouth him and chime in with your list of his annoying traits. To help you here, you can wear a rubber band on your wrist and flick it every time you give him more credit than he deserves.

On the positive front, go through your contacts and reconnect with anyone you left behind while you were lost in the whirlwind of your relationship. Hopefully you haven't burned too many bridges in this area. Of course, there is the possibility that some of your former friends have found their own significant others recently and might not be as likely to join you for a drink or a night out. An easier way to warm up these relationships is to start paying visits to those places where your estranged friends spend time and renew acquaintances. What you really want is to reinvest in relationships and friendships that you may have neglected.

DAY 5

Time for a relationship purge! You did some of this during the first couple of days. Now is the time for a proper clear out of all the breakup debris. Grab a box and methodically work your way through your house, your car, your office and any other area where such items may lie. Don't reminisce about any of these items. Quickly stash everything that reminds you of your past relationship – and I mean *everything* – in the box, then carry it to the curb. Ask a good friend to help by picking up any of your ex's belongings and dropping them off at his home. I shouldn't have to tell you that this is *not* an excuse to call him or see him.

Of course, holding onto things for sentimental reasons is not a crime, but if you are serious about getting over him quickly you must get rid of everything. Anything worth keeping, stash in someone else's house for now. It is only stuff and you do not need constant reminders of your ex aggravating the pain of your wounded heart.

Now that he and his stuff are gone, it is a good time to change your space and get a new perspective on life. Move your furniture around, now that his two bikes and workout bench aren't in the way. If you can afford it, change your bed; if not, at least get new sheets and a new duvet cover to welcome the approaching new spring in your life.

We already discussed eliminating all contact with your ex. If going cold turkey feels too hard and you find your resolve weakening, I want you to consider once again why you are doing it. You may think that a text here and there or a quick catch-up are harmless and will keep you from losing him forever, but if you have romantic feelings, they are nothing but harmful.

Cutting off all contact with the person you're trying to get over is one of the best things you can do. There are situations where it may be next to impossible, for example if you work together, but you should at least try to keep contact to a minimum, without necessarily turning and walking away in the other direction whenever you meet. This is a tricky one because your roles may bring you into contact several times a day. Act civil, but disinterested, and hopefully the two of you will become only passing acquaintances and eventually drift apart. However, if it's possible to cut off contact completely, do so. It may be best to ask for a transfer to another role or department to maintain your sanity.

DAY 6

There is a high probability that your ex will try to get in touch today to see how you are doing. This is a red herring and not a reason for you to get your hopes up. He is probably curious about your fortitude in terms of not contacting him and a little put out that you let him go so easily. Be strong, and do not respond to whatever method he uses to communicate. Your goal is to get over him as soon as possible, not to intensify and prolong the pain of the breakup. The whole thing is very much like a diet or quitting smoking: as soon as you succumb to the temptation, you will wish that you hadn't. Remember this and use whatever method works best for you. Blocking him is best, of course, because you will not even know that he is trying to call you.

So, now that we've settled that, this is how you face the day. Pull your absolute favourite, most kickass outfit out of your wardrobe. This is what you are wearing today. You will face the day like the warrior that you are. Hum Queen's tune "The Show Must Go On" and go about your day looking fab, despite feeling terrible inside. You are the star in your own drama, get some satisfaction out of it.

I have no doubt that you will do alright during the day, but then comes dinner time. You are at home…oh wait, you should not go home yet. Have dinner with friends tonight, vent some more (you still have leverage in these early days). If you can, spend tonight at a friend's or have a friend over at yours. You are not yet to be fully trusted with your devices on your own in the deep of night.

I am sure I mentioned this before, but just in case you forgot, do not – I repeat, *do not* – check his social media profile or cyberstalk him in any way. You don't want to know what he is doing without you, because he has left you and you are now living separate lives. What he does has no effect on you other than to upset you or give you false hope, neither of which you want at this stage.

If you get really weepy and feel like your emotions are choking you, I recommend that you write it all out – ON PAPER, AND DON'T SEND IT. Cry some more if it helps, you must let it all out: talk it out, write it out. Nothing helps as much as repeating your story again and again until it becomes trite.

Hopefully you will drift into a short sleep before dawn...

DAY 7

Today, grab your coffee, sit up in bed and make a list of activities you always wanted to do. Did you use to dream about creating ceramics? Playing the drums? Learning to sail? Going for a weekend in Rome? Without him in your life, you have lots of free time to fill with enjoyable new activities and interesting people.

While you are inspired, go ahead and sign up for one or more of these activities. There are, of course, multiple benefits from doing that. Setting aside the obvious, which is that you always wanted to do it, you will get out of the house, meet new people, challenge yourself and get a new focus in life.

After work, arrange to meet an old friend, maybe someone you have not spoken to in donkey's years, and hit the trendiest café in town. Talk to them about the future and the new activities you signed up for, or are thinking of signing up for. I suggest that you avoid drinking alcohol and turning this into a weeping sob-fest, you should now be looking solidly into the future. Avoid dwelling on "expectations" of how things should have been. When you catch yourself doing that immediately turn your focus to the now and change the subject.

Before you go to bed, record today in your journal and make a list of your accomplishments, even the small ones. You will drift off to sleep with a smile of contentment and anticipation.

DAY 8

Have you tried yoga yet? It is a wonderful way to centre you and bring you into the present moment. In the aftermath of a breakup, this is sorely needed, as you will probably find yourself spending a lot of time dwelling on the past or worrying about the future.

I will also make a book recommendation here. I found this book to be a life-changer and there is plenty in it to make you look at your situation in a completely different light. It is called *The Power of Now* by Eckhart Tolle. I listened to this on audio book and found stress and worry seeping away with every chapter.

A little exercise for today is to write down all your stresses and worries on a piece of paper. Read them back to yourself using the "silly voice technique". According to Russ Harris, author of *The Happiness Trap*, swapping the voice in your head for a cartoon voice will take the power away from your troubling thoughts. Release the thoughts by shredding the paper into tiny pieces. Don't you feel better now?

DAY 9

You will feel devastated if you believe you have lost your soulmate. Try to un-romanticise the way you see love. There is a saying in Greece that goes: "There are more orange trees further on that also make oranges." This is always true. Sooner or later, there will be a new man in your life and you will be marvelling that you were ever sad about your previous breakup. If you can visualise yourself finding a love that is as amazing or even better than the one you just lost, it will be easier to move on.

Here is the exercise for today. In your journal, make a list of all the qualities of your perfect mate. Imagine him in the most minute detail, inside and out.

- What does he look like?
- What does he do?
- What are his hobbies?
- What is his circle of friends?
- How does he treat you?
- What is he like in bed?
- Describe his family, etc.

You get the idea. When doing this exercise, avoid describing your ex. You of all people know that he was *not* perfect. In fact, while doing this exercise, make sure that you point out all the aspects of your ex that did not come close to your idea of the perfect mate. Visualise the person you were before you met your ex. You were pretty awesome, right? Now you can be this person again. Think of all the places this ideal guy is likely to be. Visualise meeting him. What would you talk about?

Keep adding to the description of this perfect mate over the next few weeks, as you think of new aspects of his life and personality.

While you are in this frame of mind, attack the virtual side of your ex. Delete his emails from your saved folder, delete his photos (or hide them if you can't bear deleting them), and remove all references to him from your Facebook timeline and the rest of your social media. When you are done, reward yourself with a facial or a massage and go meet a friend to discuss the finer aspects of the perfect man.

DAY 10

A very good friend of mine taught me a technique that has been a life-changer over the years. Whenever a disturbing thought crosses my mind, I ask myself: Is this True, False, or Don't Know? You will quickly come to realise that most of these thoughts are either False or Don't Know. The mind has a special way of torturing us with thoughts that are devoid of fact. So, start replacing emotional exaggerations with facts. When you think, "I'll never love a guy as much as I love him," examine the statement carefully and decide for yourself if this is True. In reality, it is either a Don't Know, or – most probably – plain False.

Another good way to banish such thoughts is with an imaginary box. In goes the troubling thought and out comes a real one, such as: "I will have a Frappuccino after lunch." Train yourself to use these techniques and soon enough you will be doing it automatically.

Today is a good day to attempt meditation. If you meditate regularly, you have probably been doing it all through this turbulent time in your life. If not, download the "Headspace" app and give it a go.

DAY 11

Now is the time to have a bit of fun. Download the "Make Me Bald" app and have a play with your ex's photos. If you come up with a particularly good look, save it for future reference. When you are feeling weepy or wistful, or even thinking of sending him a little text, retrieve the photo and the urge will pass. Another good one is the "FatBooth" app, which lets you pile as many pounds as you want onto your ex. Give this non-deserving, ungrateful ex a look that only a mother could love.

As childish as this may seem, it works. It may work less well if your ex is already balding and chunky, but console yourself; you can do better now. Of course, if you think that beauty is on the inside, this will not work as effectively...but it's still worth a go.

I hope you have not been neglecting your exercise, meditation and social life. All of these are crucial to pave your way towards healing and a new romance. You may not be ready to get back out there just yet, but keep the flame alive by downloading *Fifty Shades of Grey* and indulging yourself with a long, leisurely bath. Light candles, pour a luxurious bath oil and let your imagination take you to all sorts of decadent places.

DAY 12

I hope that you have stayed strong so far, more than one-third of the way towards salvation. Don't take your foot off the gas because here comes the next wave of feelings, fuelled primarily by anger. The best way to handle this stage is to fully express your anger towards the person who offended you. Reach for your journal and write a full account of every slight or insult you had to suffer because of your ex. Use foul language, exaggerate, let it rip. No reason not to, as you will not actually be sharing this with the offending party.

Now that your anger has dissipated a little with this creative outlet, channel your discontent into an immediate positive action – apply for that job that you always dreamed of, or volunteer at your local community centre. Focus all your energy on something you can actually control instead of dwelling on things you can't.

Reward yourself now with a relaxing sauna break at your local gym, meet your best girlfriend for dinner and a natter and sleep like a baby without a care in the world.

DAY 13

Have you admired the well-rounded behind of J.Lo? Today, you can take your first steps towards one of your very own. Download the 30-Day Squat Challenge and complete Day One. It is only ten reps, but it quickly builds up and you will soon be sporting a very pert behind.

If any thoughts of your ex are still crossing your mind, keep unloading on your journal and your best friends. A good way to do this is to start a WhatsApp group with a few of your most supportive friends and use it daily throughout your "mourning" period. It is a great way to have support 24/7 from your friends no matter how far away they live. Having your friends around you – even virtually – will keep you going even in the worst and bleakest moments of the breakup.

DAY 14

Today, we will create a reward table. Let your imagination run wild but make sure that you can afford the rewards. Here are some ideas for you:

- Subscribe to premium Spotify
- See a movie in the middle of the day
- Get tickets to a concert
- Take a cooking class
- Throw a big party
- Visit a museum
- Have a green smoothie
- Have lunch outdoors
- Eat a slice of cake
- Order a takeaway
- Spend a day with a friend who makes you smile
- Create a personal sanctuary at home
- Have a duvet day and do absolutely nothing
- Have an at-home spa day
- Light candles
- Reorganise your closet
- Book a session with a personal trainer
- Get fitted for a new sports bra
- Get a new haircut or highlights
- Buy a bottle of fancy shower gel
- Hire someone to deep-clean your house

- Meet a friend on Sunday for brunch
- Buy a special notebook or journal
- Take a guilt-free nap
- Have a massage
- Buy a new perfume
- Try a new craft project
- Wear something that makes you feel confident
- Buy a plant for your bedside table
- Buy a special piece of jewellery
- Get fresh flowers
- Go for a manicure or pedicure
- Redecorate your bedroom
- Go bowling with friends
- Have a morning walk in the park
- Organise a family picnic
- Go to the beach when no one else is there
- Book a mini vacation
- Go to a pick-your-own farm
- Go to a winery
- Watch the sunrise
- Get a session with a life coach
- Join a Meetup group and go to the first meeting

Put all these rewards in a jar and pull one out every morning provided that:

1. You have not contacted your ex

2. You have not asked anyone about him and his whereabouts

3. You have not looked at his social media

You can add some more ways to win rewards if you like. Here are some ideas:

- Had a good night's sleep
- Went to the gym or for a run
- Did not cry
- Had a healthy meal
- Did not drink alcohol
- Took care of yourself
- Organised your desk
- Spent ten minutes watching a funny video on YouTube
- Went for a swim
- Wrote a list of ten things that make you happy
- Made a new playlist that does not include any songs that remind you of him
- Went on a date
- Went on a girls' night out
- Ate a late breakfast and watched TV, while still in your pyjamas
- Took a Road Trip

DAY 15

Congratulations! You have reached the halfway point and, if you have followed the instructions so far, you must be feeling a lot better. Hopefully you have your ice cream and pizza habit under control, as well as the bouts of crying and self-pity every time his name is mentioned.

Daily exercise is probably the most miraculous medicine for all sorts of ailments, whether physical or mental. It makes you feel great about yourself and it releases happy chemicals in your body. I urge you to continue pushing yourself in this direction as often as possible.

Reorganising your environment rejuvenates you and is conducive to forgetting the past and focusing on the future. A fresh home setup will solidify in your mind that you are now leading a new life where you get to make all the decisions, free, revitalised and totally in control.

Changing your daily rituals is a great way to relinquish your joint life and launch a new you. For example, imagine a "zen" version of you, where you wake up half an hour earlier than usual, meditate for ten minutes, have a leisurely shower with a luxurious shower gel, take the time to style your hair and walk to work through the park while sipping on your latte. OK, this may not necessarily be the perfect morning ritual for you, but you get the idea. Treat yourself beautifully and do it every day and do that instead of taking care of *his* needs. You are the most important person in your life; treat yourself with love and respect, and expect the same from those who come into your life. You have no time whatsoever for anyone who makes you feel bad or rejects you.

Tonight, have a little get-together with your best friends to celebrate this little two-week triumph. Go out to dinner and catch a movie about powerful women. This is you, my dear. You are doing great.

DAY 16

I bet you are still angry at your ex, and probably getting angrier as you recall some of the low points of the relationship, not to mention the way he left without a backward glance. This is healthy and part of the healing process. The blinders are beginning to fall, and you are realising that for a good part of the relationship you may have not been yourself. You may have yielded too much, forgiven the unforgivable, and some of you may have acted like doormats for a guy who certainly did not deserve it. Through the fog of misplaced love, you may have seen him as a strong, handsome prince, riding in on his horse to rescue the princess. Now you are beginning to see the frog on the pumpkin, and it may make you laugh out loud.

Make a list of his worst traits. Did he yell at you? Cut you off mid-sentence? Ignore your feelings? Bad-mouth your family and friends? Leave the lid off the toothpaste? Going through this list will most likely make you angry at yourself. Did you really put up with all this? Who is this woman who subjugated herself to this badly-behaved brute?

Remember this moment and save it for the future. In your next relationship, keep your wits about you and make sure that your beautiful self is not lost and forgotten. To have and maintain a good relationship, you have to be the person that he fell in love with. So often, women lose themselves in a relationship and become someone not even they can recognise.

Today, give praise and recognition to the true you that is emerging once more from the ashes of your relationship. Take your journal, go out in nature and write about this person: this wonderful person who is you.

DAY 17

So, your ex was the devil and the relationship failed because of his diabolical shenanigans. Today, you will take responsibility for your part in the debacle. Trust me, it will make you feel better. To move on, you need to forgive not just him, but also yourself. Was it *really* just him?

The exercise for today is for you to imagine that you are him. Replay in your head all the scenarios where you argued. Recall the little things that he said that you dismissed as irrelevant details. Did you try to control him? Did you begrudge his nights out with his friends? Did you bad-mouth his mother? Did you whinge and whine about everything? If you did any of these things, reverse the situation and visualise your response, if you were the recipient rather than the instigator. How does it feel?

"When you lose, don't lose the lesson." – **The Dalai Lama**

This is *not* meant to be a self-flagellation session. Far from it. Its purpose is to help dissipate your anger and point out any behaviours that you should not bring into your next relationship. Your anger has served its purpose and now you must get rid of it. In large, protracted doses, it is toxic and very painful. I am not saying that you should call him and apologise or anything of the sort. This is a strictly personal process, for you and you alone.

To get rid of the poison that anger brings, you need to take some responsibility for what happened. When you are angry, you focus on another party's wrongdoings, which essentially gives away your power. When you focus on what you could have done better, you often feel empowered and less bitter. I tried it and my eyes were opened to the mistakes I made during my marriage. When I see another woman making those same mistakes, I want to shake her and tell her about it, they are so obvious to me now.

This in no way absolves my ex from his responsibilities towards the relationship, or changes the fact that he behaved in an abominable, unforgivable and cowardly way, but it does give me some explanation as to what happened with my marriage and why, and this is satisfying in itself. Give it a go and see what you think.

This exercise aims to help you focus, understand and correct any behaviours that scuppered your relationship, so that you do not bring them into the next one. Open your eyes to what women tend to do in a relationship and stop in your tracks if you recognise any of these habits in yourself.

Here is a list of the most common and deadly behaviours:

- Being needy
- Blaming and criticising
- Trying to exert control over everything he does
- Domesticating him
- Whining, nagging and whinging
- Irrational behaviours and drama
- Asking him the following questions: What are you thinking? Where is this relationship going?

- Shaming him
- Acting crazy
- Withholding sex
- Gaining weight and no longer taking care of yourself

What I am asking you to do today is difficult, but you will come out of it with a deeper understanding of yourself and what happened with your relationship.

DAY 18

Good morning, sunshine! Today is your time to start shining again. Start your day by making a list of the areas that you need to tackle before going out into the world to meet your new prince. Here are some ideas, I am sure you will have plenty to add on your own as well:

- Exercise/personal trainer
- Facebook profile
- Instagram
- Wardrobe
- Makeup
- Hair
- Lingerie
- Diet
- Facial/Botox, etc.
- New scent

Whatever you put on the list, today is the day to schedule each one in your calendar and make appointments if needed. You don't need to schedule everything in the next few days, the important thing is to schedule them. For example, make an appointment with a hairdresser, call a friend to come over and help you sort through your wardrobe, sign up for Weight Watchers or change your next grocery delivery to only include healthy foods. Today is a day full of action and it is all about YOU.

DAY 19

Now that you are taking all these positive steps to pamper the most important person in your life, do *not* pollute your day by thinking about your ex. Being human, however, he may pop into your thoughts now and again and your feelings are probably mixed. I am guessing that your emotions range from wistful to angry. You may think of him wistfully when you see a couple sitting together at a café sipping a cappuccino, or you may run red-hot when you remember how submissive you were to his unreasonable demands.

Whatever your feelings, acknowledge them, then put them in a mental box and shut the lid. If this does not work, write your thoughts in your journal instead. Both methods work extremely well for coping with stressful thoughts such as these. If you happen to be the sporty type and have the time, go for a strenuous workout when such thoughts cross your mind. This has multiple good effects, from increasing your endorphins (which make you happy) to improving your fitness while burning a few extra calories.

DAY 20

Now that you are two-thirds of the way there, it is time to start thinking of your future relationship. A few weeks ago, you created a mental picture of the perfect mate and hopefully wrote it all out in your journal. Revisit it now and see if it still holds true. You may find that, despite your best efforts, this imaginary man still has a lot in common with your ex. On this second pass, try to remove those elements that remind you of your ex.

There is a very good reason for this. Many women stay single and mourn for a lot longer than is necessary because they hardwire their brains to think of their ex's qualities as the best qualities a potential mate can have. This can go as far as to include his job, his car and his earnings. This sort of thinking is quite damaging to you and your future, and you can ruin your life fruitlessly searching for a clone of your ex. This new imaginary partner is there to help you disassociate from the one you left behind.

Have some fun with this man. Visualise waking up next to him on a Sunday morning, driving on a winding country road in a convertible, whatever rocks your boat. Write it all out in your journal and, if you are up for it, create a mood board to hang up in your bedroom. A little something to make you smile.

DAY 21

At random moments you will find your anger flaring up again. Now that you are aware of how toxic anger is to your wellbeing and what little purpose it serves, you will find it easier to banish your angry thoughts. It is not a walk in the park to get rid of this type of anger in a few weeks. Mine still flares up intensely every now and then, and it has been four years. But because I am aware, I can think it through and side-line it from my life. I have come to see clearly what it does to me and to those around me; at the same time, I know that it does absolutely nothing to him and his new squeeze. I can hate him and be angry, raise my blood pressure, be short with my family and say mean things, but he does not know, it does not affect him, and he will never know (unless he buys a copy of this book).

Meanwhile, I am suffering needlessly. I read somewhere that it is called "the second stabbing", and it is true. It hurts for a much longer period than the first one, so do your best to remove it from your life; it has served its purpose and now it is time to let it go.

I would also like to caution you to avoid the small things that can trigger such unhealthy, negative emotions. For example, if you receive a small unpaid bill from your time together, fight your instinct to contact him to pay his half. Just pay it and put it down as collateral damage. It is a small price to pay to maintain your emotional stability. Cut these threads quickly when they appear and do not give them a second thought. They are all triggers and you should avoid them.

I am not advocating to relinquish your rights to the car or the house, obviously – for those, you will fight like a tiger – I am talking about the small things, like the old T-shirt you forgot in his bathroom. Let it go! This is sound advice I learned from experience. At the height of your anger, every little stab you can give him will feel good…but in the end, the damage is all on you. Trust me.

DAY 22

All the rejection that a breakup entails can knock your confidence and your belief in yourself. This is natural and expected. Your ex evaluated the most important person in your life, YOU, and then turned his back on what you had to offer. This is why you are hurting. Today, we will work on this.

Open your journal and start making a list of your qualities. Big and small, important and insignificant, write them all out and make sure you include an example after each one. Pay particular attention to those qualities that you neglected or rejected because of your ex. Make a list of all the love you have felt, kind words you have heard, awards you won, friends that have gone out of their way to help you. Go through your photos and find those where you look your best. How far off are you from the girl in the picture? Perhaps lose a few pounds, grow out your hair – whatever it is that you liked about yourself that is missing, make a plan to regain or replace it.

You may even decide that you are a *better* version of yourself now. Recognise this and celebrate it. I am not talking about becoming a self-absorbed narcissist, what I am talking about is the ability to recognise your own good qualities and to treat yourself with love and compassion. Be gentle and don't beat yourself up over things that you would regularly tolerate in others.

This exercise will put things back in perspective. You have been loved and cared for before, and you will again.

Imagine your life ten years from now. Then look twenty years into the future, and then thirty. Realise that many of the things you're worrying about don't really matter in the grand scheme of things, and the pain you are feeling now will soon be a distant memory. The proof, of course, is in what has already passed. Bring to mind any of your previous partners, even long-term relationships – would you want to be with any of them today? What a thought, eh? It's inconceivable. This is how you will feel about this ex as well, I guarantee it.

DAY 23

Today, you may wake up with a spring in your step and feeling like a new woman. It is the three-week effect and it has been proven again and again. If you have maintained the no-contact rule, today is when the worst withdrawal effects from the love drug will subside. Because of this, it is a great day to meet your friends, go to the gym and – why not? – say hello to the cute guy at your local café.

Study after study has shown that lovers show all the same symptoms as other addicts. Craving, tolerance, withdrawal and relapse. This is why, during the breakup you experienced signs of withdrawal: lethargy, crying, anxiety, insomnia, loss of appetite and irritability. In almost every case of addiction, these symptoms subside after three weeks and you begin to feel a lot better.

DAY 24

Today, continue building on yesterday's euphoric feeling. If the weather permits, enjoy the great outdoors, go for a bike ride, a picnic or a walk on the beach. Write a poem of rebirth and revival. Go dancing with your friends. Enjoy the wonderful feeling of weightlessness.

You may even experience thoughts such as wondering what it was about your ex that held you captive and made you powerless. What did you really see in him? These types of thoughts mean that you are on the right path. Explore them further and write everything down in your journal.

DAY 25

Nothing in this book is there to suggest that getting over a breakup is easy, and that a few weeks will be enough to fully heal you and help you forget your ex. Don't have unrealistic expectations. What the guidance in this book will do, however, is prevent you from making mistakes that you will regret, help ease the pain and gently guide you towards rebuilding your life, which is what we will start doing from tomorrow.

DAY 26

Every high is followed by a low, and lovers can relapse the way drug addicts do. You may feel strong and no longer at risk of relapsing, then you hear a song, visit a place or see a friend, and this triggers memories and renewed craving. If this happens to you, divert your attention by doing something else that you enjoy but avoid activities that will make you feel bad or guilty afterwards.

Activities that work well are talking through your feelings with a friend, writing them down in your journal or, as I have often mentioned in this book, going for a run or hitting the gym. The craving will pass, and the feeling will fade.

DAY 27

I know that you are not over your ex yet, but today we will start getting serious about dating again. You may be thinking:

> ➤ It is too soon
> ➤ I don't need anybody
> ➤ I am better off by myself

The truth is – and much of the research out there proves it – you are better off *in* a relationship than without one. A great partner gives you the power to take on the world and a happy, close relationship will provide you with a longer and more fulfilling life. Even if you harbour hopes of your ex returning, you should still use this time to date a few new people to see how you feel and to rebuild your confidence.

Today's exercise is not threatening at all. Log on to the website "Meetup" and look for groups that you find interesting. It may be hiking, painting, discussing blockchain, it really doesn't matter. Many of these groups are specific to singles and are designed to help singletons meet each other without the usual awkwardness.

The best way to look at it is to think that you are only testing the water and you are not going out to find a boyfriend. This way the pressure is off, and you will have a fun evening meeting new people. In fact, this is how my current relationship started. Soon after my divorce, I went to see what was out there and just get a bit of practice after being in the same relationship for donkey's years. There were a host a hostess who introduced everyone over drinks and made sure that nobody was standing on their own with no one to talk to. I felt very comfortable and not at all awkward. The drinks were followed by dinner, one thing led to another – and presto! Without meaning to, I was dating again.

I don't need to tell you that the absolute best way to get over a man is to get another one. The problem is that you don't think you want to get another man because your ex was your soulmate and no other could possibly fill his shoes. Of course, this is not true, and to convince yourself you will need to fake it until you make it. This, my dear readers, means going out and meeting new guys – not for the express purpose of finding a mate, but for *research*. OK?

DAY 28

Now that you made the decision to dip your toe in the dating pool again, tread very slowly. There is no rush to attach yourself quite yet, you are simply window shopping.

It is not unusual for people to jump straight into the next relationship without too much deliberation, particularly men. The reason is fear of loneliness. I am not talking about the loneliness of not having friends or people to talk to; this loneliness runs much deeper. It is longing for the partner that completes you, fully understands you and loves you deeply for who you are. the one who is there for you in the best and the worst of times to support you and cheer you on. We all want this, and the fear of not having it makes many people jump indiscriminately from one relationship to the next. I get that, all I am saying is take your time and choose well.

Dating is a chore, right? Painful, expensive, exhausting, disappointing...among other things. I will venture to say that this is primarily so for those who feel compelled to get into a serious relationship as soon as possible. If you treat it light-heartedly, it can be fun, and this will come across to anyone you meet. Taking the pressure off those first dates will grant you the perspective to really choose who you want to be with; as for your date, it will be an extremely pleasant surprise. Try it, it works.

If you have trouble meeting guys, or your dating technique needs a bit of dusting off, read my first book in the Dream series, *Love is a Game: A marriage proposal in 90 days*, available on Amazon, for tips and advice.

HERE IS HOW TO GET HIM BACK. IF YOU MUST.

"Sometimes not getting what you want is a wonderful stroke of luck." – **The Dalai Lama**

Before you read this chapter, honestly answer the following:

- Was it ever great?

- Are you sure that you still love him deep down, and he still likes you? Perhaps you are so obsessed that you lost track of your present feelings and are deluding yourself about his.

- Have you moved on without even realising? Have you taken concrete steps towards a life without him?

- Will this relationship ever fulfil your needs?

- Did you at any point have shared dreams and ambitions? Do you still have these?

- Was the sex great?

- From his point of view, could your relationship problems be fixed?

- Did you break up because you wanted more commitment than he was willing to give (i.e., marriage, children)?

- Were your personalities compatible?

- Did you have fun together?

Love Does Not Conquer All

Love does not change people in the long run. Love does not change your abusive ex into a nice guy, nor your cheapskate/workaholic/jerk/flirt/narcissist boyfriend into a prince among men.

With that in mind I sincerely hope that that you have taken on board what I said in this book and what the guys themselves corroborated, and you don't want a rerun of the misery, for your own sake. If I have failed thus far, this chapter is for you.

If your ex has any lingering feelings for you, getting him back is relatively straightforward. Keeping him once he is back is the tricky part. Many exes get back together, only to separate again shortly thereafter (think Elizabeth Taylor and Richard Burton). The problems that tore you apart do not simply disappear. You will need to do some work if this reunion is to survive.

But first things first, here is the failsafe way to get your ex knocking on your door again.

Practise Abstinence, Retain Your Dignity

"And ever has it been known that love knows not its own depth until the hour of separation." – **Kahlil Gibran**

Nothing – and I repeat, *nothing* – is more effective in getting your ex interested in you again than giving him the time and space to contemplate what he lost and realise that it may be gone forever.

During "the talk", he will expect your pleas to stay together. What if, instead of crying and appearing desperate, you keep your cool and say something along the lines of being sorry that things did not work out as you hoped they would. He will not be expecting this; it will get him thinking that perhaps he doesn't know you *that* well after all and he may be making a mistake.

He expected to have to deflect your arguments for staying together and gently push you away; yet, you are walking away on your own. Is it possible that he did not have such a hold on you after all and you are willing to let him go and retreat in dignity? An important point here is to emphasise that you are sad about the breakup and you wish that it had not happened because you are soulmates, but you are not going to stand in the way of his decision. You don't want him to think that you don't care. It is a delicate balance you will be navigating.

So, following "the talk" you disappear from him and all your common friends *for at least one month*. He should have no way to find out how you are doing or where you are. This means silencing your Facebook and other social media as well. Do not block him, just avoid posting any clues as to where you are, what you are doing or how you are feeling. The only exception to this rule is to post something that is truly new and out of the ordinary. For example, you tried skydiving or met a celebrity, had a makeover or went on a pilgrimage to Thailand. Even then, post it without much commentary but do make sure that you look your best. This is very important. If he sends you any messages, don't respond unless it is something practical that requires a response. In those cases, your response should be warm and polite, not weepy or pathetic. Do not say you are missing him or anything of the sort.

The idea here is that you are doing exciting things, perhaps reinventing yourself and certainly not crying into your soup. As time passes, he will start recalling and missing the girl he originally fell in love with. He will wonder if the problems between you were as serious as he made them out to be and whether they can be fixed after all. Perhaps your absence and silence mean that you are working on just those points. In the meantime, you are inaccessible and giving no clues as to your emotional state.

No contact means, no calls, texts, emails, Snapchat, Facebook, etc. No running into him "by accident", no going to parties and events where he is likely to be, you get the picture. What this will do is protect you from your worst enemy during a breakup: *yourself*. Freshly-dumped women go a bit crazy and say and do things they later regret. The no-contact rule will prevent this humiliating stage that is guaranteed to drive him further away, and give you time to revert to the true you – the one he originally fell in love with. This time will also give you perspective on the relationship and the reason(s) he decided to call it quits.

At the same time, he will miss you and the bad memories and reasons for the breakup will fade into the background. The bickering, whinging, nagging, or whatever else drove him away will become less significant after he starts waking up in an empty bed, watching TV on his own and eating frozen dinners while trawling through Tinder profiles.

Everything hinges on the "no contact for a month" rule. If you truly bump into him by accident before the month is up, keep it short, smiley and positive. Don't mope, don't bring up the breakup or the relationship, don't brag, don't give him any real information, don't appear jealous, accusatory, nasty or desperate, and for god's sake *do not under any circumstances go to bed with him*. Have a ten-minute chat and then say your goodbyes.

If you find out through friends or otherwise that he is dating someone new, don't panic. It is probably a rebound relationship. Many guys respond to a breakup this way and these relationships rarely last. Chances are that he will not date seriously for at least a couple of months, so keep your cool.

So, what should you be doing during the no-contact month? We discussed many strategies in the previous chapters of this book. Most of these will be beneficial to you whether you get back together with your ex or not. In fact, the no-contact month is as much about him missing you as it is about you rediscovering yourself and finding out if you indeed want to get back together. Once the fog of habit and everyday routine has lifted, you may find that you are enjoying your freedom and looking forward to finding a new man – one who will treasure you and is better suited to your interests and personality. To take full advantage of the no-contact month and the "me" time that you are having, don't disregard this option.

Once the month has passed it is time to make your move. The best way to do this is to engineer an accidental meeting. You already know his friends, his hangouts and his hours. Arrange to get invited to a dinner or party that you know he is attending, or maybe you know that he goes running in the park every Saturday, or to the gym on Wednesday evenings and you can bump into him there.

Pay attention to your appearance for this meeting and try to look as similar as possible to the girl he originally fell in love with. Some tantalising details should be different, to demonstrate that you have moved on and there is a new part of you that he knows nothing about. At this meeting, be warm and funny and gently remind him of some of the great times you two had together. Assure him that you are doing well, and have done a lot of thinking and growing since the last time you saw him.

Don't reveal all. You want him to suggest a catch-up. He will be curious, after all. More than likely he will do so on the spot. If not, he will probably get in touch over the next day or two. If you don't hear from him, send him a message along these lines: "Great seeing you on Tuesday, you're looking well. Shall we meet up for a coffee to catch up on old times? I'd really enjoy that."

If you follow these steps and your ex has any remaining feelings for you, you will almost certainly hit your target. A word of caution: *Treat this relationship as a new one and go through all the steps of proper dating.* This will indicate to him that you are indeed a different person and the relationship will not drift into the old patterns that caused the breakup. Good luck.

A FEW THOUGHTS ON DIVORCE

"Being divorced is like being hit by a Mack truck. If you live through it, you start looking very carefully to the right and to the left." – **Jean Kerr**

I don't feel like this book would be complete without briefly discussing divorce. In this I am sort of an expert, having gone through not one, but two divorces. Divorce is a breakup on steroids. What makes it so traumatic is what surrounds the emotional breakup. Kids, money, housing, lawyers – all these are aspects that make divorce a true nightmare to behold. For us women, it is an extra difficult time, as it tends to happen when things get complicated or difficult at home.

So, how is a divorce different from a regular breakup? For starters, there is the formal aspect of the union. There is the engagement, the bridal shower, the hen "do" and of course, the wedding. Wearing a big, white dress, you stand in front of all your friends and relatives and swear loyalty "till death do you part" (at least in

55% of cases, 88% if you are Syrian). This is forever, and you want the world to know.

It is absolutely not the same as a regular breakup. You have to go to a lawyer to break up a marriage, you may have to pay alimony and your finances are inextricably wound together. You may have acquired kids, property, assets and common bank accounts. But above all, in a marriage, you have his formal promise and assurance that this is meant to be *forever*. Over the years you have made choices secure in this "forever blanket"; choices that you may not have made otherwise. When it all comes crashing down, it is catastrophic, devastating and completely life-altering. Second only to the death of a loved one, divorce is the most traumatic life experience.

When you break up with a boyfriend, you can both walk away and start rebuilding your lives relatively quickly. Divorce proceedings, on the other hand, can last for years and during that time you may be constantly afraid that the man you once trusted with your future is trying to ruin you financially. You will need to go to court, spend money you don't have on lawyers, lose some or all of your common friends and admit to yourself and others that you failed. It is a long way from simply moving your stuff out and changing your address.

The death of a marriage can be brought about in many ways and I will not delve too deeply into the subject. After all, this book is about getting over a breakup, not detailed divorce advice. What follows, rather, is a collection of my musings on the subject based on personal experience. Please take it for what it is and use only what applies to your situation. Having said that, most things discussed elsewhere in this book apply to this type of breakup as well.

The modern man wants it all and his expectations are high. The wife has to be a perfect mother with a body to die for, ideally earning her keep, but also ready for a wild shagging on the kitchen table while the kids are angelically asleep. She keeps a tight ship, meals are served on time, laundry is done, and the home environment is tidy and inviting.

The perfect wife also has the time to carefully listen to her man. Guys do not take kindly to babies and toddlers monopolising a mother's attention, nor are they willing to compromise for a wife who has let herself go. It is a sad state of affairs, but if you are unattractive and inattentive you are at high risk of divorce, despite the years spent taking care of your man, his needs and the children.

Much of this dissatisfaction coincides with the time in most women's lives where they may be getting on in years and have sacrificed their careers for the kids. They are financially vulnerable and stupidly feel secure in their relationship. It can look like this…

While you are knee-deep in changing nappies or soothing teenage angst, out of the blue your husband starts being irritable and angry without justification. He may say that he is depressed and nothing makes him happy. His hours can change, and you may find that his overnight work trips increase. He snaps at you for no reason and you find yourself walking on eggshells around him. He is spending more money on himself and he is no longer satisfied with any of your decisions.

This is an extremely painful time and my heart goes out to you. I wish I could give you more hope, but when this happens, things snowball quickly and all the talking or counselling makes very little difference. He perceives your efforts at this stage as manipulation, and your power over the relationship is mostly gone. Everything goes from bad to worse until he says something along the lines of, "I am unhappy, I want a divorce." Or, as in my case, "I want to find my path to happiness." Needless to say, his path to happiness does not include any obligations to his wife or his family.

I am not suggesting that you should not try to reconcile or work things out – by all means do, especially if there are children involved – but also prepare. Since my divorce, I have been advising women to keep a separate bank account and, if possible, to never end up 100% financially dependent on their spouse. It is all well and good to say that you are entitled to 50% of the assets, but when you find yourself with an empty bank account, abandoned with a mortgage and small children it feels like you are a long way from getting your hands on any financial support. In most cases, he has been planning for this moment; you will be caught unawares and it will happen quickly. Keep something on the side for a rainy day, even if it is all rosy right now.

You may say that your divorce is very amicable, and you intend to stay friends. I will suggest to you that your friendly feelings may evaporate once he starts parading his new girlfriend in front of your kids and common friends, you are left out of family gatherings, your couple friends cut you off or you get screwed financially. There are simply too many points of contention when it comes to divorce, and you will be very lucky if you remain civil to each other and manage to forge a business-like relationship with each other (especially if there are kids involved).

This book is not meant to discuss divorce in detail; but, should you find yourself in this unpleasant situation here are my top tips from my own experience. They are not all-encompassing and they don't apply to everyone.

- When you see the first signs of anything being amiss, get your finances in order.

- Find out everything you can about the family's bank accounts, insurance policies, loans and investments. Make copies of everything, including payslips, bank statements and bonus payments.

- During divorce proceedings, the most important thing to remember (so that you are not surprised) is that you will not be dealing with the same man you spent years of your life waking up next to. This new man is selfish, he can be cold, calculating, ruthless and unrecognisable. He may feel a little guilty very early on, but this tends to evaporate quickly. Get as many concessions as you can at this early stage – *in writing*.

- Get the best lawyer you can afford very early on and provide her with all the financial information at your disposal. Many women lose out by not fully understanding what they are entitled to. UK law dictates that assets be distributed 50/50 but this varies wildly based on your individual circumstances, especially if there are kids involved. Do not start any negotiations without first getting legal advice.

- Your ex will try to convince you to go to mediation, as it dramatically reduces the cost of the divorce. Mediation, however, systematically disadvantages women and it is a great way for you to get less than your share. Women are generally at a disadvantage when advocating for themselves as, by nature, we are conciliatory and want to please. Furthermore, women are more risk-averse and will tend to settle for the proverbial "bird in the bush". I am not saying to avoid mediation, but if you do attend, go with your eyes open and consult your attorney beforehand.

- Money will rear its ugly head before, during and after the divorce. Write down all your financial needs in detail. Think of the unexpected and make sure that you are covered. For example, what happens if the kids need braces, a private tutor or money for a school trip? Make sure everything is agreed in advance so that you can minimise future contact and conflict.

- In terms of the kids, I assume you will want to have custody. The standard arrangement is for your ex to get one night a week, every other weekend and half the holidays. This works quite well because it will give you time to date, go out, and start rebuilding your life.

Contact

As discussed previously in the book, no contact is a must when you are trying to get over a breakup. Unfortunately, contact is unavoidable during the long divorce process or when there are kids involved. During a divorce, in addition to all your heartache you have to navigate complicated legal and financial arrangements that bring you into regular contact with your ex. During that time, you cannot practically eliminate contact. I found the best way to keep your sanity is to do everything in writing and stay on topic during communication. This way, you will also have a written record of everything that transpires.

If you find it impossible to face him, use your most capable friend as a go-between. They will have a cooler head than you and it will protect you from some of the heartache and the worst of the recriminations. In my case, negotiations had reached a standstill until my best friend stepped in and negotiated on my behalf. After many months of legal fees and no progress, he sorted everything out in less than a month. If you know someone who can do this for you, I strongly recommend you consider the option.

By all means, block him from all your social media and unfriend him. What was discussed previously in the book still holds. To heal, you need to create and maintain distance. When you must retain contact, do so in a way that is the least damaging to you. No reason for you to be crying over his pictures with his shiny new girlfriend or the huge house that he bought. Stay away from anything that rubs this sort of information in your face.

I find the description below to be both accurate and inspiring.

"Early in the process, my lovely therapist helped me articulate a metaphor: I was trapped in a dark and twisty forest, but on the other side of a thorny wall was a beautiful meadow with butterflies and flowers. I wasn't afraid of life after divorce, just afraid of the pain of getting to the other side of the wall: telling my parents, finding a lawyer and walking into an empty house. Keeping that hopeful image in my head made it easier to cut through the barriers one at a time, because I knew freedom and joy and peace were on

the other side. One year out, I'm grateful to say that life in the meadow is lovelier than I dared to dream it would be." – Janelle

FINAL THOUGHTS

"Never allow someone to be your priority while allowing yourself to be their option." – **Mark Twain**

Breakups suck, there is no way to dress this up and most of us will go through at least one bad breakup in our lifetimes. As much as you are unable to avoid the breakup, it is within your control to minimise the pain and maximise the opportunity. And there is certainly an opportunity within every significant emotional event.

The period of introspection that follows a serious rejection such as a breakup is always one of intense personal growth, and one of the best opportunities you will ever get to re-examine where you are going and change direction if needed. You may discover a new life through your new-found freedom, one far surpassing the one you gave up.

Use this time between relationships to work on your initiatives and discover who you truly are, what you really want and why you are worth having.

Of course, you can spend the time crying, shutting yourself away from the world, lamenting your bad luck, getting fat, sinking into depression and wallowing in self-pity. Many women do, and it is a real shame and a wasted opportunity. The choice is yours. Do remember, however, that the man you are crying over may very well be a fabrication of your wounded heart, and not so very irreplaceable or amazing in real life. Because he rejected you, you may have elevated him on a pedestal where he does not belong. Hopefully working your way through this book and re-reading the sections most relevant to you will teach you how to break free of this illusion. Your love addiction can be cured.

You are an amazing woman, the best one you will ever meet. Love this woman and treat her with warmth and kindness. She is worth it.

ALEXANDRA FILIA

"I love helping women find happiness. This is my passion. Admittedly, I went through several careers and had many adventures before I finally settled down long enough to write The Good Breakup and Love is a Game. On a small sailboat, I explored the world for 7 years, married twice and founded and sold a successful business in the City of London.

What I am most proud of, however, is the many women I have helped in their search for their soulmate. In one year alone, I was maid of honour in 14 weddings and in my book, I will teach you all the techniques you need to come out of a breakup whole, excited about life and ready to find your own fairy tale romance."

Alexandra Filia was born and raised in Athens, Greece before moving to New York to complete her studies. She worked as a stockbroker, banker and in professional publishing before selling everything and moving onto a boat. She sailed the world, writing about her adventures in a series of articles published in a cruising magazine. When she arrived in London on her boat "Nikia", she founded and sold an award-winning business while raising two toddlers.

She has married and divorced twice and her expert advice has helped several people get over their heartbreak, leave a toxic relationship behind and find the love of their dreams. She and her partner share their home in London with her two amazing teenage daughters.

Alexandra has published two books in the Dream Series: "Love Is A Game: A Marriage Proposal in 90 Days", and "The Good Breakup: Take a Deep Breath and Remember Who the F*** You Really Are". The third book in the series: "Forever Young: An Anti-Aging Guide for the Terrified" will be available soon.

www.loveisagame.net

Continue the discussion at the *Love is a Game Facebook Group* (women only) at:
http://bit.ly/joinloveisagamegroup

Also by Alexandra Filia

Love Is A Game: A marriage proposal in 90 days

A Book About Finding "The One"

Love is a Game is a no-nonsense book about love and relationships. It is a guide on how to land the man of your dreams, where to meet him, approach him and make him want to marry you.

22278473R00069

Printed in Great Britain
by Amazon

The Upfold Farm Mystery

A Chief Inspector Pointer Mystery

By A. E. Fielding

Originally published in 1931

The Upfold Farm Mystery

© 2015 Resurrected Press
www.ResurrectedPress.com

Published by Resurrected Press

This classic book was handcrafted by Resurrected Press. Resurrected Press is dedicated to bringing high quality classic books back to the readers who enjoy them. These are not scanned versions of the originals, but, rather, quality checked and edited books meant to be enjoyed!

Please visit ResurrectedPress.com to view our entire catalogue!

For news and updates, visit us on Facebook! Facebook.com/ResurrectedPress

ISBN 13: 978-1-943403-01-1

Printed in the United States of America

Other Resurrected Press Books in *The Chief Inspector Pointer Mystery* Series

RESURRECTED PRESS CLASSIC
MYSTERY CATALOGUE

Journeys into Mystery
Travel and Mystery in a More Elegant Time

The Edwardian Detectives
Literary Sleuths of the Edwardian Era

Gems of Mystery
Lost Jewels from a More Elegant Age

Anne Austin
One Drop of Blood
The Black Pigeon
Murder at Bridge

E. C. Bentley
Trent's Last Case: The Woman in Black

Ernest Bramah
Max Carrados Resurrected:
The Detective Stories of Max Carrados

Agatha Christie
The Secret Adversary
The Mysterious Affair at Styles

Octavus Roy Cohen
Midnight

Freeman Wills Croft
The Ponson Case
The Pit Prop Syndicate

The Uttermost Farthing: A Savant's Vendetta

Arthur Griffiths
The Passenger From Calais
The Rome Express

Fergus Hume
The Mystery of a Hansom Cab
The Green Mummy
The Silent House
The Secret Passage

Edgar Jepson
The Loudwater Mystery

A. E. W. Mason
At the Villa Rose

A. A. Milne
The Red House Mystery

Baroness Emma Orczy
The Old Man in the Corner

Edgar Allan Poe
The Detective Stories of Edgar Allan Poe

Arthur J. Rees
The Hampstead Mystery
The Shrieking Pit
The Hand In The Dark
The Moon Rock
The Mystery of the Downs

Mary Roberts Rinehart
Sight Unseen and The Confession

Dorothy L. Sayers

Whose Body?

Sir William Magnay
The Hunt Ball Mystery

Mabel and Paul Thorne
The Sheridan Road Mystery

Louis Tracy
The Strange Case of Mortimer Fenley
The Albert Gate Mystery
The Bartlett Mystery
The Postmaster's Daughter
The House of Peril
The Sandling Case: What Would You Have Done?

Charles Edmonds Walk
The Paternoster Ruby

John R. Watson
The Mystery of the Downs
The Hampstead Mystery

Edgar Wallace
The Daffodil Mystery
The Crimson Circle

Carolyn Wells
Vicky Van
The Man Who Fell Through the Earth
In the Onyx Lobby
Raspberry Jam
The Clue
The Room with the Tassels
The Vanishing of Betty Varian
The Mystery Girl
The White Alley
The Curved Blades

Anybody but Anne
The Bride of a Moment
Faulkner's Folly
The Diamond Pin
The Gold Bag
The Mystery of the Sycamore
The Come Back

Raoul Whitfield
Death in a Bowl

And much more!
Visit ResurrectedPress.com
for our complete catalogue

FOREWORD

The period between the First and Second World Wars has rightly been called the "Golden Age of British Mysteries." It was during this period that Agatha Christie, Dorothy L. Sayers, and Margery Allingham first turned their pens to crime. On the male side, the era saw such writers as Anthony Berkeley, John Dickson Carr, and Freeman Wills Crofts join the ranks of writers of detective fiction. The genre was immensely popular at the time on both sides of the Atlantic, and by the end of the 1930's one out of every four novels published in Britain was a mystery.

While Agatha Christie and a few of her peers have remained popular and in print to this day, the same cannot be said of all the authors of this period. With so many mysteries published in the period, it was inevitable that many of them would become obscure or worse, forgotten, often with no justification other than changing public tastes. The case of Archibald Fielding is one such, an author, who though popular enough to have had a career spanning two decades and more than two dozen mysteries, has become such a cipher that his, or as seems more likely, her real identity has become as much a mystery as the books themselves.

While the identity of the author may forever remain an unsolved puzzle, there are some facts that may be inferred from the texts. It is likely that the author had an upbringing and education typical of the British upper middle class in the period before the Great War with all that implies; a familiarity with the classics, the arts, and music, a working knowledge of French and Italian, an appreciation of the finer things in life. The author had also traveled abroad, primarily in the south of France, but probably to Belgium, Spain, and Italy as well, as portions of several of the books are set in those locales.

The books attributed to Archibald Fielding, A. E. Fielding, or Archibald E. Fielding, are quintessential Golden Age British mysteries. They include all the attributes, the country houses, the tangled webs of relationships, the somewhat feckless cast of characters who seem to have nothing better to do with themselves than to murder or be murdered. Their focus is on a middle class and upper class struggling to find themselves in the new realities of the post war era while still trying to maintain the lavish lifestyle of the Edwardian era. Things are never as they seem, red herrings are distributed liberally throughout the pages as are the clues that will ultimately lead to the solution of "the puzzle," for the British mysteries of this period are centered on the puzzle element which both the reader and the detective must solve before the last page.

A majority of the Fielding mysteries involve the character of Chief Inspector Pointer. Unlike the eccentric Belgian Hercule Poirot, the flamboyant Lord Peter Wimsey, or the somewhat mysterious Albert Campion, Pointer is merely a competent, sometimes clever, and occasionally brilliantly intuitive policeman. And unlike, as was the case with Inspector French in the stories of Freeman Wills Croft, with the Pointer novels, the emphasis is on the mystery itself, not the process of detection.

Pointer is nearly as much of a mystery as the author. Very little of his personal life is revealed in the books. He is described as being vaguely of Scottish ancestry whose father was a Coast guardsman on the Devon coast.. He is well read and educated, though his duties at Scotland Yard prevent him from enjoying those pursuits. He is fluent in French and familiar with that country. In an early book in the series it is revealed that he spends a week or two each year climbing mountains, his only apparent recreation, though in an earlier book it is revealed that he had once played forward for the All-England International football team. He is unmarried except to his job, while his most endearing quirk is a tendency to look down at his feet when thinking. His success as a detective depends on his willingness to "suspect everyone" and to not being tied to any one theory.

The Upfold Farm Mystery involves the murder of Walsh, one of a party of artists that has taken up lodgings at the farm of the title. A number of possible motives are presented, none of which are particularly persuasive, involving artist rivalries, the affections of the farmer's two daughters, and the large inheritance that the murdered man had recently received, but in the background is a mysterious brass box that had disappeared, only to reappear just prior to the murder, and then disappears once again. No one seems to know why the box is so important, but it clearly is as subsequent events show.

One intriguing feature of the Pointer mysteries is that they all involve an unexpected twist at the end, wherein the mystery finally solved is not the mystery invoked at the beginning of the book. *The Upfold Farm Mystery* is no exception to this rule. Not only does Fielding introduce the usual red-herrings and subplots to confuse the reader, the real mystery of the book is not so much who committed the murder, but rather why is the mysterious brass box so important. *The Upfold Farm Mystery,* published in 1931, is the eleventh book in the series featuring Chief Inspector Pointer. With it, Fielding decided to depart from her standard formula of the earlier books wherein a crime is committed, Pointer is called in, and through sound but routine police work the case is solved. The bulk of the book is taken up with a first person narrative of the events before and after the crime as written by one of the boarders at the farm, a writer of mystery plays as he tries to assist the local police superintendent in solving the crime. Included in this narrative are a number of asides as to how solving a "real" crime is much more different than his own fictional portrayals. Chief Inspector Pointer, himself, doesn't show up until near the end of the book whereupon he almost immediately comes up with a theory solving the crime. It is interesting to speculate whether this unusual structure was the result of the author having become bored with the conventional formula, or whether it was an attempt to stand out in what was becoming an increasingly crowded field of detective fiction.

Despite their obscurity, the mysteries of Archibald Fielding, whoever he or she might have been, are well written, well crafted examples of the form, worthy of the interest of the fans of the genre. It is with pleasure, then, that Resurrected Press presents this new edition of *The Upfold Farm Mystery* and others in the series to its readers.

About the Cover

The cover of this book contains a re-worked portion of the original dust jacket for the first edition of the book, published in 1931.

About the Author

The identity of the author is as much a mystery as the plots of the novels. Two dozen novels were published from 1924 to 1944 as by Archibald Fielding, A. E. Fielding, or Archibald E. Fielding, yet the only clue as to the real author is a comment by the American publishers, H.C. Kinsey Co. that A. E. Fielding was in reality a "middle-aged English woman by the name of Dorothy Feilding whose peacetime address is Sheffield Terrace, Kensington, London, and who enjoys gardening."

Research on the part of John Herrington has uncovered a person by that name living at 2 Sheffield Terrace from 1932-1936. She appears to have moved to Islington in 1937 after which she disappears. To complicate things, some have attributed the authorship to Lady Dorothy Mary Evelyn Moore nee Feilding (1889-1935); however, a grandson of Lady Dorothy denied any family knowledge of such authorship. The archivist at Collins, the British publisher, reports that any records of A. Fielding were presumably lost during WWII. Birthdates have been given variously as 1884, 1889, and 1900. Unless new information comes to light, it would appear that the real authorship must remain a mystery.

Greg Fowlkes
Editor-In-Chief
Resurrected Press
www.ResurrectedPress.com
www.Facebook.com/ResurrectedPress

CHAPTER ONE

MR. Hillock leaned on the gate and, folding his powerful arms on the top bar, looked meditatively about him.

His face was weather-beaten and healthy looking, in spite of its suggestion of a man who might at times take more whisky than was good for him. But if the eyes were not as clear as they should have been, they were resolute. Indeed his whole face was resolute, with its large nose, close-shut mouth, and heavy chin.

It was emphatically the face of a man who could only be keenly interested in his own concerns. Nothing altruistic would easily move Mr. Hillock. On the whole it was a hard face, and Mr. Hillock would have remarked, with one of his tight-lipped, faint smiles, that he had need to be hard in order to live. For Mr. Hillock was a farmer, a man, moreover, who had bought his land when the big estate was broken up on which he and his forefathers had been tenants for five generations.

It was a beautiful evening, towards the middle of April, fresh and cold. None of your summer nights for Mr. Hillock. He liked things cool and frosty. His eyes would have told you that, and yet there was in them, when he was angered, a look that had made more than one man back down hastily.

It was getting dark, well towards seven. The peace of the twilight was on the land. Mr. Hillock took off his hat and let the cool breeze play around his thick dark hair. His land, as far as he could see it in this light. And, if Lily would only be sensible, it could be passed down to his grandchildren. He himself could never clear the land of the mortgages. There was a heavy sum due this coming week, and how to meet it would tax the farm to the utmost. His son might have won through, but there was no son. Only Lily and Verbena, and Verbena was blind. True, young Chapman was in love with Lily, or had been until lately, and young Chapman was the one man who could pull Upfold Farm through and set it on it feet again.   Chapman needed a wife, but if Lily kept on flirting with Walsh, one of the girls at Frayle's farm would get Chapman instead. They were fine-looking girls. Far prettier, every one of them, than his Lily.   And Chapman was the type of man who refuses to be kept dangling by any girl. Fortunately Chapman's farm and his own fitted into one solid block.

That ought to weigh, and did weigh, Chapman had said as much. Sensible young fellow, Chapman—never likely to do anything wild, but the sort to plod on steadily and surely to his goal.

A step sounded on the road behind him. A step as firm as his own, a stride as long. It was Superintendent Gibbs, a friend of his. A moment later and the trim figure of the police officer stood beside him.

"Monarch of all you survey?" Gibbs said pleasantly, after the usual greetings and remarks on the weather.

"Umph," was Hillock's only reply. It was his favorite answer.

"I was coming up to see you," Gibbs began again, joining the other along the gate. "There've been some car robberies over at Northwark, and I'm to forward information concerning all newcomers to these parts. Now, about those people you have staying with you at the farm."

"Mistake," Hillock said curtly.

"Oh, I don't mean for a moment that one of them is suspected—"

"Having them down here at all is the mistake, I meant. Never ought to've let them come."

"Well," the superintendent said in the tone of a busy man used to combining pleasure and work, "we must just run them over. Of course, I don't count young Mr. Abbott, nor his friend, young Mr. Richardson. We know all about them. I hear his cousins at the rectory are nearly over their mumps, so I don't doubt the two young gentlemen will be back there very shortly. But the others?"

"There's Mr. Scullion," the farmer began slowly.

"We'll hope it isn't him," the superintendent said, with another of his cheery grins. "Shouldn't care to tackle him single-handed." Then he went on in a burst of unprofessional enthusiasm. "But how he can paint! I saw that Adam and Eve of his. The less said of Eve the better. Just as well Adam couldn't make comparisons; but the orchard in which they're standing!" Gibbs waved his pipe in the air to express unbounded approval.

"Ah!" Mr. Hillock's tone too was warm—then he went on more critically— "but, there weren't any Blenheims in those days. Looks foolish to me, Gibbs, to see Red Blenheims supposed to be growing in the Garden of Eden. Looks like a man who doesn't know what's what."

"Why didn't you suggest to Mr. Scullion to paint crab apples," asked the superintendent; "at least I suppose the rector would say there were only crabs in those days. Wonderful man for learning is Mr. Abbott."

Hillock only said, "Humph," and smoked on.

"Drinks like a fish, I'm told," Gibbs added.

"Humph" again was his only reply to this true bit of gossip, which, as both knew, referred to the artist, not to the parson.

"Then there's the other artist, Mr. Walsh." The superintendent had his note-book out. "I've spoken to him once or twice. Pleasant chap, seemingly."

"Rich waster!" There was something grating in Hillock's hard voice.

"Don't think much of his painting myself," Gibbs went on, "but I always meet him with easels and such like hanging all over him."

"He may call his daubs painting, and Mr. Scullion may swear it's painting, but it isn't." The farmer spoke venomously, and for a moment Gibbs lost his cheery smile. He had just recollected hearing some gossip about Walsh, the man in question, and Lily Hillock. Gossip that had evidently reached her father's ears.

"Well, I've got him down on my list all right. Distant connection of the rector's, isn't he?"

"Believe so. Very distant. Every family has some blots on it," grunted Hillock.

"Well, now," Gibbs decided that he had better hurry on to the next boarder at Upfold Farm, "what about the third of your painting lot. What about that dark-eyed little chap who looks like a gipsy. Squints a bit, too?"

"McKirdy? He may squint, but he's nearly as good with his brush as Mr. Scullion. Or—well, perhaps not that. But he's damned good."

"Where does he come from?"

Hillock shook his head. "Mr. Scullion picked him up in India somewhere. He's half a nigger, my daughter Lily says."

"Ah, not gipsy." The superintendent made a note. "That's your painting lot, isn't it?" he went on, consulting his book. "Those three—Scullion, Walsh and McKirdy?"

"That's them. Then there's Mr. Maltass, who writes—"

"We're not interested in Mr. Maltass. His brother's at the Home Office. Who else is staying with you?"

"There's only Smallwood left, a chap who spends his days and nights practising the piano. Thank God he's off in what used to be a loft over the stable. Funny sort of thing for a man to do, it seems to me." Gibbs was refilling his pipe. "Sort of thing for girls at school, but a stout young chap!" He shook his head.

"Lantern-jawed young fellow, isn't he, always whistling and singing?"

Hillock nodded. "He's the son of Sir Quentin Smallwood, the Wimpole Street surgeon. The parents wanted him to be a surgeon too. A friend of his, who ran down to see him the other day, told me he had taken every sort of medical degree, but has thrown it all up to become a pianist. Funny world!"

"Son of Sir Quentin Smallwood," wrote the superintendent in his neat precise writing, and with a nod as though the parentage were eminently satisfactory, and settled all doubts as to the son's taste for looting cars. "That's the lot, isn't it?"

"It is. And I'm going to give 'em all notice," Hillock said grimly. "I don't mean the two young chaps from the rectory, who're only staying with us until the rectory mumps are done with, but the others. Excuse of rebuilding that part of the house. I can't let Walsh go because of the rector, without letting all go. But I shall drop a word to the rest, that if they care to run down after a fortnight, they'll find their old quarters ready for 'em again. But there won't be any room for Mr. Walsh. Not ever again!"

The superintendent put away his note-book as Hillock said a brief good night, and stumped up a path that would lead him to his farmhouse, a long, rambling building full of quaint corners and little, crooked passages. He stood a moment looking up at it, before he went on into the big square lounge that had been a parlor in his grandmother's time. At first he thought the room was empty, then he saw that in the corner sat his blind daughter, Verbena. It seemed odd, even to her father, to hear a leaf turn in that darkness. Verbena was reading a book from the Braille library in town.

"You're planning something, father," she said, from where she sat. "Something you don't want to do."

Verbena Hillock not only could tell any footstep without mistaking it, but she generally knew the mood of the walker with extraordinary correctness.

"Where's Lily?" her father asked, instead of replying.

"She's not in."

Hillock made a movement, as though to say something, and then stopped. From the long passage outside came voices. One was Scullion's great booming tones, the other the soft, drawling voice of Mr. Maltass, Painter, and author were evidently having a discussion.

"I tell you he's a second Gauguin," came in the former's room filling tones "But the finest butterfly in the world has to pass through the chrysalis stage. Walsh is passing through that stage now. But he's a great genius. Nothing less than one of the greatest."

"Well, certainly you ought to know," came the reply.

"I do know," Scullion roared confidently. "I knew when I first saw him painting in Vevey. Why, the place is in darkness!"

The lights were switched on. Stalking up to the fire, Scullion stood on the rug before it, hands in his baggy trousers, the long Savoyard trousers he affected, and as the workmen there carry their tools inside their long bags, so did Scullion carry palette knife and tubes of paint in his. He was a huge fellow with a great flaming red beard and a mop of dark-red hair that looked at times like thatch. Maltass on the other hand was neat and small, and rather precise in appearance, with a pair of very bright, light eyes that had a swift, sweeping way of looking around a room.

As the lights went up, Hillock, turning to say something to Scullion, suddenly took a stride forward and snatched a burning brand from the hearth, beating it out on the bricks, and stamping on the spitting flames.

"Who the devil brought this in?" he asked. "It's elder! Elder!" He repeated the name in something like horror. A horror which he evidently expected the others in the room to share.

"Well, what if it is?" Scullion asked. "Walsh broke off a few branches to paint, and I suppose flung them on the fire here when he had done with them. Why not? What if it is elder, Hillock?"

"Mr. Walsh, eh?" The farmer stood quite still. "Just the sort of thing—just the sort of thing Mr. Walsh would do," he said under his breath. "Where is he now?" he asked fiercely.

"Out," Scullion said carelessly. "What's the matter with burning elder, Hillock? Is the wood valuable? If so, he'll make it right with you."

"Ask the first tramp you meet whether he would burn elder wood on the coldest of nights, or wouldn't rather, shiver. Ask the poorest gipsy if he would let a twig of elder be thrown on a fire. Why, man, we don't grow it in our hedges because some of the trimmers won't trim it. To burn elder!"

"He and McKirdy brought some in," Scullion said vaguely.

The farmer did not hear him. "He's called up the devil, has Mr. Walsh. Well, let's see what the devil will do to him?" With that Hillock turned on his heel. He left something violent behind him.

"I knew I'd never smelled it before," Verbena said "Elder berries have a beastly smell, I think. And yet, somehow—it attracts one. As though it has a sort of power over you."

"Rubbish!" Scullion boomed "Superstition always is rubbish. Elder wood is just as good to burn as oak or pine."

"Father's not superstitious about many things," Verbena said at that. "Peacock's feathers in the house, and breaking off elder branches are the only things that upset him. Of course no one ever heard of burning a branch of elder before. It's worse than burning mistletoe." And she swept her fingers over the page of her book again.

"And you think this means bad luck to Mr. Walsh, Bena?" Maltass asked.

"We'll have to wait and see." Scullion gave his great laugh.

Maltass turned swiftly to the blind girl.

"Did you speak, Bena?" Bena did not shake her head—she never made those signs, that a normal person would have made—nor did she lift her face when she spoke.

"No," she replied, out of the depths of her big book, "I didn't say anything."

Rather an odd silence fell on the little group.

"It's pleasant out of doors," Maltass said finally, almost under his breath. "What do you say to taking a turn down to the orchard gate?"

"Don't mind if I do," came in Scullion's stentorian tones, and a minute later the two men walked off together.

"Poor girl," Maltass said as he had done many times before, "what a fate to be blind. Barely twenty years old and very pretty."

"Ugh—I can't bear deformed things, maimed things." Scullion spoke with careless loudness.

"Hillock told me this morning that he's thinking of making some alterations in our wing." Maltass hurriedly changed the subject. "Has he spoken to you on the subject?"

"He has," Scullion said, carefully putting his foot on a worm. "He has. I told him it wouldn't suit me to move till May. I don't mind what happens to the house then."

"I, too, would rather leave in May. I'm very comfortable, life down here is peaceful. I have an idea that Hillock's really only anxious to get rid of Walsh. And I wondered if, supposing you spoke to Walsh, he might not either leave the farm, or cease his attentions to Miss Hillock. He told me that he had not the slightest intention of marrying the girl. I think it's because of Lily that Hillock wants us to clear out. I can't think he has any objections to you—or me—staying on."

"I don't see myself interfering with Walsh," Scullion bawled. "Why should I? She's an ugly little devil, but Walsh is doing good work in his painting of her."

"Maybe. But it's not decent to make open love to the girl under her father's roof. Walsh is behaving like a cad, and you ought to pull him up. You brought him down here."

"He brought me," came from Scullion. "He came down to visit a new relation, the venerable, rector, and I came along to paint with him. As to making love to the girl— come now, Maltass, hasn't she asked for it? Doesn't she throw herself at the head of any one of us?"

"She's a young girl," Maltass said in a distressed voice. "Up to the moment when she met Walsh, she lived the usual life of girls of her class."

"You bet she did," came unpleasantly from Scullion.

"She's only just back from that agricultural college, and was half engaged to young Chapman, Hillock himself told me as much. That's all off now. Walsh is acting like a cad, I repeat. The girl has lost her head over him. He ought to've stood off, since he's no intention of marrying her."

Scullion turned to him with a note of savagery in his voice.

"You're talking like what you're not, Maltass, and that's a fool. An artist has to live—hold life close to his heart. An artist is not to be judged by your sniveling little prayer-book rules, by God, he's not! Laws aren't for the artist. Except laws of painting."

"Walsh is a rich man," the author went on doggedly, "and wealth can turn any one's head in these cursed times. Hillock is hard up and so Lily has to earn her own living, or work hard at the farm dairy for less pay than she would get from an employer. Walsh's money, with its promise of ease, has dazzled a silly, but, until she met him, innocent country girl."

"Oh, do shut up, Maltass," Scullion yawned rudely. "Silly and innocent! Have another look at the wench. You must be as blind as a bat, if you call her face either of those words. It's a clever young devil that lives inside Lily Hillock. Clever and ruthless. Walsh is a harmless rabbit compared to her—"

"Well, between young Chapman and Hillock himself, I think Walsh is in for an unpleasant time, unless he pulls up, and I do dislike unpleasantness. It's simply fatal to writing." Maltass ended on a plaintive note.

"Violence is life!" Scullion said, with almost ogreish enjoyment, blowing out a great breath "The more violence, the more life. You don't get violence from dead things, do you? Well, then, that's the proof."

"Scullion, you ought to be the King of the Cannibal Isles," came a young man's voice from farther down the path. Edward Abbott, the rector's son, staying temporarily at Upfold Farm until some little cousins should have finished having mumps, came into view. He was a good-looking young man with an air of finding life very jolly, provided one didn't look at it too hard.

His friend, Richardson, who had been staying with him when the mumps interlude occurred, joined him and looked an equally cheery soul, but with rather a predatory jaw and inscrutable eyes.

"Why were you chanting the praises of violence, Scullion?" Abbott asked. "Any one been trying to dun you?"

"Maltass is worried," Scullion roared. "He wants to save Walsh from the fate that's bound to overtake him. For Walsh, mark you gents both, has burned a branch of an elder tree." Scullion's tone was hoarse with mock horror.

"Oh?" Richard son's tone was cool. "Walsh? And what, pray, is about to overtake him? McKirdy, I fancy, would hope it's the steam-roller," he added under his breath.

Scullion gave his enormous laugh. "That's what we don't any of us know, but are all looking forward to seeing."

"Verbena Hillock would know," Abbott said lightly; "she knows everything, the little witch."

"As to McKirdy," Scullion seemed to have turned Richardson's words over in his mind. "McKirdy perhaps doesn't love Walsh. But then we artists are a jealous lot."

"But McKirdy won't allow that Walsh is an artist," Richardson said, with open malice. He liked to tease men and animals.

Scullion's very neck seemed to swell. "McKirdy," he yelled, "would still be in some Indian gutter but for me. I found him painting post cards at Delhi. I've taught him all he knows of his job. All that he can ever learn. But, by God, if McKirdy thinks he can measure genius better than I can—"

"You'll explode on the spot," finished Richardson promptly and as though the prospect amused him. Linking arms with his friend, the two younger men departed whistling.

"If those two make another apple-pie bed for me tonight," Maltass said, with determination, "I shall lie in wait for them, and pour a jug of cold water over each when they're fast asleep."

But Scullion was looking at a tree caught by a shaft of moonlight, and had for the moment forgotten Maltass and all the household at Upfold Farm.

CHAPTER TWO

AS Maltass and Scullion returned to the house a figure rose from a lounge chair in the hall. A comical figure, Maltass thought, was Herbert Walsh, attired in a smock and huge fisherman's boots, a sou'wester almost sitting on the back of his flannel collar. With the addition of a cloak with a cape, this was his usual painting costume, and one much appreciated by the villagers.

"Miss Abbott is here, Scullion," Walsh said eagerly, "I've asked her to come up to the studio and see how my picture's getting on." Walsh had watery green eyes and a blotched skin, and looked as though a cake of soap would be a novelty to him. Just now he was smiling broadly, with a pleased vanity that made Maltass long to kick him.

Laura Abbott detached herself from the corner where she had been sitting chatting to Bena Hillock over the latest book that the blind girl was reading. Maltass's heart beat faster as she came up to him.

She was not pretty. Thank heaven, no. None of your rose and lily beauties here. Her charm was rarer, deeper, more lasting.

"Yes, come on up to the studio," Scullion roared hospitably, leading the way. "We've installed daylight lamps, you know. At least Walsh has—the bloated millionaire. I only left off work because I couldn't stand the ruddy row that Smallwood was making on his tin pan of a piano. How can I try to paint mimosa with that crimson din in my ears?"

"This is my picture," Walsh said importantly, as the four—for Maltass accompanied them—walked down a passage on the first floor that led into a big, square, north room, and then continued on to a landing some distance beyond. It was this room that was dignified by the name of studio. The two doors leading into the passage could be shut, and were generally kept closed. Maltass's rooms opened off the passage on one side of the studio, Walsh's rooms off the continuation on the farther side.

In the studio stood three easels. The best one, and in the best lighting, was Scullion's. The second best corner was the one to which Walsh now led the way.

"What do you think of it?" he asked Laura. She said nothing. "Bickersteth of *The Palette* spoke of it as the greatest masterpiece since Whistler's day," Maltass prompted her in a stage aside.

A low laugh came from the least lighted corner of the room, where in front of a shabby, rickety old easel a lanky figure was standing with its back to the others. The figure turned now and came forward, palette still in one brown, slender hand. It was McKirdy. He, too, stood looking at the canvas, through his large, dark Eastern eyes behind thick-lensed glasses. He was extraordinarily ugly, with a meek, almost ingratiating smile that showed his retreating gums. Though slender, he was ungainly in everything except his walk. He moved now across the bare boards without a sound, though he was not wearing carpet slippers. From the picture his eyes went swiftly, almost furtively to Scullion, then back to the picture. Then with a final look at Walsh, he laughed again and turned away.

"Good work, Walsh," Scullion approved. "Look at that middle distance, Maltass. Once Walsh gets out of his swaddling clothes, by Jove, we shall see something worth seeing." Scullion's great voice roared out almost a note of reverence. Stepping back to get the thing into better focus, he all but trod on McKirdy, and turned to curse him.

"Have you taken those boots of mine to have the caps stretched?" he asked sharply.

"No, Mr. Scullion, I didn't think you wanted them done at once," murmured McKirdy in a deprecating, reed-

like voice, taking off his overall with almost feverish
haste.

Maltass watched him curiously. Would nothing make
the man rebel? True, if Scullion chose to make a valet of
him, perhaps he had the right to do so. The right of power
over powerlessness Maltass had been about a month at
the farm, and even in that time he had noticed the
deliberate pushing of what had been the pupil into the
place of the servant and the installing of Walsh in the
favorite's empty position. Yet McKirdy never murmured,
never even looked protest. Only when it came to admiring
Walsh's canvases did he show spite. Maltass, who wrote
plays, detective plays, had been studying Scullion with a
view to working him in as the villain, now, suddenly
decided to take McKirdy instead.

"If you're going to the shoemakers," Walsh called after
the hurrying McKirdy, "I wish you'd take a pair of mine,
they need stretching too."

McKirdy did not seem to hear.

"Hi! McKirdy," Scullion called, and Maltass's blood
boiled at the conscious crack of the whip in the voice.

Just for a second McKirdy hesitated Then he turned
his quiet, meek, dark face "Yes, Mr. Scullion?"

"Didn't you hear what Mr. Walsh said? Take his
shoes, too, down to old Brown and have them put on
stretchers."

"Yes, Mr. Scullion."

"Awfully good of you, McKirdy," Walsh said carelessly.
McKirdy flushed. He seemed about to speak. Maltass
waited with intense curiosity. He knew what he—
Maltass—would have said and done, especially with a
pair of boots in his hand. But the man turned and almost
ran from the room.

Maltass shot a glance at Laura Abbott, but she
evidently had not heard what had just passed, she was
standing as though entranced in front of Scullion's
painting. He joined her and also came within the spell.

It was a true Scullion. A child holding out a bunch of wild flowers. The child was peculiarly ugly and repellent. But the flowers! They seemed to go beyond nature itself, to have a beauty transcending reality.

"Good stuff!" Maltass said to Scullion. You could not say more of such work. Nor to such an artist.

But Scullion was still standing before Walsh's easel.

"They're like the flowers of heaven," Laura said, with a catch of her breath.

Scullion heard her and came across.

"There aren't any flowers in heaven, there's only gold in heaven, Miss Abbott."

She looked perplexed, as though a joke had escaped her.

"Haven't you ever noticed that there's not a flower in heaven? Streets of gold. Gates of precious stones. Of such is the Kingdom of Heaven in the Bible. Not a flower, not a blade of grass. Not a shadow of a tree falling across a green stretch." He laughed almost spitefully. Laura looked hurt. Really hurt. She moved away.

"Fact, Miss Abbott. St. Paul—it was St. Paul who wrote about what heaven is like, wasn't it?—knew what means heaven to most people. Jewels and gold. That's about it."

She turned to leave the studio murmuring something about speaking to her brother downstairs.

"You don't seem very enthusiastic over my picture," Walsh said peevishly.

She gave a rather awkward smile. "I'm not a bit artistic. I can't bear Epstein for instance, nor even the Italian Primitives which my father loves so much."

"Yet you like Scullion's thing over there."

"I love his flowers," she temporized, and left them.

"You need more life in that figure," Scullion said to Walsh after another dose inspection of the painting. "Get Lily Hillock to sit for you again."

"Lily Hillock!" Walsh burst out into a torrent of abuse against all women. Some of the words he used had an Old

Testament ring that made Maltass look along the passage
to see that Laura Abbott was safely downstairs. Then he
settled himself on the arm of a chair to study Walsh in
quite a new character. That of a declaimer against
woman the ensnarer—the vamp. But Walsh did not
regale them long with his blistering words. Still mouthing
a few choice epithets he flung his hat on his head again,
thrust his arms into his cloak and was off.

"Let's hope he meets Miss Hillock on the way and
succumbs once more," Scullion said, picking up his
brushes.

"On the way where?"

"To the nearest pub, of course. And after a halt there,
on to Latimer's Oak."

"At the risk of becoming your echo, why Latimer's
Oak?"

"Because that's where he painted that." Scullion's
voice changed as he pointed to the canvas which Walsh
had just brought forward. "It's there that Miss Hillock is
posing for him swathed in muslin and a sunshade. I can't
think why the villagers should tittle-tattle. Perhaps an
umbrella would have been still more of a chaperon."

"Where's my sister?" Young Abbott stuck his head in
at the door.

"Looking for you. So probably is Lily Hillock." Scullion
gave that laugh of his that was said to loosen windows
from their settings.

Abbott's nostrils quivered. For a second the cheery
good nature of his face changed to that of a quick, hot
temper.

"Some day you'll get badly hurt, Scullion," he said
quietly enough. "I hope it will be damned badly. But what
was Walsh rowing about?"

Maltass wondered that Edward Abbott should care—
care enough to ask the question in spite of his resentment
at Scullion's not entirely unmerited gibe. For of late Lily
Hillock, Abbott and Richardson had made rather a
frequently met trio.

"The wiles of woman," the writer now put in, "and their exceeding costliness to helpless man."

Abbott burst out laughing. Rather an odd laugh. He stood looking out of the window on to the path down which Walsh could be seen hurrying with his knock-kneed gait. His slouch hat flapping in time to the cape of his coat. "Where's he off to?" he asked half of himself.

"Eventually to Latimer's Oak," Scullion bawled in repetition of what he had just said to Maltass.

"Is that a second pub?" Abbott asked in a sham ignorance.

Scullion chuckled. As a rule he and Abbott got on well together. "As to his outburst"—the painter used his thumb to lift some painted ivy bodily from a stone —"I behold in it the hand of an all-seeing father." He intoned unctuously.

"You think Hillock's been hauling him up? High time!"

"Walsh hasn't any sense, except when he's painting," grunted Scullion, his mouth full of brushes, "and then it's not sense. It's genius."

Richardson, never long away from Abbott, now came on up to fetch the other for a round on the links. He, too, stood a moment in the studio.

"How clearly you can hear Smallwood. He seems to be improving muscularly—by leaps and bounds. Is that what's meant by ringing the welkin? I think it must be."

A particularly banging bit of playing, noisy and turbulent, filled the room.

"I can't stand it much longer." Scullion went over to a window, threw it open, and flung a paint tube in at the window of a wing running at right angles. The window was open and instantly the pianoforte stopped. A rather long-haired young man stuck his head out.

"Want me? Well, I'm finished for the time being," came in benevolent tones. A minute later Smallwood himself stood in the doorway. He was a tall young fellow with glasses and a stoop, and a friendly eye. With hands in his pockets, he lounged across to the artist.

"How do you suppose I can paint with you banging away in my ears?" Scullion asked wrathfully.

"It was Schubert-Liszt's setting of 'Hark, hark the Lark,'" grinned the pianist; "very suitable accompaniment to that sort of thing. I can't think how a rough-neck like you, Scullion, can paint as you do. Extraordinary case of dual personality, or something of that sort."

"Not much lark about the din you were making." Scullion was by no means placated. "Unless it was a shooting party having pot shots at it, and the damned bird yelling *'Tweet! Tweet! Missed me! Missed me again!'* in the intervals."

Smallwood's grin grew broader, as without a word he had a look at the two other easels.

"What's come over McKirdy's painting lately?" he asked after a moment. "He's gone off tremendously. All the life is out of it. His mind's on something else." Smallwood bent closer over the painting.

"I like McKirdy's work. It has life. What have you been doing to him, Scullion?"

"Nothing," came a grunt.

"You're his sun. If you shine on him the poor devil lives and blossoms. When you hide your lace under a cloud, he droops and withers."

"Ha, ha!" roared Scullion, as though well pleased. But he repudiated the words with a wave of a palette knife. "Ask Lily Hillock what she's been doing to him. Or—for Lily won't tell the truth, it's not in her —ask that twisted little witch Verbena—you can hear McKirdy talking to her now. Can't think how he can bear to. I can't stand the sight of her listening face myself."

"Poor kid," Smallwood said pityingly, "it's all wrong. Pretty and young, and blind. But where's Maltass? I want a word with him—"

"Can't say. Maltass never is where you think him. Sly little devil, Maltass."

"Maltass? Sly?" Smallwood repeated in surprised tones.

Scullion nodded, combing his great red beard with his painted fingers until it parted like a Sikh's. "Knows just the sort of pebble that will make the kind of splash he wants to observe," boomed Scullion. "And why does he hate Walsh? And if he hates him, as he does, why doesn't he let it be seen?"

"Rot, Scullion. Why should he hate Walsh?"

"Lily Hillock, perhaps. How can I tell why?"

"My dear fellow, the only woman whom Maltass knows is in existence at the present moment is Miss Abbott."

"Present? Ah, but the verb 'love' consists of future and past tenses too. Quite particularly so."

"Still, you're about as wide of the mark in linking him and Lily Hillock as when you speak of his slyness."

"Look here, Smallwood," Scullion stopped his painting for a moment. "Where do you think Maltass is? I'll bet you a bob—my betting limit—that he isn't there."

"Can't take you on, for I know he's writing in his room. I've just remembered seeing him go into it."

"A telegram come for Mr. Maltass," came the voice of Arthur the farm's man-of-all-work, whistling cheerily as he tramped through the studio. Arthur's manners were affability itself, and without more ado he opened a door in the corridor and peered into the sitting-room beyond.

"Ah, not there. Gone on out," Arthur murmured, passing on down the other corridor.

"But how could he have got out without our seeing him?" Smallwood puzzled.

"Through that door at the end of the passage," Scullion pointed.

"Does that lead out?" Smallwood asked in surprise, gazing towards it. "I always thought it led into a cupboard or something of that sort." Opening it now, he saw that stairs led down to the ground floor hall.

"Lovers' Lane many a time I'll be bound. You never noticed it?" Scullion looked at him contemptuously. "Maltass wouldn't be two minutes in the place without noticing it. Bet you a bob. But I've chattered enough. I want to work." And with that he turned his back and became absorbed in his painting.

CHAPTER THREE

Being the diary of Eugene Maltass, arranged to run consecutively, with the dates omitted, as well as all purely personal matters, and with certain passages amplified, but not altering the conclusions formed at the time from what he saw and heard.

THE day after the burning of the elder-wood I had to take a parcel of manuscripts to catch a certain train. Arthur was out, and it was absolutely necessary that certain alterations should be in my manager's hands that night. I took a short cut across some fields, and there, in a lane almost hidden by banks and hedges, high as any Devonshire could show, I came on Walsh and Lily Hillock.

Lily is a tall, well-made young woman, with a plain face, not improved by the paint she uses, but lit by rather an unusual pair of green eyes. I hold no card for, or against, the tint. It all depends on the shade. Lily's eyes reminded me of a clever black cat's. And at times I had seen a look in them when they rested on Walsh that was distinctly reminiscent of pussy and a mouse. Her straight, very fine black hair, which she wore exceedingly short, added to the impression.

I would have turned back, but time was too important. And, as I came nearer, I saw to my relief that I was not interrupting a lovers' tryst. Instead, a row of the first order seemed to be on.

"Not a farthing!" he was saying angrily. "And as to my playing with you, deluding you—" Then he caught sight of me, and gulped like an angry turkey cock. "Wait a moment, Maltass!" he called shrilly. "I'm coming along."

But I shook my head. He had his painting things with him, and that gave me an excuse.

"Too many stiles for luggage," I called back, as I hurried past. I had no intention of helping him out. If Lily was telling him off, so much the better. And if a few, home truths came her way, it would do no harm.

I mounted a tall stile and looked back with not altogether unmalicious amusement. Walsh was shouldering his painting kit in a way that meant moving on. And even as I watched him, he hurried off. He was barely out of sight, when Abbott appeared with a suddenness that looked as though he had been waiting around another bend. He and Lily stood talking very earnestly indeed.

"Confound the minx," I thought. It was extraordinary how she, with plain face, attracted men. It was as though the will of the woman conquered even her own drawbacks. I had no feeling of spying. That only came after a full minute or two. For Lily had assumed an attitude that meant but one thing—raging fury. I expected her to shake her fist in the direction Walsh had taken. And there was more than that. She was not only pouring out molten anger to Abbott, but inciting him, or taunting him, at any rate egging him on to do something. No film played by the greatest stars could have been clearer. Finally she said something that was evidently rather too loud in tone, for Abbott put out a warning hand in a swift admonitory gesture and, turning, stared hard along the lane that had swallowed up Walsh. Neither saw me, for the stile on which I was standing was some distance away, and only used when Hillock's big bull was in the field. I climbed down and hurried on. But the scene had made an ugly impression. More than could easily be accounted for. I decided that there was something secretive and peremptory about the gesture of caution made by young Abbott. Or was it rather the raging fury that even from a distance seemed to radiate from the young woman as light does from the saints in the early masters? I decided that if Abbott was going to make a fool of himself over Lily, life would indeed be pleasant at the farm. His sister would expect me to help keep him out of mischief. Hurrying on, I mused that I would never have expected Edward Abbott to fall for Lily's wiles. Nor Richardson either for that matter. But these last few days one or both were always hovering round her.

I posted my packet, and retraced my steps, but by another road.

I love an oak wood in April, even an old one like this with lichened and gray trees that the woodpecker laughs at loud and long as he flips past. But the nuthatch shared my affection for them. And as I stood a moment, a brown owl hooted so softly in the sunshine where he was taking a surreptitious sun-bath, that it sounded like a bird's ghost.

I smiled a little at the old superstition that the sound is unlucky, or rather foretells trouble. He had chosen a very good spot, I decided, on a bough close to the big bole of a tree that had once been a monarch of the forest. This was the Latimer's Oak which, according to Scullion, Walsh was painting, and under which Lily Hillock, clad in a sort of white puritan frock and with a vivid orange sunshade had posed for him with a basket of flowers on her arm.

As I got near the farm, I saw Walsh ahead of me, his ridiculous cloak flapping like the wings of a big bat. I waited a while, and then followed him in. Bena was sitting by the window of the dining-room, the clicking sound of the Braille that she was writing coming in sharp taps. As a rule, she sat and worked in a corner that no seeing person could have used, it was so dark and shadowy.

She rose as I passed her and came out into the hall to meet me. "You've got your gray tweed coat on now, haven't you, Mr. Maltass?" she asked. I thought she looked puzzled.

"Yes, I changed into it before going out. How did you know?"

"It smells of your pipe much more than your brown one does." Somehow, for some odd reason, I thought my reply pleased her.

"You're awfully clever," I told her truthfully.

"I have to be!" she retorted bitterly. "But you're worried about something."

I had a feeling that she was watching me intently with the eyes of that quick mind of hers.

"Did you smell that, too?"

She laughed.

"No. Your step told me that. You're walking twice as heavily as when you went out. Yet you're not carrying anything."

"How do you know I'm not?"

"When you opened the gate, both your hands were free and your arms too."

"I'm tired," I retorted.

"No. You're walking even quicker than usual. You're not tired—you're displeased—irritated about something."

"Verbena, you'd have been burned as a witch in the old days," I told her severely.

She looked at me with her large, beautiful, vacant eyes.

"They could tell the future, couldn't they?" she murmured. "They could tell what was coming to people. I can't. I wish I did know." She passed her tongue, long and thin and pointed, over her lips. "I wish I did know," she repeated broodingly, then she went back to her chair, took up her little Braille punch again, and adjusting the double brass ruler on her board which clipped the paper ready for her, went on with the little dots that would stand out on the wrong side and be read by clever finger tips. Bena contributed to a Braille weekly paper. She wrote notes on birds' songs and the sounds of the seasons.

I went on up to my rooms. Evidently Smallwood was in, for the sound of his piano reached me clearly. Great rippling chords. As I opened my door Scullion called out to Esther, the one maid of the farm, who was washing up the passage with much clattering of pail and sloshing of water. He put his head out of the door that, as usual, closed the end of the passage to ask her to be careful about letting any water get under the door as he had some canvases standing there. Over his shoulder I saw Walsh half-way down the continuation of the passage on the other side of the studio. His hand rested on the door knob, he still wore his hat and cloak, but it was the curious expression on his face that caught and held my attention. The light from the corridor window was full on his features which wore a look of fear, or, perhaps, apprehension is a better word. Then Scullion shut the door between, and I closed mine.

"Can anybody tell me the time?" came in a loud hail from Richardson below in the garden. "My watch always stops an hour after winding."

His answer came from the rather harsh and strident grandfather clock in the hall that struck the half-hour, half-past five. And as though connected with the clock there came first, a curious sound of glissading outside in my corridor and then a fearful yell from Scullion. I hurried out to find him nursing his foot and using language calculated to set the old rafters on fire. He had slipped on the soap left behind by Esther, he said, or rather, I interpreted his language to mean that. Esther, hurrying up at the noise of the crash and Scullion's voice, assured him and me that this was not her scrubbing soap. She pounced on it and eyed it closely, or as much of it as was left after Scullion had finished with it.

"Why it's Mr. Maltass's! That's whose it is. No one else uses this kind but him."

She held it out to me.

"When did you miss it, sir?"

I had no idea that I had missed it. I never do miss things of that sort until months have gone by, when a dim idea begins to shape itself in me that it's some time since I last saw a particular brush or strop.

Scullion explained at great length, in what might be called the language of hyperbole, that he did not care whose soap it was, but it had broken his ankle. And, in fact, his foot had already swollen up to quite a formidable size. I helped him cut his boot off and bandage it with strips of linen produced by an indignant but rather alarmed Esther, helped her get him settled into a chair, and then went off for a long walk. It was quite dusk when I returned and let myself in by a side door. I had had a supper of bread and cheese and good bottled beer—none of your home brewed ales for one who knows the average innkeeper's idea of brewing, so I settled down for some hours' writing. My first pipe was hardly going when Esther slipped in to say that Mr. Gibbs, the superintendent of police, was below and wanted to see me.

Her manner suggested that she was giving a hunted man a last chance to escape. I told her to show Superintendent Gibbs up. He was a pleasant-faced, tall, soldierly-looking man, whose only army training had been in camp just before the armistice, but even that had left its mark in carriage and bearing. He looked around the little room approvingly.

"Nice quarters, sir, if I may say so. Nice and quiet, I mean. Away from the rest of the house."

I told him that I was a writer and needed quiet, which was why I had come to Much Widham. I ought to have known when I made the remark what was coming, what was bound to come. How many detective novels and short stories have I not read beginning with some one remarking on the peace of the place? Where afterwards a homicidal maniac is found to be living and pursuing his hobby?

As I say, I ought to've known when I made the remark that I was asking for trouble. Well, I got it.

The superintendent nodded to my words. "Can't hear the talk that goes on in the house, I suppose, from this inside room?" I said that was so.

"And the others don't hear your typewriter either, I'll be bound." Again I agreed, and asked him to sit down. Obviously the superintendent had not come in to discuss the acoustics of my sitting-room at nine o'clock at night.

He declined a chair.

"I'm in a hurry, sir." His manner was that mixture of straightforwardness and civility which, as a rule, distinguish our police officers. Bending forward slightly, he gave me a rather keen look.

"It's this way. Our chief constable, Captain Murgatroyd, is on sick leave. Mr. Spencer is his deputy. Well, Mr. Spencer knows your brother, Mr. Maltass of the Home Office—"

"Ah, yes, my brother Laurence," I murmured. "Well?"

"And he also told me in strict confidence, Mr. Spencer did, that—well, that you're really the man who writes the Michael Hare plays, sir." He had dropped his voice to a whisper. Rather an awestruck whisper.

"Did you believe him?" I asked with some curiosity, for the superintendent's eyes were running over me curiously.

He flushed. Quite a nice, boyish flush. Evidently I did not quite come up to his idea of Michael Hare's parent.

"The chief constable is a great admirer of yours, sir. So's Mr. Spencer. As for me, I think them the cleverest plays ever put on the stage."

"Oh, come!" I said, with a fatuous smile. "Not quite that, Superintendent."

"Oh, but they are," he replied almost indignantly. "Michael Hare, the deaf detective, who can't be misled by what people tell him, but only goes by what he himself sees, he—well, he's a wonder. I don't mind telling you that I got my promotion because of solving one little puzzle just by going by him. It was only a smallish case in a way, but important to us down here, and I had just been to see one of your 'melodramettes' as they call them on the bill-heads. So I thought, what would Michael Hare do now? And I tried to act as he would have done. Not paying any attention to anything but what his own eyes saw and his own fingers touched. It brought me home a winner, sir."

"Good!" I began in gratified tones, "but—"

"Excuse me, sir," he interrupted. "But I've come to you with a message from Mr. Spencer. A man has just been found murdered in the woods near by. Will you help us in the investigation?"

My heart swelled with gratification as I said as briefly as possible that I would be glad to be of any use. I did not pretend that I could not be of the greatest help, for obviously the writer of detective fiction, or rather of a play, is quite clearly a born detective himself. To me, that point does not seem worth laboring. All this talk of working backwards from the clues to crime, of knowing and choosing the clues, is such twaddle. For my part, in my playettes, I stage a crime, true. True, also, that I know who the criminal is, but as to how Michael Hare is to find the guilty one, above all how he is to bring home the guilt, is quite another matter. I repeat, that obviously only a writer who is himself a born detective can do that.

"Who is the man, and exactly where was he found?" I asked now.

"It's Mr. Walsh. He's just been found lying close to Latimer's Oak with the top of his head battered in. Doctor says it must have been done some hours ago, but all he can say for sure is not less than two and probably not over six."

He had to repeat his news a second time, before I would accept it.

"But, good heavens, I saw him here at his room door at half-past five. He was just going out again."

The superintendent's bright eyes brightened still more.

"That's what I call luck!" And he asked eagerly for particulars.

As I gave them, there rose before me again Walsh's face as I had had that one swift glimpse of it with the head turned a little sideways, eyes downcast, and that look of dread on his features. There was another point where I might help. While I had bandaged Scullion's swollen ankle, I had been close to the windows in his rooms. To the best of my belief had Walsh gone down either of the paths which they commanded I should have seen him. That left only one other possible path. And it happened to be the one leading directly towards Latimer's Oak. Smallwood's window commanded this path. But, unfortunately, Smallwood had been playing, which meant that he had been probably, or almost certainly, too absorbed in his music to look out of doors.

"Still, you never can tell," murmured Gibbs hopefully. "And did you stay in the house after this, sir? Not that we suspect you of a hand in a murder," he finished, with a genial smile.

"That's fortunate. For I went for a long ramble and met nobody. It's the sort of day that tempts one to take advantage of it out of doors. And the sort of work I'm on, writing, doesn't incline one to choose out crowds when you want to think. By the way, who found Walsh?"

"A gamekeeper. One of Mr. Binyon-Slaney's men. Or rather, his dog found it. The body had been rolled into a bed of bracken very close to Latimer's Oak, and enough of the bracken had been pulled around the body to quite conceal it."

"And when exactly did he make the discovery?"

The superintendent looked at his watch. "It's ten past nine now. He came to the station at a quarter to. Found the body at just before the half-hour."

"Has he any idea how long the—eh—body would have taken to hide?"

"Not long. Say, five minutes at the very outside."

I had noticed how thick and high the ferns, as I called them, grew around the oak in question.

"But," I put in suddenly, "whoever did it must have had daylight. What time was sunset today?"

The superintendent had thought of that too. "Sets at a quarter to seven. But by that oak it would have been darkish around about ten minutes earlier. Certainly at a quarter to seven no one could have closed that bracken stuff around the body as they did, so the gamekeeper says. And he I knows."

"I saw him alive at half-past five. The keeper says a quarter to seven would be the latest possible moment for his body to have been hidden as it was. That sets a very sharp limit, Superintendent."

"And one we can narrow down still further by questions doubtless. Just as we can narrow down the suspects by leaving you out, and the two young gents from the rectory," he agreed.

The superintendent made careful notes.

"It's a most tremendous help this, Mr. Maltass, I mean your having actually seen Mr. Walsh leaving. I'm going to be quite candid with you—I know nothing I tell you will go any further."

"It certainly will not, without your express permission."

I'm not a talkative man at the best of times, and have even been called a silent one.

"Chapman had a rare quarrel with Mr. Walsh only yesterday. Chapman's considered a quick worker in everything. Not that I say or think he did this murder, but there was the quarrel. He ordered Mr. Walsh out of his orchard. No reason whatever for his behavior, Mr. Walsh wasn't offering to hurt his cherry trees, but I'm told Chapman went fairly wild at sight of him."

I pushed back my typewriter and looked around for my spectacles. I am somewhat short-sighted. Where the deuce had I laid them?

"Looking for anything, sir?" the superintendent asked in the tone of a man in a hurry to be off. I could hardly tell him that I, Michael Hare's author, mislaid my glasses on an average once an hour, and usually took another hour to find them.

I mustn't let Michael Hare down like that.

"I want a book that will serve for notes," I temporized. "This will do." By luck I had caught sight of my, glasses. Thrusting the case into my pocket, I picked up the first note-book I could lay my hands on and with a curious feeling of elation and expectancy turned.

"Can I see the body?" I asked.

"It's at the station. The police car's outside. What's the quickest way out of the house from your rooms, sir?"

I led him through the studio into the passage, where Walsh had stood so short a time before with that intriguing look on his face, and opening what looked like a cupboard door, led the way to the floor below. Here I cautiously opened a side-door and motioned him to step out into the garden. As I did so, a door near us creaked slightly. Instantly the superintendent's torch was on it. It seemed to quiver as we looked. Some one was closing it noiselessly. But in a flash the superintendent's hand opened it. Before us stood Verbena Hillock. She looked into the beam of the electric torch with a pitiful unconsciousness of its blinding powers.

"I heard steps. It's a policeman, isn't it?" she asked under her breath. Her face very pale.

"It's me, Superintendent Gibbs," that officer said gently. "I'm sorry if I disturbed you, Miss Bena. I called in for a chat with your father, but he's out. So Mr. Maltass and I are going for a spin together." He spoke as to a child. But the face still looking unwinkingly into the light was not that of a child. In years Verbena was around twenty, I fancy. But there was a look of tragedy and resignation on features that should have been lovely and gay, which robbed them of youth and charm.

"How did you guess it was a policeman?" he asked again.

"I know the sound of your car."

"When's Mr. Hillock expected back?" he asked her, as he had already asked Esther.

"Any moment. But what's wrong, Superintendent Gibbs? What has happened?" She was trembling. He took her hand.

"Now, Miss Bena, listen to me. You go to bed and I'll drop in in the morning and tell you all about it. There's been an accident to a man in the spinney. You shall hear all about it in the morning."

She turned without a word. We watched her silently climbing the stairs before we closed the house door after us. It struck me as odd that she did not press her question further. Was she afraid of what she might hear? For I had a certainty that she knew or guessed something that made the presence of the police officer in her home at that hour have a meaning for her. And I had a further certainty. She was glad. Under all her tremors she was glad. Whatever it was that she thought had happened, pleased her. Well, loving her sister as she did, for the two girls were devoted to each other, if Verbena thought Walsh a danger to Lily—I dropped the thought. Here were deep waters. Thank God, none of us can be judged because of our emotions. But how could she have any idea of what had happened? Walsh often stayed away from dinner, often came home later than the hour was now . . . I must be wrong. Bena could have no faintest notion of the tragedy.

The superintendent drove me swiftly down to the station, and within a minute or so I was bending over the stretcher on which lay the dead body of Walsh.

Poor Walsh. Weak, but good natured, and capable of real kindnesses. Oddly enough, this showed in his face when dead clearer than I had ever seen it in life. Even though his head was half-battered in.

I looked the body carefully over. Or rather, I let Michael Hare look him over. Except for the battered head, there were no marks to be seen. Apparently there had been no struggle. His hands were unmarked, so were his wrists.

"Did the doctor find any signs of violence except these?" I asked, pointing to the head.

Gibbs said that the medical man had found nothing else.

Then I turned to the clothes. I had often noticed that Walsh carried a very imposing-looking wallet. It only contained a couple of pounds. Some small change was in his pockets. A couple of letters of no apparent importance were on him, besides his well-filled cigarette and card cases.

"I don't think he's been searched," Gibbs said. "I should say those pockets and their contents were as he left them himself. His gold watch is all right, cuff-links and so on, too. Good stuff all of it. No, I shouldn't think he had been robbed. Not unless he was carrying something special we don't know about."

I turned my attention to the long top-boots, fisherman's waders almost, in which Walsh had so loved to array himself. Down the backs, running from the heel to. half up the calf were long streaks of earth. It needed no especial gifts of deduction to know that the body had been dragged where it was found.

"See the coat and trousers." He pointed to the earth marks down one side of them too. The clothes told us nothing fresh. Except that Walsh had, apparently, not been carrying a weapon.

"What sort of thing was he hit with?" I asked finally, studying the head, and making, truth to tell, very little of it.

"Doc says something small but heavy with a sharp, but not actually cutting, edge. Only about two inches long. Sharp cornered. Right-angled corners."

"Sounds like the base of a candlestick," I murmured.

"That's just the sort of thing he suggested. Small paper-weight or candlestick. The odd thing is"—Gibbs too bent over the wounds—"that he is certain there were two, what shall I call them, instruments used. One two inches long, the other about an inch and a half. Roughly speaking only, of course. But he is sure of his ground.

"And also sure that the smaller one was of the same shape, similar in all respects except size and weight to the larger. Both were used at the same time. That's what's so odd, Mr. Maltass. And both were used with tremendous force. Now I've seen a man struck down once with handcuffs, an escaping prisoner's trick, and his head was rather like that." He bent over the body while I shuddered and turned away, glad that Michael Hare had no further need to linger in the mortuary.

CHAPTER FOUR

IT was far too late for me to see the place where Walsh had been found.

"Bit of luck detectives must have up in Lapland and that part of the world," Gibbs said enviously, as we drove back to the farm. "Seven months daylight or so would let you put in some really good work." Like most of us, Gibbs only saw one side of it. What detectives did during the winter did not occur to him.

We learned at the farm that Mr. Hillock had not yet returned. Arthur had told us at dinner that Mr. Hillock was taking his daughter to spend some days with his sister. As her house had no telephone, the superintendent had already sent a telegram asking Hillock to return with Lily at once.

I confess it was with a thrill that I entered the dining-room, where the superintendent had decided to get together all the people staying in the house, and tell them the news, before questioning each one separately.

Scullion came in first, looking as angry as one would expect him to be when fetched from bed, for he had turned in early. Smallwood came next, his pleasant face showed only lively curiosity. Abbott and Richardson were last. They looked more than curious, they looked amazed, but they also, both of them, looked very pale. The superintendent had not asked for Verbena. He had an idea that a blind girl could tell him nothing of what he wanted to know first of all, and that was when, and by whom, Walsh had last been seen in the farmhouse, but Bena came in dressed in a close-fitting black dressing-gown that gave her rather the air of a very young seminarist. As usual, she slipped into a dark unobtrusive corner.

The superintendent explained just where and how the body had been found. But he made no mention of the peculiar character of the cuts, simply telling them that the death was due to blows on the head. This meant, of course, that all the gentlemen present must remain at the farm until the inquest, which would probably be the day after tomorrow. If possible, he would of course prefer them to remain until the dreadful affair had been thoroughly sifted. As no one had signified any intention of leaving the farm, this would presumably be no hardship. He excepted the two young gentlemen from the rectory. They were at liberty to transfer themselves to the other end of the village at any time, but he would be much obliged if they would stay at Much Widham as long as possible.

That is the worst of local police. There was no reason at all why Richardson should go back to the rectory. Of course he should have been told to stay on at the farm.

Scullion roared out a string of amazed questions. Smallwood in his usual quiet voice expressed shocked horror at the superintendent's news.

Three of those present were quite silent—Abbott, Richardson and Bena Hillock. The girl leaned back in her corner wrapped in her black cloak, its hood, for there seemed to be a hood to it, half pulled up over her head, till now she looked like a young monk fast asleep. But she was not fast asleep. I could almost feel her mind rushing to and fro in the room.

"But—but—" Abbott said, finally rousing himself from his apparent stupor, "but the motive?" His voice was flat and toneless.

"Walsh was bound to have heaps of enemies," Richardson said suddenly. "Thick-skinned egoist." There was no regret for Walsh in those venomous tones.

"He was rather by way of being a friend of yours?" Gibbs turned inquiringly to Scullion who shrugged his huge shoulders. It was a continental trick of his.

"Walsh was a god-given painter in the rough. But as to being my friend?" Scullion seemed to turn the word around, and view it from every possible angle before rejecting it. "Walsh, the man, must have had, I should think, a host of enemies."

"I don't agree with you," Abbott said to that, speaking very swiftly, his words almost tumbling over each other. "I don't think Walsh was the kind to make bitter enemies. He was too weak. You couldn't hate Walsh—which means that you couldn't kill him."

"You could for gain!" retorted Scullion. "As to not hating him"—he gave one of his great roars of laughter—"all depends, my friend, all depends."

There was a very peculiar silence after the words.

The superintendent broke it by saying that he wanted to hear from every one present when they had last seen Mr. Walsh, and under what circumstances.

Esther and I appeared to have been the last. I had already told of the glimpse I had had of Walsh leaving his room. She had nothing fresh apparently to add to my account, but Gibbs now had the room cleared of all but himself seated at the table, myself in the window, and Esther nervously balanced on the extreme edge of a chair facing him.

Had she seen the face of Mr. Walsh, she was asked. She had. What was his expression?

"As though he was surprised to see that there little lion again, and I didn't care for the look of him."

The superintendent might be pardoned for staring with goggling eyes. "What little lion?"

"Little brass lion with wings on a box, sir. Mr. Chapman brought it from his last holidays for Miss Lily. He had his paw on a book, which got loose and dropped out with polishing. But you must polish, so what's the good? It gave him a friendly look," Esther went on, "his paw, half-raised as though to shake hands. Took a lovely polish he did. Like gold, as you might say. But Miss Lily wouldn't have none of him after he got damaged. So I put it on the table in the passage beside Mr. Walsh's door. Many a joke he used to make about it. Then it got lost over a fortnight ago. I was no end pleased to see it again beside Mr. Walsh's door."

"And Mr. Walsh was looking at it, you say?" groped the superintendent.

"Standing looking hard at it," she repeated, "as though he didn't half like his looks."

"Had I noticed the box with the lion on the lid?" Gibbs asked me.

As a matter of fact, now that Esther had mentioned it, I saw again the face of Walsh in the dark passage, his features brightly lit by the western sun. At the time it had been the look of apprehension on his face that had alone riveted my attention, and therefore had remained most clearly in my memory, but now, I did remember also that something had gleamed on the table beside him. Something on which, certainly, his eyes had been fixed. And as I thought back harder, I too recollected quite clearly the little lion box . . . but surely that little brass box . . . could it be its reappearance that had caused that strange look?

It seemed a fantastic thought. True, in my last playlet a candlestick standing on a man's desk had meant a sentence of death, a sentence from which Michael Hare had only just saved him. But after all—a playlet! This was a very different thing.

What sort of a box was it? the superintendent asked us. We described it in a duet as about the size of a cigar box with a lion standing on the lid.

"It was the familiar St. Mark's lion," I told him.

"I was that surprised to see it again standing by Mr. Walsh's door. And so was he," Esther put in. "If I hadn't been trying to finish the passage, I'd have spoken about it to him, seeing him standing there taking such notice of it."

The superintendent rose. "Suppose we go and have a look at it, too, Mr. Maltass. Lead the way, Esther."

We followed her up the stairs, along the passage out of which my room opened, on through the studio, and down the continuation of the corridor to the first door. A little table stood always beside this. Its polished top was bare.

Esther, who was ahead of us, gave a little squeak.

"Why, it's gone again? Mr. Walsh must've took it—"

She actually brushed her hands over the top. "He took it," she repeated in bewilderment. "Whatever for? He must've been the one who took it in the first place, then." It was a bizarre touch. This brass box lost, seen for a moment, and then gone again. It was not in any of the rooms around. Finally, we gave up the search for it and went downstairs again.

"Now, was it something inside the brass box itself?" Gibbs murmured. "Or was it stood there as a message?"

"Precisely. That is the question." My tone was dry.

"Fortunately you're helping on this, sir," he said pleasantly. "Looks to me rather a mix-up."

Bena was asked to come in next, since she had chosen to be present. She said, without being asked, that she knew nothing of Mr. Walsh since exchanging a word with him at lunch.

Gibbs passed at once on to what interested him most. The little brass box.

A look that I thought rather wary came into her face. She spoke as though the superintendent's interest surprised her. The box which he described was, she said, a gift to Lily which Mr. Chapman brought back from Venice. But it got damaged in cleaning, and Lily had it taken out of her room. As to where it stood after that, Bena gave her twisted melancholy smile, how should she know? Questioned further she said that Lily never used the box in any way; it had stood purely as a mantel ornament in her room until the lion's gospel got loosened and finally lost.

Her face was in shadow where she sat, but when the interview was over and she rose to go as I opened the door for her she passed out quite close to me. The superintendent murmured that he would be glad if she would let him know at once should she, on thinking things over, remember anything that she had not mentioned which might, however remotely, bear on the tragedy. His tone did not suggest that he thought this at all likely. It might have altered had he seen her expression as she passed on out saying that she did not think she would have anything to add to what she had just said. I had a sudden sharp shock. I felt a sudden certitude that, mad though the thought seemed, Bena knew who had murdered Walsh, knew it absolutely without a shadow of doubt on her own part.

"She knows!" I murmured, coming close to the superintendent. "That girl knows the truth."

He stared at me. I tried to put into words what I had just seen. It did not impress the police officer much.

"I hope you're wrong, sir," he said frankly and promptly, "as I'm afraid that would mean that her father was in this. And I can't think you're right. How could she know anything! Why, she's blind! Oh, I think you're wrong in your guess, Mr. Maltass."

I let the matter drop, but I knew that I was right. None of the others could apparently add anything to Esther's and my account of the box. Like us, every one said that they always thought it was empty. That they had never seen any one put anything in, or take anything out.

Smallwood had noticed that it was gone from the table some time ago, about a week or more, but had not seen it today.

Scullion was the last to come in. He stared at me.

"Hallo! I wondered where little Maltass had got to. You seem to be enjoying a sort of favored nation clause. Why?"

Gibbs said shortly that I was assisting the police in their inquiry.

"Paul among the prophets, eh?" Scullion had a fondness for misquoting scripture. "How nice for Paul! Well, hurry up, I need some sleep even if Walsh has been murdered. It's your job to find the murderer."

"How did you meet Mr. Walsh in the first place, sir?" Gibbs asked unhurriedly.

Scullion seemed to think back.

"He came to make a sort of duty call on the old lady in Switzerland whose gardens I was painting. Old Miss Smythe. By Jove—" Scullion paused and his eyes widened. "By Jove, little Smythie inherits now, doesn't she? I shall double the price of the pictures I'm to paint of her gardens next month. Lucky they're not started yet," he murmured half to himself.

"He was calling on Miss Smythe?" Gibbs recalled the wandering sheep with a peremptory rap of his crook.

Scullion eyed him angrily. "Haven't I just said so? Look here, Superintendent, where's the shorthand writer to take notes. I'm blowed if I'll recite all this twice over."

"I'm taking all the notes that are necessary at this stage of the proceedings," Gibbs said coldly. "I should like to know just how you met Mr. Walsh."

"I was painting in Miss Smythe's garden as usual. I paint there every spring. Her gardener plants what I want, and as I want 'em. She was showing Walsh over the house she has near Vevey. He told me he painted too. Would I care to see any of his sketches. The cheek of the remark amused me. He was in Montreux. A few days later, Miss Smythe asked him to stay a few days with her. He brought his sketches with him. Came down to where I was working and started showing them to me. I gave them a look, intending to tell him what I thought of them—" Scullion's great laugh roared out—"but I got the surprise of my life. I saw a man who was a genius and didn't know it. Didn't know it," he repeated seriously. "He actually thought his work was all wrong because it was different from others. Heaven help us others! I told him all he needed was diligence, and me to show him how to

get out of the bad mannerisms he had picked up."
Scullion paused. "I think the next thing was that he—or
was it Smythie—I can't remember, suggested Walsh
coming down here to see the rector, a distant connection,
whom he'd never met, but from whom he'd just had some
charming letters, he told us. Then I think he, or the
rector, arranged for rooms with Mr. Hillock here.
Anyway, Walsh asked me to come along with him, and
put in a couple of months painting my own stuff, and
showing him how to handle brush and paints. I think
that's the whole story," he wound up meditatively. "I
helped Walsh, not with his painting, but to get his
painting out of himself. It was all in him, you know.
Genius was in Walsh." There was something, as always,
rather fine in the impressive, because impressed, way
that Scullion, usually so brutally frank, spoke of Walsh's
possibilities.

"And this brass box that we're trying to find out
about." Gibbs went on to ask Scullion what he knew of it,
and whether he had ever noticed Walsh use it in any way,
or pay especial attention to it. Scullion could not at first
understand what box we meant. I was not surprised. He
never noticed things of that sort. Finally, when he
grasped what article we were interested in, he had to
confess that he had no idea when he had last seen it
himself, much less when Walsh had last seen it.

He remembered, he said, Walsh making various
jocular remarks about shaking a paw, but Walsh was for
ever making silly speeches of that sort. Scullion was
immensely interested, however, to hear of its supposed
connection with the murdered man, with his having been
last seen looking attentively and rather apprehensively at
the brass lion on the lid.

He explained what I knew to be the case, that he
himself had not seen Walsh then. He had heard his door
close, however, and had rushed out to speak to him,
choosing my passage as the one that led quickest to the
front door, had tripped on a piece of soap "placed there on

purpose in my opinion," he roared, and how his ankle still prevented him getting a boot on.

"Maltass's soap," he wound up, with a most unfriendly eye on me; "deuced odd altogether. Right in front of his door."

It took a minute or two to explain to the superintendent that I was not sure either when I had last used, or seen, the left-over of the cake in question. Esther had put out a new cake of the soap I preferred a day or two before, leaving the thin remnant beside it in the dish. Personally, I said, I thought that Esther had carried off the old one that morning and had probably dropped it in the passage.

"You didn't see it lying there when you came and went yourself during the day, did you?" the superintendent asked. What a tiresome question. Michael Hare would have seen or rather observed and drawn all possible conclusions from a dropped pin, let alone a quite visible slab of soap.

"If I had, I should have put it down to Esther washing up the passage," I replied with dignity. "Today is her afternoon for it."

The superintendent made a note of the fact that it is my bedroom, not my sitting-room that opens off the passage, that my wash-stand is close beside the door, and the soap dish on the side of the door. So that a hand inserted could have "borrowed" the soap.

Gibbs thought a moment before turning to Scullion again.

"Might I ask you, Mr. Scullion, just how Mr. Walsh's death affects you—financially, if at all?"

"I lose my bread and butter," Scullion said gloomily. "You see, he naturally made it worth my while to stay with him. Unfortunately, I didn't get it set down in writing. So now I'm in the soup. I'm a perfect babe in business matters," he boomed. "How could I dream that this was coming? The devil only knows what I'm to do about it." he growled half to himself. "I don't even know whether he made any arrangement with Hillock about me. I don't even know if he's paid up to date. A nice thing if he's behind hand with his payments." Scullion for the first time looked really moved at Walsh's death. "But, of course, he has!" He drummed on the table with his fingers. "And he may have left me something in his will," he said in a more cheerful tone.

"I thought Mr. Walsh had no power to leave any money away from the next-of-kin to the late Mr. Carlisle," Gibbs said.

Scullion looked black. "He told me he had a small, very small, fortune of his own. Couple of thousands or so. Surely he could dispose of that as he wished! And he always expressed a very proper recognition of the fact that he took up a lot of my time, and that my time was valuable. I expected quite naturally that he would have made some provision for me as a token of gratitude."

Scullion eyed us both as though daring us to suggest differently.

"How about Mr. McKirdy," Gibbs asked next. "Did your arrangement with Mr. Walsh, whatever it was, cover him too? I mean, to put it bluntly, was Mr. Walsh paying for him here too?"

"Certainly not!" Scullion looked scandalized. "Poor old Walsh! We aren't blood-suckers, Superintendent. Of course McKirdy pays for himself. He has a small room away off in an attic, and Hillock makes some small but quite sufficient charge for it. McKirdy is doing quite well with illustrating books and magazines, I'm glad to say. But for me he'd still be coloring post cards in some Indian bazaar."

"He is in your employment in some way, isn't he?" Gibbs asked.

"He's my apprentice in the good old way, only I haven't asked any premium," Scullion roared in tones of magnanimity. "In return he, of course, renders me such slight services as he can. Small enough return for what I've done for him."

"How about the Brussels Exhibition?" I asked. "Wasn't there some talk of your getting the committee to exhibit a couple of his etchings?"

"That fell through," Scullion said negligently. "I couldn't be supposed to nurse two cubs. Walsh and McKirdy. Naturally, as McKirdy had had the best I could do for him, it was Walsh's turn to take up my time. There's only so much time any man can spare," he finished truculently. "I've spared all I can, for instance, at the moment." He rose, "And, as I say, McKirdy had naturally to give place to Walsh. Each in his turn."

Gibbs made a note or two, then he said to the giant who was evidently making for the door:

"Just a moment, Mr. Scullion, can you tell me where you were this afternoon from, say, half-past five on?"

"Of course I can," roared Scullion contemptuously. "You mean, will I? I will." And he related very much what I had already told the police officer. Scullion had been painting around half-past four when Walsh put his things up, and looking at the clock on the mantel hurried away. "He had an appointment," Scullion said firmly. "Quite clearly so."

"How do you know that?"

"Because I'm not absolutely an idiot. Any one would know that an artist doesn't leave his painting at the stage Walsh had got his to. He was upset about something. Has been upset for a couple of days. Or nearly a week. And this afternoon he ruined as good a piece of work as he had yet done. Muddled it hopelessly. Started quarreling about Lily Hillock before he went out, and finally flung out of the studio in a black rage. Came stamping through again after half an hour or so. I never notice time when I'm hard at work, and I heard his door shut, after a couple of minutes, as though he had merely dropped in to fetch something or leave something. I thought of a word I wanted to say to him and hurried to cut him off." He repeated again the story of the dance on the soap and its consequences, and again hinted that I knew more than I had told as to how it came to be in front of my door.

Asked by Gibbs, who paid no attention to this ridiculous gibe, whether he knew of anything in the dead man's past that might explain such an end, Scullion looked at him derisively.

"Walsh was the gayest of Lotharios, or the dullest of 'em, but a Lothario all right. Must be dozens of men thirsting for his blood, I should say."

"But you know of no particular case?"

For a second Scullion hesitated, then he said shortly, "no," and yawning loudly left us.

A moment later the door was hurriedly opened and Hillock came in. He is the type of man who does not show when he has had a blow. Perhaps his tanned face had more gray and less red in it than usual, but had I met him, and known nothing of the tragedy, I should not have noticed it.

He said that he had not received any telegram, but was on his way home after driving Lily over to her aunt's for a visit, when a constable in the garden had stopped him and told him of the tragedy.

I admired the way Superintendent Gibbs handled the interview. Not a look, not a word was different from usual, yet he was most emphatically the police officer, not the friend of some years' standing.

As to when he had last seen Walsh, Hillock said that it was on the previous afternoon or evening, when he had spoken to him about throwing elder-wood on the fire. Walsh had taken the farmer's remonstrances as a joke, and Hillock had evidently let himself go a little in return. He could not, or would not, repeat exactly what had been said, but conveyed the impression of anger on both sides. But he maintained that Walsh had told him, without any request on his own part leading to it, that he intended leaving the farm next week. "Gave me the usual seven days' notice, in fact," Hillock said grimly, "and told me that he might be moving out much sooner.'Day after tomorrow,' which would now be tomorrow, was what he said," Hillock did not disguise the fact that he had informed Walsh that as far he was concerned, the sooner would emphatically be the better.

As to this afternoon, and his own movements from half-past five on to seven, Hillock said that he had gone the round of his pig-sties, walked over a couple of fields and had a look at a couple of his cows, and meeting his daughter Lily, had taken her on in his car. He had started for the sties around four and had met Lily over on the road, the other side of Much Widham, around six or thereabouts. Then he had driven off with her and reached his sister's at about a quarter to seven. His sister or her servant lass might know the time more precisely. As to people whom he had met, Hillock gave the names of two of his men on the farm, and a name or two of acquaintances whom he and Lily had passed while driving. Altogether it looked as though he might have a patchy but fairly plausible alibi or series of alibis for the danger period, the time from half-past five to sunset at seven.

"To get to your piggeries did you take the shortcut through the spinney, past Latimer's Oak?"

Hillock said that, as usual, he had done so.

Had he seen Mr. Walsh? He had not. He had already told the superintendent that he had not seen Walsh today at all.

Questioned about the brass box, Hillock showed a complete ignorance of it, which might be genuine.

On this, he was allowed to hurry off to fetch his daughter home again. She might have some really useful information to give the police.

Abbott was next asked to come in. He seemed unable to give any help whatever. Acknowledged that he had seen the brass box in question when he first came to the farm about a fortnight ago, standing outside Walsh's door in the passage, but had not noticed that it was gone, far less seen it again today. As for his own movements, he and Richardson had gone for a long ramble, getting in late for dinner. He mentioned, vaguely, the round that they had taken, but much of the time had been spent lying out on their coats on the grass smoking and talking. They had met no one they knew, except on the way home about half-past seven, when they had all but run into the postman.

Mr. Walsh was a relation of his, was he not?

To which Abbott replied that he was something like a fiftieth cousin fifty times removed, and that until a year ago when another distant connection, a tea planter in Ceylon, had left a fortune to his next-of-kin who chanced to be Walsh, he, Edward Abbott, had never heard of the chap. Nor had his father. Walsh had written from town, and again from Switzerland, suggesting a desire to call at the rectory and a second letter saying that he and Mr. Scullion, the well-known artist, were coming down to Much Widham for a couple of months' painting, would, or could, the rector suggest suitable accommodation. Abbott's father had arranged with Hillock to take the two, or as it turned out three artists, and in due time Walsh had called at the rectory and dined there at intervals.

"To whom would the money go now?"

"To an old lady called Smythe. A dear old maid who lives somewhere on the lake of Geneva."

"And after her?"

After her, it would come to his own father, supposing the rector outlived the lady, in which case, the money would eventually be divided equally between his children, which meant between himself, Edward, and his sister Laura.

Abbott had already told us that he had last seen Walsh in the studio during the afternoon. Gibbs now asked if he could tell us about a meeting with Lily Hillock immediately after she had been seen, or heard, quarreling with the dead man.

Abbott said promptly that he had chanced on Miss Hillock who was naturally in a very indignant mood because the painter, after getting her to promise to stand for him in his picture of the oak that he was painting had put her off with neither apology nor explanation. Walsh had simply told her that she would not be wanted any more. Lily, who had made her arrangements to continue to stand for him, was naturally vexed. The more so, because up till two days ago Walsh had been much too attentive to her. Miss Hillock, very naturally, Abbott said, resented her dismissal almost as much as she had done the artist's effusiveness before. She had asked him, Abbott, to speak to Walsh at once, but he had preferred to keep out of the dispute. That was all. After a short talk with Lily he had gone on his way, met Richardson and spent the remainder of the day as he had said.

I thought the explanation might explain the little scene that I had watched. Naturally Abbott had not said anything about it until pressed, as it had nothing to do with Walsh's murder, and more nearly concerned Lily Hillock than it did himself.

Nothing different or more detailed could apparently be learned from Richardson, so Smallwood was next asked in. As I expected, he was no help at all. He had never heard of Walsh, until being recommended to try the farm for quiet practice by a friend of his, who had stayed there often in the summer, he had come on down and found the three artists just installed. As to this afternoon—he bore out my own belief as to his whereabouts. He had been trying to learn a new Debussy, and as he could only learn by ear he had worked hard at the music roll on his player piano, afterwards trying to reproduce it. I knew, we all knew, of this peculiarity of Smallwood's. Even the superintendent, like all the village, knew that he practised with feet and bellows until he could play the piece with his hands.

As to any confidences from Walsh about anything in the man's past which would explain his murder,

Smallwood only shook his head. He knew nothing whatever of Walsh's past life. The man had quite definitely not attracted him in the least.

This finished the private sitting for the moment, since McKirdy had not come in. We adjourned for drinks all round. I was just finishing mine when McKirdy hurried in. Met by us all in a body he looked startled. Scullion pounced on him as might a Colonel of the Foreign Legion on a frustrated deserter.

"Where the devil have you been? Why the hell couldn't you be here when I wanted you?"

McKirdy looked past him. He said nothing. I think he would have gone on up the stairs without a word but for the superintendent.

"A word with you, Mr. McKirdy, please."

McKirdy seemed to see him for the first time, to see any of us for the first time. Without any sign of surprise or interest he followed Gibbs and me into the dining-room and let us close the door. I stared hard at him. What had happened? Something had. He was not the same man who had left the farm this afternoon with two pairs of boots to be stretched. There was in him now something—I tried hard to get the word—I could only think of the French *exalté*.

Told of Walsh's murder, he only shook his head and murmured indifferently: "Very terrible indeed. Most shocking."

"Now, merely as a matter of course, we must know where every one staying here at the farm was this afternoon from half-past five on till seven. Would you mind telling us where you were?"

McKirdy took quite a moment before replying.

"I went to the shoemaker's first of all, and left a couple of boots to be stretched for Mr. Scullion, and for Walsh." A faint smile, rather a cruel one, flitted across his thin lips for a moment.

"Then—well, it was a lovely, warm afternoon. I had been working very hard. I went for a walk. I wanted to tire myself out. I walked on and on until finally I found myself at Larkhall station just as a train passing this way was expected. So I took it. It was the nine, and I walked slowly back here, taking my time over it."

Had he met any one on his walk? McKirdy did not know. He had been deep in his own thoughts and had not noticed where he went, except that he avoided the main highways. At Larkhall station he had spoken to a porter.

It was an eminently reasonable tale, and yet I doubted it. I found in a few minutes that the superintendent doubted it too.

However, the mere fact of a murder happening in one's own circle is so unusual that it has, must have, strange reactions. As to when he had last seen Walsh, it had been when the now murdered man had asked him to take his boots to Brown. Again that flickering smile came and went.

As to his acquaintance with Walsh, it had begun when he was helping Mr. Scullion with the flower studies that the great man made annually at Bois Riant outside Vevey. A Miss Smythe owned the house and gardens. Walsh was a kinsman of hers. McKirdy went on to tell practically the same tale that Scullion had already told us. He repudiated the idea that he had ever had any confidences from Walsh which might explain his end, or throw any light on the dead man's circle of friends elsewhere, or on his life before he met him.

About the brass lion box, McKirdy was equally vague. But I thought he followed with very close, though secret, attention every word that Gibbs had to say as to its reappearance this afternoon. He himself, he said, had noticed it on the table in the corridor many times, but had lately missed it. It made a bright note in the passage. He had asked Esther what had become of it about a week ago, merely from vague curiosity, but he had not seen it at any time this afternoon. As he had left with the boots before Walsh, at a time when I felt sure that the table was still bare, this answer was only to be expected.

Finally, McKirdy left us, still looking like a sleepwalker. For the news of Walsh's murder had not removed the peculiar absent look from his eyes.

"What do you think of the man, Mr. Maltass?" the superintendent asked when the door closed behind him. "You know him fairly well. He strikes me as though he had been drinking heavily, but is the kind of man who doesn't show his liquor."

"McKirdy is bowled over by half a glass of claret, superintendent," I told him. "He is full of something though, potent as new wine. I wonder what it is! Of course, it may have nothing to do with the crime. He may have got religion."

The superintendent laughed. "Do you know, Mr. Maltass, now you mention it, he's not unlike Cobbler Joe, a gipsy, hereabouts, who got converted, and now goes around the caravans preaching. But it seems a bit odd. To happen just this afternoon."

"He may have got an inspiration for a picture," I pondered aloud. "I like his work immensely. It's not in the same street with Scullion, of course, but it's very good too in its own way."

"He certainly doesn't waste any words of regret over Walsh's murder," Gibbs said, sorting out his papers. The superintendent shared, in common with most of his cloth, a liking for things to be done in order and more or less according to rule. Order and rule demanded expressions of shocked horror on hearing of the violent death of even a detested fellow creature, and McKirdy had not produced this expected small certificate of respectability.

"Naturally he didn't, couldn't, love him," I replied. "But I don't think he hated him. There's a lot of the fatalism of the East in McKirdy. What will be, will be, is his motto, with the rider, I fancy, that it's sure to be something no one wants."

Gibbs gave his quick chuckle. Then his face grew grave. "It's that box that beats me along with other things. That brass box placed where Mr. Walsh, and he alone, would be sure not to miss it. And which he seems to've taken away with him, but which isn't on his body. The size of it sounds too large to've been the thing that killed him, but it might have been.

Gibbs sank into deep thought to stare up finally at me expectantly.

"What does Michael Hare say, sir?"

I knew it was coming. I could have let Michael Hare say a couple of quite unexpected words. But I bit them back.

"That if the box held a message, or if its mere reappearance stood for something, there must have been some previous use of it. Unless Walsh received a letter telling him what to look out for—" It was no use pretending I was not as puzzled as Gibbs was.

"Perhaps Miss Lily can throw some light on it," he suggested finally and not very hopefully.

"Can, or will?" I asked pertinently, and we both fell silent.

What did Bena know, and how did she know it? Had she a tangible clue, or was her knowledge intuitive, or was it founded on deduction?

I would have given a good deal to have answered these questions.

CHAPTER FIVE

IT was around half past ten that Lily Hillock came home. Superintendent Gibbs and I rose as one man as Hillock's car could be heard outside. We both wanted to see the girl. But if we expected to see her looking any different from usual, we were mistaken. Lily swept into the hall head up, shoulders back as usual. As I have said she was a plain young woman with something in her that drew men in spite of that. There was a quality in the girl that rose above looks and birth, something conquering. Something that refused to be kept down. Call it insolence, call it arrogance, it was native, not acquired, and would have persisted under any circumstances. I had finally come to the conclusion that it was the girl's own will-power that one felt. That Lily Hillock was one of the few people who knew what they wanted and how much they were prepared to pay for it.

"Well, Miss Lily," the superintendent began a little awkwardly. "This is a dreadful business—this murder of Mr. Walsh. Can I have a few words with you alone? Alone, that is to say, except for Mr. Maltass who's helping the investigation."

"I don't mind," she said curtly, and led the way into the stuffy drawing-room. There she stood, one hand on the dingy marble mantelpiece.

Her green eyes rested on mine for a moment. I felt that she was summing me up, and as an antagonist, not as a friend. Lily had tried to make a fool of me shortly after my arrival, and how nearly she had succeeded only I myself knew. After a very short time, however, she had given me up and turned her attention to Walsh. He was a wealthier man than I, and I think she divined where my interests in Much Widham lay.

After that one long probing look she faced the superintendent entirely through the interview.

"Now the first question," Gibbs began, stroking his mustache and looking at her thoughtfully, "is, when did you last see Walsh?"

"This evening. At half-past six," Lily said composedly, and, as far as I was concerned, unexpectedly.

"Half-past six this afternoon," Gibbs repeated.

"Would you mind coming down to the police station tomorrow, Miss Hillock, and letting us have that as signed evidence? Of course, you know that all this affair concerns you very deeply. Concerns every one in the farmhouse very deeply."

"I don't see that," she replied swiftly; "that's the sort of talk I expected to hear from the cottagers, Mr. Gibbs, but not from you. Mr. Walsh had just come into a big fortune. He's a man who always tries to flirt with every woman who'll look twice at him—poor shrimp." There was no mistaking the contempt in her tone. "Of, course this murder has nothing to do with us down here."

"I'm afraid it's anything but 'of course,'" Gibbs said slowly. "Now where was it that you saw him at half-past six today?"

"Under Latimer's Oak," was the quiet reply. I frankly gasped. Gibbs stroked his mustache as though it were a cat's head, over and over, fast and furiously. Then he asked swiftly:

"Did you speak to him?"

"I think I gave some exclamation of surprise," she answered slowly, as though thinking back. "'You, Mr. Walsh!' was exactly what I said, I think. Or, 'You here!' Something like that."

"And he?"

"He didn't answer." Her voice was quite level and composed. "He was standing under the tree as though deep in thought. He didn't see or hear me. I was hurrying along to meet my father. I was late. I had been picking daffies for my aunt, and here and there some primroses,

and had spent much more time over the basket than I
thought. So I only hurried along the path that goes near
the oak. I really called out whatever it was I said in
surprise, as I went on."

"Where did you meet your father?"

The rest of what she had to say tallied with that we
had already learned from Hillock.

"Now as to a brass box which Mr. Chapman is said
to've brought you from Venice with a St. Mark's lion on
the lid."

She professed to complete ignorance of it after
refusing to have it in her room once it was damaged. That
was a month or so ago. We did not detain her, but all
three walked into the hall where her father and sister
were waiting for her. The two girls went upstairs
together. Hillock stayed on by the fire, staring into the
leaping flames on the hearth where only the evening
before he had rescued the burning elder branch.

We said nothing. Neither, for a moment, did he.
Finally he roused himself.

"I'll go to bed, too." His speech was thick. So he had
been drinking again. A pity. I had found that he took far
too much of an evening as a rule.

"I'll go to bed," he repeated. "Lily has played with fire
and will have to pay for her playing." He nodded gloomily
to himself, and strode on up the stairs.

Arthur came in to put the lights out and lock up. It
had been his evening out and he had only heard the news
a few minutes ago. He was one mass of exclamations and
queries, but he was unable to help us any. Except that he
was positive, like Esther, that the brass lion box must
have been taken away by Mr. Walsh himself, for he,
Arthur, had dusted the passage only half an hour or so
after Esther had scrubbed, and had seen nothing of it
then, nor was it, he was quite positive on both points—on
the hall table later on when he took a jug of hot water
into the murdered man's room at half-past six. In fact, he
had not seen the "lion" for about a fortnight. He had

never noticed Walsh, or any one else, using the box in any way.

Gibbs finally got rid of him, and he and I went up to my sitting-room for a last word.

"Most extraordinary thing that about that box!" he muttered, motionless in the room. "Not that I doubted what Esther told us. She's a sensible body. Not given to imagining things. You yourself were struck by the expression on Mr. Walsh's face. Just caught sight of the box again, evidently."

"Yes I think very clearly it couldn't have been there when he went into his room." I was only too well aware of the fact that the superintendent expected better things from Michael Hare than that, but that damned lucky man had never had a tangle like this to solve. What was the meaning of that brass box? What did it stand for—or contain?

We arranged to be up at dawn so as to inspect the place where the body had been found, and then we parted. I tried to sleep with a brain seething with facts, ideas, and surmises.

Suddenly I sat up. I have a memory like a sieve, but unlike a sieve it is capable of suddenly flashing a picture before me of something which I had completely forgotten. The picture that now whizzed across my mind was that of Hillock offering Walsh the use of an old, built-in bureau in the dining-room. You opened a cupboard door to the right of the fireplace and, instead of shelves, found the lower half of the cupboard to consist of a bureau with drawers and a let down flap of the usual type.

I saw again Hillock detaching a key from his chain, and telling Walsh that it was the only one in existence, and therefore, to be careful not to lose it. I recollected now that Walsh had complained that his painting things filled his rooms to overflowing, and that he would like some spot for his correspondence. I remembered now, that I had known Walsh from time to time to stay behind in the room "to write a letter," or be there ahead of us.

Undoubtedly he used the bureau . . . Gibbs had locked himself into Walsh's two rooms, preparatory to a careful investigation, but no one had thought of the bureau below—or was it only that no one had spoken of it? I decided to have a look at it. A tap, cautiously low, on the rooms that Walsh had occupied, received no reply. I could hear nothing within. Perhaps the superintendent did know of the bureau. Taking my electric torch, I went as I was, down the stairs.

I had no reason for being barefoot, except that it is a custom of mine, I love the feel of boards or carpet under my soles. Turning on my light, I walked quickly down the passage to the dining-room. The door stood nearly a foot ajar. I was not surprised, for it had a defective catch that refused to stay shut. It was in darkness. So Gibbs was not here. Even as I thought this, I heard a sound from the farther corner of the room, the corner where stood the bureau which was in my thoughts.

What I heard was the crackle, the quite unmistakable sound that Bank of England notes make when handled. I stood rigid. In the first shock of surprise I had not switched off my light. Yet the rustling continued. A mouse in the paper-basket, I asked myself? For whoever first coined the phrase, "quiet as a mouse" has never heard the creature among paper. I turned my torch on the corner where was the bureau. Some one in a long dark cloak with a hood was just closing the cupboard door. I called out and dashed into the room. At the same moment a terrific blow crashed on the top of my head. When I came to, I was surprised to find myself still in this world. I felt like one vast headache sprawled on the floor. My torch had fallen near me. I groggily turned it on. I was alone in the room, except that there was something on the carpet not a foot away—a thick blackthorn cudgel which generally stood in the hall, and was supposed to be reserved for any entering burglar. It had always seemed to me that it might come in as handy, for the transgressor as for the defender of the hearth. As I pulled it towards me, and supported myself to my feet with its help, I realized that I was lucky to have escaped at all, considering its size and weight. Or had it been laid near me as a warning, as that lion box seemed to have been placed outside ·Walsh's door? But his seemed to have been, or contained, a summons. I felt my head cautiously. There was a large bump and a cut on top. Here again was a similarity. My injury, though slight in comparison with his, was similar—a blow, ferocious and swift, on the head. For the first time I realized that with reason a detective's life is classed among the risky professions; that whatever the motive that had caused Walsh's murder, spent though it might be, supposing it to have been jealousy, the criminal would want to escape detection And he had already taken one life. Who was it who had stood in the darkness by the bureau counting, or at least handling, bank notes? I felt sure that it was the blind girl. To any one standing there with eyes to see my light would have given ample warning of my coming I had obviously taken the watcher or guardian behind the door by surprise, but then he had a thick, half-closed door between himself and me, and my torch had not shone full on him. Yes, Bena was the hooded figure, of that I felt sure, but what was she after? For whose sake was she there? Father? Sister? Or for some one else? How had she opened the bureau? As to my assailant, of one thing I was certain, he was a tall man. But then Hillock, Chapman, Scullion and even quiet Smallwood, were all tall. Possibly, too, even Abbott and Richardson had they brandished the club might have got in that blow. I myself am below the medium height. By this time I was feeling better. There was some water on the sideboard. I took a glass and had sense enough to leave spirits alone. Feeling better still, I finally managed to get up to my room with the help of the cudgel and the banisters.

As I halted a moment outside my door to get my breath, again sounds reached me from within the room.

But not of papers this time. Nor was the door ajar. What I heard was the careful moving of a chair.

I peered through the keyhole feeling as though I might fall through it, for stooping was agony, and the keyholes at the farm were of a Merovingian size.

There was nothing mysteriously hooded or cloaked about the figure that was staring into my wardrobe. Scullion's huge hand just reached up a pair of shoes. My shoes. Now Arthur himself says that he has a fondness for "manana, as the Spaniards call it." As he learned the expression from a film caption, and pronounces the word to rhyme with banana, a Castilian might not recognize that racial trait, but there is no doubt as to Arthur's meaning, and that he in no wise overstates his case. It is his custom only to take away in the morning when he brings me my early cup of tea, any boots and shoes used on the previous day.

Scullion, therefore, was now examining the ones that I had worn for my ramble in the late afternoon. Even as I peered at him with an eye that seemed to be elongating itself like a snail's in order to see round the cut of the keyhole, he gently scraped some mud off one of the insteps with his thumb and then stood making dabs at it with a forefinger. He put the shoes back where they had stood. Then he passed from my range of vision. I waited. In a minute he came into view again with my shirt in his hand, and examined the cuffs and the front with care. He looked gloomily dissatisfied, stepped to my wardrobe again and returned with my coat, subjecting it to the same scrutiny before replacing it. Then he stood as though listening. I decided that he was meditating a return to his own rooms, should the coast still seem clear. So I turned the handle briskly. On the instant he tried to switch off the light, but only succeeded in upsetting the reading lamp, which, fortunately, lit the room as well on its side as upright.

"Scullion? Dropped in for a chat?" I asked pleasantly.

"Yes." He grunted like a surly Bill Sykes. "Just that. For a chat." And he sat down and eyed me with those bull's eyes of his. I said nothing, and waited with throbbing brows for the "chat" to materialize.

"Hallo!" he cried in unmistakably genuine amazement, "why your head's—good lord! What's happened now?"

It was not Scullion who had whacked me on the head. I had been sure of that before, but apart from my own belief, there was too much of a swift rush of speculation—surmise—in his eye. Like a flight of birds they rushed across his mind. "Who did that?" he asked with breathless curiosity, but entire lack of sympathy. "Why, it looks for all the world as though whoever did for Walsh had been practising on you—had it only come first."

"I slipped on the stairs as I was going down to the dining room just now." Even as I spoke I sank into a chair. The room was rising and falling around me.

"What did you go there for at this time of night? We finished the whisky." He helped me bathe my head, and bind a towel round it, with surprising deftness.

"It's easy to slip in the darkness," he muttered. "Playing Nosey Parker at night is apt to be dangerous."

I did not intend to quarrel with Scullion.

"You haven't explained what you are doing here," I said instead.

"Oh, that—" He nearly put my eye out with a gesture signifying that his presence needed no explanation.

"It's Walsh's death," he said finally, seeing that I intended to have one. "I loathed the blighter as a blighter. That's granted. We all did. But as a painter—my God!" There was a pause. "Where were you yourself this afternoon?" he barked suddenly. I knew what was in his mind. I had known since I had seen him examining my boots and garments. And I could have laughed aloud. Scullion to turn detective! A bull in a china shop, a bull among cobwebs, a dozen comparisons swept through my mind. A criminal would have an easy task, I reflected, to outwit such a trailer.

"I was walking, and walking through woods. My shoes would probably, therefore, show the same kind of leaf mould as that around Latimer's Oak. But the shirt and coat I was wearing, will, I fear, not be of any help as far as bloodstains are concerned."

His jaw dropped. He stared at me with such comic amazement and chagrin on his face that I had to laugh.

"Come, Scullion," I said on that, "as a flower painter you head the list, but as a detective you don't stand an earthly."

"But how did you know," he stammered in a small voice that I had never before heard from him.

"Deduction," I murmured hardily. But his eye shifted to the keyhole, and he threw back his great red beard. "Oh, I see! As you saw!" Then his face darkened, and getting to his feet by the help of his stick and the table, he looked at me with something very like open suspicion.

"Why are you working along with the police? You didn't care a hang for Walsh. You're the sort of lazy chap who wouldn't stoop to pick up a thousand pound note. Then why go to so much trouble for a man you didn't know well? It looks damned fishy to me. You were out yesterday afternoon."

"Oh, go to—bed!" I said rudely, "and wake up with some sense." I flung the door open for him, and with another hard stare at me, as though hoping to read my guilt in my eyes, he limped off.

So Scullion suspected me of murdering Walsh. At first I tried to find it funny, but it was a chill thought. I mean the suspicion. And there came with that a sudden distaste, a faint horror, at the realization that we each and every one of us in Upfold Farm that night, except the criminal—supposing him to be one of us—was suspecting all the others. Not that I suspected all. Two only, in my mind, or three if I reluctantly included Hillock, might be guilty. But we were, one and all, ready to suspect any one—on the watch for any slip.

I felt a sudden need for company. For some one friendly and outside the circle of possible suspects. There was Smallwood. His piano playing constituted a perfect alibi. I would go and talk things over with Smallwood. He had never mixed himself up in any way with Walsh, or with Lily Hillock. I made for his room. It was down a flight of stairs, and formed part of what had once been a hay loft. He was on the present first floor, and a little used path ran past his sitting-room window sloping precipitately down to the ground level. His door I found locked. I expected Smallwood to have nerves. Something about his light eyes suggested the possibility of them. I knocked discreetly. Loud enough to be heard if he were awake —not loud enough to wake an ordinary sleeper. And I confess I wondered if I were suffering from *idée fixe*, when once again I heard a sound from inside a room. This time also there was no mistaking it. The plop of a person jumping lightly to the floor. Then I heard a window shut and fastened, and a curtain drawn. All with great care to make no noise. I knocked at once. I had been attacked. The sounds I heard might not be made by Smallwood but by an intruder. There came an instant cessation of such little noise as there had been. I called softly:

"Smallwood! Smallwood!"

A moment later I heard a sleepy "Who's there?" in the tone of one roused from deep slumber. The voice came from where the bed stood. "I want to speak to you," I said urgently.

"Half a sec," came the reply in a more alert voice. I heard the faint swish of a stiff garment, yet, when rather surprised at Smallwood's ceremony, I waited another minute, he opened the door clad in an old bath-gown that could not have produced a swish had it tried for a week. He ran his hands through his hair. Running them up, not running them down.

"Anything wrong?" he asked. "Good heavens, you've been injured!" I had forgotten my Indian turban. "Is anything else wrong?" he asked as I came on into his room, pushing past him to do so.

I would have given a good deal to have answered that question. Who had plopped into that room?

"I came just to talk things over," I said now; "but as I tried your door I distinctly heard your window shut and some one drop on to the floor. Better have a look around together. Some one may be hiding in here."

"But your head?" he persisted. Apparently more concerned for me than to find out if any one was in his room.

"I hurt myself on the stairs—" I had to stick to the same lie—"but you've several fitted cupboards. Suppose any one got in while you were asleep. You'd better look through the room I while I'm here."

He did so, but insisted that I had heard his bolster drop off the bed and his window closing itself, as it also did frequently. The weights were out of order, and the lower sash had a way of descending like a guillotine. The latter was true, I knew. The bolster, too, really did lie out on the floor. My hearing, excited as I was, with an injured head, might have played me false, might have translated these commonplace facts into something sinister. And yet . . . suddenly I noticed that as he hurriedly opened a cupboard that served as a wardrobe, a raincoat hung right in front. Hung on a nail though all the rest of the clothes were on hangers. Smallwood was very particular about his clothes. And as he walked to another corner of the room I noticed another thing. He left the damp outline of his shoe on the wooden, stained floor. He had already explained that he had thrust his feet into the first thing that came to hand, which were the shoes in which he had walked in the garden in the evening, but, looking sharply, I saw that they were still oozing not damp, but water. Had he taken a bath with them on? Those wet shoes and that swish of a stiff garment . . . that plop . . .

that sound of a window cautiously closed . . . I suddenly felt disinclined for any chat. I wanted to get out of the room. Was it possible that that dark raincoat had been worn by whoever had rifled the bureau? That it was not the blind girl at all? But how could I get away? Suddenly I asked him to play for me. Most people would have treated this request as a sign of lunacy or raging fever, but not so Smallwood. He was always ready to play for any one at any hour. Opening the piano he played something gentle and soft. It should have soothed my mind to quiet, but my mind was like a rush of leaping salmon.

"You play jolly well," I said, as he finished. He gave a smile that suddenly reminded me of Bena's twisted one.

"Just good enough not to be better," he said shortly.

"What the hell!" came in a stentorian tone from outside. "Who the devil is playing at this hour of night?" No need to speculate as to the speaker. Almost with thankfulness I realized that here was no room for suspicion as to the owner of the voice, or of the mighty fist that smote the door before Scullion glared at us from the threshold.

"Are you mad, you two? If you don't want any sleep I do. Touch that tin pan again, Smallwood, and I'll rip its notes out and fling them out of the window."

Smallwood only laughed. He and Scullion got on well together. I got to my feet. Glad of Scullion's appearance as an excuse to leave. I had an idea that Smallwood was equally glad to see me go. I do not envy those who have to pretend friendliness where they feel doubts and perplexities. Smallwood could have nothing to do with Walsh's murder. The idea was preposterous even if Smallwood had not been heard hard at work on his piano during the time that the murder was done; but why had he come back into his rooms in that extraordinary way? We all had latch keys. No one at the farm inquired into the hours we kept. Smallwood could have come in with the morning paper had he chosen. Then why the window?

There seemed only one reply. Tonight, for the first time, Superintendent Gibbs was in the house, and I knew also that a constable was watching the farm outhouses. Yet to give that as an answer to any action of Smallwood's?

I walked very slowly. My head still hurt badly and I felt as though the carpet were a snake twisting round and round. It was not eavesdropping, but merely the ordinary use of one's ears that made me hear Scullion's stentorian, "I'm damned if I don't think it looks fishy, Smallwood, and so I tell you straight. I never could see the use of beating about bushes. I tell you he had the same muck on his shoes as under Latimer's Oak. And then to get himself hand-in-glove with the police."

I confess that I stood still then. This much had been involuntary, but now I stopped where I was and deliberately listened.

"Rubbish, Scullion! What would his motive have been? Or is Maltass a homicidal maniac?"

"Motive? How should I know," roared Scullion contemptuously. "Lily Hillock, probably. I don't say he did kill him, mind. I only say he could have, and that he's no right to be given extra advantages."

I turned back. I did not intend to, but I opened the door on that.

"What do you mean by extra advantages?" I asked. "I couldn't help hearing what you said, or rather what you bellowed, Scullion. What extra advantages have I, pray?"

"Being allowed to run with the hounds," he said, with a grin. I always knew that Scullion's bark was worse than his bite. "We're all after the criminal. At least we three are. Supposing you to be all right, Maltass, and the criminal is all out to get off with it. But come to my rooms and have a drop," he finished hospitably. 'Smallwood'll never get any further if he works on water."

"I'll join you in a bottle of beer," Smallwood said, closing the piano.

I said I would take neither beer nor spirits as I wanted a clear head in the morning.

"And what the devil's the use of a clear head in the morning?" roared our host, leading the way down a flight of stairs to his rooms, where he poured out a glass of whisky that would have sent an elephant reeling and proffered it to me. "Who wants the morning, anyway," he persisted as I waved it away. "The beer's over in the coal-scuttle, Smallwood. Help yourself. Yes, who wants the morning—except the dawn." Scullion combed his beard and suddenly strode over to a pile of canvases, pulled one out, and stood it in front of us. "Dawn," he repeated briefly. No need to name it. Dawn itself, it was. Rosy. Vague. Timid. Translucent. Unearthly. I saw it on the flowers by the river. A bunting on a branch in the foreground was singing it. I could almost hear his light, cheery titter like breaking glass. I could all but feel the water rippling, beneath the first pale gleams.

"Dawn," roared the painter again, taking the canvas away; "but you can have the rest of the day until evening. What was I saying? Yes, we're all detectives. Except the criminal. And why should you be given such an unfair start? I still don't see. Smallwood here says you've a brother in the post office or the lost dog's home—I don't see what difference that makes. My own brother is a purser in a P. and O. Why didn't the police let me in?"

"They were afraid they wouldn't be able to hear your whispers," Smallwood said, bursting out laughing as he drank his beer.

"Still," Scullion boomed on, "there's one thing I know about Walsh that you don't, Maltass. As for Smallwood here, he doesn't count."

"What is it you know?" I asked promptly.

He roared in amusement. "Think I'm going to tell you? You have your advantages, however you got 'em. I keep mine. Yes, Maltass, I don't believe you'll get the criminal as quickly as I shall. Maddening thought, eh? Well, do you good." He turned morosely back to his own big tumbler.

Smallwood and I both knew him in that mood. The pianist rose to go.

"What do you want to hound him down for?" Scullion suddenly demanded. "Why shouldn't he have his chance to get way, if he can beat the police? He had his reasons. They may have been good ones."

Smallwood took his departure now. He looked his thorough disagreement. I lingered.

"Knowing what I know, and what you don't," Scullion went on, pouring in more whisky, "I think he had *very good* reasons. Benefactor in a way, except that Walsh painted as none of us will ever paint. But the man in question didn't—" He pulled himself up. "No use sitting there watching me drink, and having none yourself," he announced with his engaging candor. "I never get drunk. Can't. And if I did, I wouldn't tell you the one thing you must know, before you can even begin your hunt. So good night to you, Mr. Sleuth—Mr. Policeman's Hangman."

I too left. Scullion could be a foul-mouthed brute when he was what he called "comfortable," and "half-drunk," but his words stuck most annoyingly. He did know something. Something that to him, at least, seemed a good clue. What could it be? I sat with my aching head propped in my hands. Scullion's very certainty that neither Smallwood nor I, nor, the police, knew it, looked as though it were something that Walsh had told him in confidence. Scullion had met Walsh in Vevey. Was it something that had happened in Vevey? Yet, Scullion showed no signs of going back there to pick up a trail. Whatever it was, if it was something told him, it seemed to be something that could he as easily followed up at the farm as anywhere else. Unless, of course, Scullion made for some fresh spot after the inquest. I decided that a very close watch should be kept on his movements and correspondence. Yet the idea of Scullion as a detective was as comic as ever. I wished the superintendent would show himself. On the wish the door opened and Gibbs himself came in softly.

I told him what had happened to me, and what I had heard outside Smallwood's door, winding up with the caustic comment that the eye of the law, in the person of his constable outside the farm, seemed to have closed early and tightly.

Gibbs shook his head. He looked as trim and neat as though it were noon.

"I'll explain that later. I want to see the dining-room and the bureau first of all."

Making no noise, we hurried down the stairs. Gibbs left me for a second to have a word with his constable outside as to keeping an eye on Smallwood's window. Then he opened the dining-room door.

All looked as usual. Gibbs and I inspected the cupboard. It showed no marks of any kind. The key, as usual, was in the lock. On opening it, the bureau looked quite untouched too. Gibbs studied the lock very carefully. So did I. It showed no signs of having been forced. He inserted the key from Walsh's bunch which he had with him, and turned it to and fro gently. "Nor, I think, has it been picked. Feels smooth and turns sweetly. Well, now for a look into the empty stable." He opened the flap. Inside was a largish, envelope addressed in print characters to Herbert Walsh, Esq., Upfold Farm."

Gibbs took it up. It was sealed, but one end had been slit open. It still seemed full of papers. He drew out a wad of Bank of England notes, and counted them. There were ten, of one hundred pounds each.

We stared at one another.

"Very" I agreed, answering his stare. He placed the envelope and contents on one side and went carefully over the rest of the bureau's contents.

"Nothing but silly letters from silly women," was his comment when finished. "Lots of things relating to this money he's come into, which I shall have to go through with his solicitors. Nothing that sticks out as a clue or a motive." He took up the envelope again. "Except this. By Jove, this! Not come by post, you see. Handed to Walsh, and evidently locked by him for safe keeping here in this bureau."

"Or found by him in the brass box outside his door," I said. "The envelope has been folded, and would, I fancy, fit the box, as I remember its size."

"Ah!" He made a note in his book; "but however it came to him he evidently preferred not to have it on him when he went out to the meeting when he was killed. . ."

I was studying the envelope. It was printed in a neat and, I should have said, not a disguised hand. It was sealed with ordinary red sealing wax. The seal used was a shilling with this year's date on it, and a deep mark right across it as though some one had tried to chop it in half.

"What I heard was something being taken out of that envelope," I said slowly. "I heard the rustle of notes first. But then I heard the sound of some paper being carefully extracted from a long envelope."

"There's no other long envelope but this," the superintendent said, "and the pigeon holes don't look to me as though they had been searched or interfered with in any way. Nor the little drawers, either. If you think something was taken out, it must have been pretty valuable for them to take it and leave the money."

I stood silently thinking.

"I'm not so sure that we haven't here an act of restitution," I said finally. "I still think it was little Bena I heard and saw at the desk. I think she was putting these notes back into the envelope, counting them possibly. But certainly she took out a paper. Or, rather, whoever was at the bureau took it out. If it was Bena, for whom was she acting? Lily? Her father?"

I had asked myself the question many times.

"—Or Chapman," finished the superintendent under his breath. "It's a shame to drag her secret out, but in strict confidence, Mr. Maltass, it's my belief, has been for a year or so, that Verbena Hillock is in love with young George Chapman."

"And he's in love with her sister?"

"More or less. Chapman's out for money. Means to rise. I think his fancy was caught by Lily Hillock all right, but whether he himself is caught—ah, that's another matter. Close fish, is George Chapman."

"And he never cared in that sort of way for Bena?"

"Not as far as I know, or ever heard suggested. Pitiful." Then the superintendent shook sentiment from him as a dog does water. "Now, where exactly were you when you were hit?"

"Immediately, I stepped into the room. Some one leaped at me from behind the half-open door and felled me like an ox."

"You had your torch on. You don't think it was a woman who struck at you with that cudgel?"

"Lord, no!" I almost laughed. "That was Samson's blow, not Delilah's, Superintendent. I went down as though I had been kicked by a field full of mules."

We examined the carpet carefully.

"Here's a lump of garden mold." I pounced on it. "And here's another." I picked up a second crumb. "Whoever hit me came in here over those beds outside."

"That means he didn't slip in through these windows," Gibbs said to that; "there's only the gravel path outside here, but came through the next room. Mr. Hillock's own room. . . . And he often stamps across those beds. I've seen him go and come that way many a time. So as to save a corner. He doesn't lock his door." We were talking in the lowest of tones, and now crept out into the hall, and Gibbs delicately turned the knob of a door some distance away. He opened it and waved a hand to where a steady sound like the sawing of wood told of, apparently, undisturbed slumbers.

And undisturbable. I remembered the thick speech of the farmer last night.

"Yet supposing he had wanted to strike such a blow, it was exactly such a blow as he would be expected to

strike," I said, as we closed the door again and returned
to the other room.

"Verbena at the desk . . . she wouldn't need a light.
Any one else would have had to have one. Doubleday was
patrolling, and these curtains are a trifle thin. The light
in here might have showed through. . . ." Gibbs was
talking half to himself.

I nodded. "Quite so. Daughter at the desk and father,
behind the door. Not probable, but possible."

"Well, at any rate, it's certain, not merely probable
nor barely possible, that if so, that haughty piece Lily
Hillock was in the center of things, though she's much too
cautious to come here herself."

"You don't like her?"

"I don't want to like her," I he replied candidly. "She's
the kind you're apt to like too much, if, at all.
Fortunately, she's above any policeman. Her idea is a
chap who'll take up politics later on, Labor Party of
course, and stand for some Socialist borough. However—"
He was looking the floor over as I was, inch by inch, I
don't know whether he or I first noticed that it had been
swept. We had had dinner in here as usual, and, as usual,
Arthur had dropped something while waiting on us; it
was a boiled potato, I remembered now. Not a crumb was
to be seen. And, moreover, I could have sworn that the
stained-oak floor had not been nearly as polished last
night as it now showed itself. I was certain that there was
a new dent in it, too, very close to where I had fallen.

We finally agreed that there was nothing more to be
seen in the room and made in silence for my own part of
the house. When we were there Gibbs ran a hand over his
neat parting. "That desk wasn't forced, yet I met Mr.
Richardson last night with a first-class chisel up his
sleeve making for that same dining-room."

"What?" I stopped pouring out a siphon and wheeled.
"What?"

"Just so, Mr. Maltass. But first, as to how I didn't
hear your fall nor know anything about the attack on you

in the library. Doubleday, the constable outside, wasn't asleep. He had caught sight of a man, doubled in half, creeping along a hedge and hailed him. The man took to his heels. Doubleday couldn't follow, because he had been told to keep the farmhouse in sight. But in the course of his rounds, half an hour later, he saw the same figure, slipping through a hedge, on the other side of the farm this time. Doubleday had the sense not to make a sound, but to obliterate himself in the shadows. The man came on at a swift run, clambered lightly over the orchard gate, and then—well, Doubleday waited, but no one reappeared. After a while he threw some gravel up at Mr. Walsh's windows where I was working, and I joined him outside. We investigated the orchard. But to search even a small orchard at night with a couple of electric torches is most difficult. Still, I don't think the man was on the premises. And the only way he could have got away, would be up that little steep footpath and in by Mr. Smallwood's window.

"Speaking of Mr. Smallwood's wet shoes," Gibbs said, as no light or leading came from me. "There are only two places where he could have got them in that time. Unless he stood in his bath, of course. One's the duck pond, only a few yards away from where Doubleday first saw the crouching figure."

"And the other?"

"On your way to Latimer's Oak you have to pass over a little brook. In the dark it's very easy to step into the water."

I reflected. "Could it be reached in the time?" It could, the superintendent thought, by any one in a hurry.

"You think Smallwood may have some idea of his own, and want to see the place?"

"Well, no, that's not what I thought," Gibbs said frankly. "My idea was rather that some one—not necessarily Mr. Smallwood—I'm with you there, but some one had left something behind on the scene of the crime, and that Mr. Smallwood was trying to retrieve it."

"Perhaps he did," I suggested.

"You don't know Bones. Bones is my Airedale left on guard. No one put a foot or a hand over the circle of cord I left him to guard, and I roped in a nice large amount. That's why I say Mr. Smallwood might have got as far as the cord—and Bones—and yet be back in the time. He wouldn't stay long with Bones there!"

I felt quite incapable of making any sensible comment on what I had heard so I said feebly instead:

"And Richardson and his chisel?" Here I felt on firmer ground, for in my sober, quite unbiased judgment, Richardson alone of all those in the farm, was capable of a crime. I would not go so far as to say that I had hitherto thought him capable of murder. But if one had been committed—

"Richardson . . ." Gibbs grinned a little. "Well, it was like this: coming back after my fruitless search of the orchard with Doubleday, I heard some one slipping cautiously down the main stairs here. I waited in the dark at the foot, with outstretched arms, and folded Mr. Richardson a moment later to my heart. As my arms closed around him, I felt the steel in his sleeve. It was a chisel."

"And he was making for the dining-room?" I asked.

"He was making in that direction. His story was that he wanted to open a case of wine, which he had had sent along from the rectory, and had gone to the kitchen for a screw-driver. Couldn't find one and took a chisel as next best. He was now on his way to replace it, so he said."

"Had he opened the case?" I asked. "I know one came for him a couple of days ago." I was determined to be fair.

"The case was open all right, but had not been opened with a chisel."

"Did the chisel you found on him belong to the house?"

"I can't be sure till morning. I went down with him and he showed me where he had taken it from."

"He seems to be a very tidy young gent. Put the box of tools back and shut the cupboard door most carefully. Extremely so."

"You mean? Remember I wasn't there and didn't see it."

"I mean, Mr. Maltass, that Mr. Richardson had left things in the kitchen so that if any one went in there, they'd never think he had been to the tool box. He said he had slipped the chisel up his sleeve so as to have both hands free, as he had no light, and didn't want to wake any one up. The lights go on on the stairs with a tremendous click."

"What did you do?"

"Let him think I believed him, of course. Saw him to his own room after putting the chisel back again." Gibbs grinned reminiscently. "Talk of a dog with its tail between its legs! But, of course, I didn't know then about that desk with a thousand pounds in it, waiting to be collected. Hillock has not a safe that I did know. Funny." And he looked to me to say the magic sentence that would clear these events up. I began to wish I had never written a word about Michael Hare and his silly triumphs. The village idiot could have solved his problems, I felt viciously. Whereas this: "And now, Mr. Maltass, what does Michael Hare think of it all?"

What he thought was that Superintendent Gibbs was asking a fool's question. I only looked very wise, or at least as wise as possible, and said portentously:

"Not yet, Superintendent, wait until I've looked the place over." And with that I made for bed, while Gibbs again stole away to try to catch more of the household stealing about with burglar's tools up their sleeves.

CHAPTER SIX

THE beauty of the morn got little notice from us, I'm afraid, next day, as Gibbs and I made off at dawn. At Latimer's Oak, a delighted Airedale leaped at his master. Bones—a delicate allusion to his shape—did not bark, but he was almost as noisy with his tail. The superintendent had a couple of men with him, and they began to detach the rope that marked the place where the body had been found from the circle of cleft sticks into which it had been dropped, and which Bones had been told to guard. In winter, Bones, on such occasions, was accommodated with a portable wooden kennel inside which, in bitter weather, hung a tiny stove of the miner's lamp variety, brother to the one that kept the police car's radiator from freezing.

Together with the police I studied the ground. We had drawn galoshes over our shoes, one of Michael Hare's invariable precautions which the superintendent told me he had at once adopted. I had quite forgotten all about it. As I studied the ground now I became ever more uncomfortably aware of the concentrated police gaze riveted on me, and on my every action. It was quite a horrid position.

In my last play but one, the wretched Hare had deduced heaven-only-knew-what from a patch of grass where a dog had lain. By an effort of will I banished him from my mind and, adjusting my glasses, bent down, determined to see all that there was to see.

Fortunately, without working what Rouletabille called "the little gray cells," it was quite clear that this man had been dragged the few feet from the oak to the ditch where the bracken grew thick and high. The ground told the same tale as the boots had done. And the ditch repeated again the story. But as to anything fresh—! We hunted for a possible weapon. Bones helped us with an enthusiasm that produced seven separate old boots, quite a pile of bottles, and two broken umbrellas, but he also first found the blood-stains and sniffed them over so continuously as to attract his master's attention. But for a few dark spots on the thick moss nothing in the place suggested a tragedy. Nothing on this side of the tree even looked like a struggle, yet apparently here was where Walsh had been killed.

"Why, here's a tin box!" came from the constable who was on the other side of the gray old bole. Joining him we found him holding a lid in one hand that bore a label of a well-known biscuit-maker, while he stared down at the tin it fitted, which had been buried in the earth at his feet, the top a bare two inches below the ground. It had been freshly put into a hole neatly prepared with a trowel. The curious thing was, that no attempt seemed to have been made to cover up the lid, yet there was a piece of sod which had been neatly cut to mask the hole, and from the marks on the lid, the sod had evidently been over it at least once, yet the total absence of rust showed that the box had only very recently been put in its place. Was the fact that the lid lay bare due to the haste of a murderer?

Again I heard the slight crackle of bank notes. Saw the hooded figure doing so neatly and accurately in the dark that for which most of us need eyes. That largish envelope which we had found empty—had it lain here? Michael Hare, I thought resentfully, would have found it with a small piece torn from one corner. The corner would have been caught in the lid. The link would be clear. But I had no such help. I decided afresh that in my next play, Hare should have something really stiff to get his teeth into. Something like this puzzle at Upfold Farm. . . .

"Lovers' post box?" the superintendent asked finally.

"Why covered with a sod?" I asked. "Dirty thing to handle, especially in wet weather. There are plenty of hollow trees around. That sod top looks as though the box was only intended for one especial occasion." Suddenly I felt a glow.

The three eyed me as Bones would have done a biscuit.

"One of Mr. Walsh's finger-nails was black. We took it for paint. What if it proves to be earth—earth he got when removing this sod, or trying to replace it?"

"Was he leaving or taking something?" wondered the superintendent.

The question was a facer. And then I remembered Scullion's statement about being in possession of the clue that would lead him home, while we others scuffled around vainly trying for foot- or hand-hold. Was it a love affair, and had Walsh gone here to fetch or post a letter from or to a lady as Gibbs had wondered? Now, elastic though the dead man's affections were, he had really been, for the time, deeply occupied with Lily Hillock. Thinking back hurriedly, 'I felt sure that he had not been away from the farm for any unaccounted hours, long enough that is, for him to have a second affair running at the same time. Nor would a love affair account for Scullion's words and air of triumphant certainty. But what about another reason for that buried box? What about blackmail? A summons to Latimer's Oak to pay for some past folly, that box having been hidden there to serve as the bank? And the thousand pounds in that envelope fitted here. It looked as though Walsh had shown some unexpected flash of sense, and had dropped the sum which he had got ready for the blackmailer back into security before leaving the farm. This idea fitted the look I had seen on his face, the look of apprehension.

The murderer, finding perhaps a valueless envelope where he had expected a nice sum, had, in a fit of fury, killed the man who doubtless threatened him with exposure. Walsh had all a weak character's skill in vituperation. All went together with the known facts. And the idea went with Scullion's words. Supposing that Walsh had given him definitely to understand that he was being blackmailed. Yes, if Scullion knew that much, and knew who the blackmailer was, or at least for which affair it was that Walsh was now being asked to pay, that would explain his air of being on to the winner that had struck we so unpleasantly last night. And it might explain Bena's look, supposing Walsh to have confided in her too.

I now imparted my idea in pontifical tones. The only pity was that Gibbs claimed to have thought of it too. But we all agreed on it as the most likely solution of the box, Walsh's presence under the oak, his murder, and the finding of the notes in the bureau.

"And," I went on, "it might account for the fact that no effort was really made to hide the body. For any length of time. As by burial. That bracken could only be an affair of days at most. No effort was made to account for Walsh's absence from the farm. Even apart from the finding of those notes in the bureau, I should say that the murderer didn't get what he wanted, and struck in fury. I don't think this was a premeditated murder, in other words."

We were talking while hunting for the weapon. Nothing but the fact that, using the rope which had, made the circle last night as an ever-lengthening radius, we all four worked quarter by quarter found it at all. It was the last cast we were making. On its very edge the same constable who had first seen the tin lid lying as he thought on the ground, came on something which he at first looked at in perplexity, and then came brandishing towards us with a splutter of, "Look at this, sir! Here it is! This is what done it. That's where. I found it. Never thought what it could be for a moment."

What he held were two kitchen weights fastened together by a short length of stout cord.

We looked at the affair in silence for a moment. One was a pound, the other a hall-pound weight. There was blood and hairs on the bottom edge of one. The other had been buried in mud or soft earth and showed no such marks. But the hairs were of the same fawny-brown as those on Walsh's head. His hair, stains of his blood, without reasonable doubt.

"That's clothes line, that is!" said the second constable suddenly. "Leastways it's just the same as my wife uses, which is what every other woman hereabouts uses." He was the only married man amongst us, and as such was listened to with respect.

Kitchen weights—clothes line supposing it to be one. . . . Suddenly I stiffened. A conversation, a description recently heard.

Edward Abbott, Richardson and I had dined with the rector last week, and Richardson had talked of his brother who was llama ranching in Peru. This brother had just been home, and had brought with him some of the balls used in Paraguay by the Indians to kill or snare animals or enemies of all kinds. One stone at the end of a rope, or two stones fastened together by rope, one of which is held in the hand while the other end is twirled around the head until it is let fly as a sort of lasso, killing, strangling or breaking a hind leg, as wished. The length of rope can be anything up to eight feet, so Richardson had quoted his brother as having said. The rector had gone to his shelves, to come back with a volume of Darwin's Voyage of Discovery, and read us, from its pages, an account of the native Bolas. The next day, at dinner at the farm, I had referred to the talk, Richardson had again repeated what his brother had told us, again we had discussed the idea. Some one, Walsh himself, I thought, had suggested that it would make a capital weapon with a short length of rope. I decided to tell Gibbs of this double talk later. We were going on to the rectory in any case. The relationship between Walsh and the Abbotts, though slight, made this necessary.

The woods yielded no further discoveries of any kind, and we parted. I to return to the farm where Doubleday would be shortly relieved, and Gibbs to go to his station for breakfast and a glance at the necessary affairs of the day.

I usually breakfast in my own room. To my surprise, Lily knocked almost as soon as it was served. She looked plainer than ever this morning, sallower probably, and tired. But her green eyes had not lost their brightness.

"Oh, what has happened to your head?" was her first shocked exclamation.

I told her the same lie as I had told Smallwood and Scullion. She seemed quite surprisingly sympathetic, for Lily Hillock, who had always struck me as rather a hard damsel. She insisted on undoing the bandage, and seeing for herself what damage had been done, and cut me a fresh plaster with quite a pretty air of fuss, asking innumerable questions as to where and when I had fallen.

I told her that I would rather not talk about the matter. She gave me a very straight look, but after a second, began to discuss Walsh's murder. What did I really think? What did the police really think? How much more savage tramps were getting nowadays than they used to be. . .

In short, I thought Miss Lily had come a fishing. Well, it's a poor stretch that doesn't have room for more than one rod. I spoke on an impulse.

"Are you quite sure you don't know anything more, anything that might help us to find Walsh's murderer, Lily? You and he were on good terms, he must have spoken of many things to you."

"He never told me anything that would be of use to you," she said at once, and very firmly. "But according to his own stories, he always left out names. Of course, he had had no end of love affairs—some with married women. . . . I think the police ought to go through his desk." She leaned eagerly forward, her green eyes shining. "I'm sure they would find something among his papers that would help." She sounded very urgent, very sincere. Yet if it had been Bena at the bureau last night, then surely Lily must know something more.

"Lily," I said urgently. She had asked me early in our acquaintance to call her by her first name. "What about the brass box? I think there's more to it than we yet know."

This time she laid a hand on my arm.

"There's nothing to that box," she assured me. "Nothing whatever. It could have no more to do with Mr. Walsh's murder than the table on which it stood, or the bath tub. It's ridiculous to suppose that Mr. Walsh ever gave it a second look."

There was nothing for me but to leave it at that. I did not believe her, but I could hardly say so outright.

I tried her on another subject.

'When I came on you both yesterday afternoon, Walsh was saying something to you about 'not a farthing.' That seems rather an odd remark for him to have made." I looked at her inquiringly.

"He was always talking about doing me a really good turn"—she spoke contemptuously now—"and I had had an offer, weeks ago, of a nice little florist's shop—quite cheap too. Really cheap. Mr. Walsh had talked a lot about getting it for me, and I quite thought the loan was as good as settled, but day before yesterday he refused to discuss it at all, and was most frightfully rude about it. And as to yesterday" —her face flushed darkly—"you heard yourself how he spoke to me." She bit her lips hard. Something in her eyes made me think of a cat about to spring. Lily Hillock could be a dangerous woman, as most people of marked character can be. Gibbs sent up word that he was ready now to go on to the vicarage.

As we drove through the village he gave me a meaning look.

"Those weights came from the farmhouse kitchen, sir, and were missed yesterday morning. The clothes line there has had an end cut off quite recently. It's only used on a Monday, so Esther can't say for certain when it was cut, except that it was not done a week ago."

I felt relieved and said so.

"No one living at the farm would have used the weights, they would know it would be found out too easily."

Gibbs did not agree with me.

"Whoever threw it away may well have thought it would never be found," he argued.

"He didn't need to've thrown it away near the spot at all," I insisted. "Five minutes' walk would have made all the difference. Whoever threw it into those bushes hoped it would lie concealed, but didn't really care. It's not a vital point. In other words, it can't lead us to the criminal."

Gibbs still shook his head.

"Whoever threw it away may have done so under some panic—heard a footstep—saw some one coming, and hoped to retrieve it later. Perhaps tried to retrieve it later." He looked at me again with that kind of a look that is as clear as words.

"You mean Smallwood?" I laughed. "Not on your, life, Gibbs! Whatever he went for last night, it wasn't to get back the instrument with which he had murdered Walsh, or any other man."

"You think you can be sure of that?" Gibbs clearly was not impressed. "Murderers are just ordinary people, Mr. Maltass."

"Not a bit," I maintained. "There never was a murderer yet whom every one didn't dislike. They're people without any real friends."

"Well, sir, in your play, that rich young fellow, I forget his name for the moment, Marsh, that was it, Julian Pedigree Marsh, he was the murderer and every one liked him, you remember."' Gibbs evidently.

I thought he had me here. And I considered it a very unfair blow.

"Of course, in plays and books you have to twist and hide. They're but cross-word puzzles, you know. Unless you write the blood curdlers, the easiest staff in the world to write, where you put yourself into the criminal, and just write plain crime psychology. But in detective writing, you must give just that one twist to nature. Hide the fact that your murderer isn't made of ordinary stuff, isn't like the usual run of men and women, but has something inside himself, in his soul, I suppose, or his lack of it, that puts a barrier, unseen but by no means unfelt, between himself and all other people. Now there's one man—"

I stopped myself.

We were driving up to the rectory. "Look here," I asked, "would any suspicious circumstances make you suspect the rector?"

"Well," Gibbs temporized, "that's different. There's his life-time spent amongst us here. We have all tried him and never found him wanting. He's different. If he ever went in for crime, we should all know that he had' lost his mind. That he wasn't himself. That's different. Besides, blackmail alters things, Mr. Maltass. I think this was a murder in desperation, perhaps. Some one meant only to threaten, and found they had to go further than they meant. Anyway, those weights bring the thing home to the farm in my opinion, and to nowhere else."

I hardly listened. Smallwood, and those bloodstained weights! It was utterly impossible. It was preposterous to try to find a link between the music-lover and this ugly crime. He had never exchanged a dozen words with Walsh, I could swear. Nor could I associate him with blackmail. As I had said to Gibbs, the very fact that the farmhouse weights were used meant, to me, that the user—the murderer—was not an inmate of the farm household.

Yet Smallwood had been out last night, and had refused to acknowledge the fact . . . what chivalrous or unselfish motive had taken him out by his window and back by his window? We were drawing up at the rectory.

News travels quickly in the country by bread post and milk post, as well as postman post. The maid who opened the door knew what had happened to Mr. Walsh. For:

"Why, it's Mr. Maltass! My goodness!" she murmured aghast, staring at me in horror.

"Why not?" I said easily. "We want a word with the rector, Doris, if he can spare us a moment." She looked both relieved and disappointed. "Is Miss Laura up yet?" I went on.

"She's gone to town. Went late yesterday afternoon. Master Johnnie nearly cut his foot off at school with a scythe he got hold of. Just like Master Johnnie, isn't it? He's in the school hospital. The master can't go. But Miss Laura hurried off. But is it true that one of the gentlemen up at the farm has been murdered?" She was showing us into a room and drawing up the blinds.

"Which one?" Gibbs asked.

"Lawks, has more than one been killed?" Her eyes popped. "Mr. Walsh was the only one I was told of."

"Mr. Walsh is the only one I was told of, too," Gibbs assured her, with a faint grin. "But weren't you told who did it? Come now, Doris, surely you were told that, too."

"No, sir." She took him quite literally. "All we know is that it was one of the other gentlemen as done it."

"Too bad. No help from you evidently. Now hurry, and give the rector our message."

Doris, half-indignant, half-amused, hurried away.

Mr. Abbott came in at once. He was one of those men still to be found, though in diminishing numbers, among our country clergy. Of good family, fair means and solid scholarship, he loved his rectory, and loved the life with its opportunities and duties. He was all sympathy as to my "accident on the stairs" last night, and then said:

"You've come to tell me that Herbert Walsh is dead. I was told by Doris that he was murdered." He smiled faintly, the smile of a man who knows how to take what he heard with plenty of salt. "But what brings you, Superintendent, along?"

"He was murdered, sir," Gibbs said at once.

The rector's mouth, opened for an invitation to us to be seated, remained open for a full second.

"That sounds quite incredible," he said finally, in the shocked tone of a man far removed from crime.

Gibbs went on to tell him of the place where the body had been found. No one until the inquest was to know by what weapon we were now certain that the murder had been done.

"As to Mr. Walsh himself, Mr. Abbott, could you tell us all you know about him, his people, his home?"

The rector could tell us little. And that little he had only learned from the dead man.

Herbert Walsh was the son of an architect in a London firm that had been moderately well known in its day. He was an only child, and was apprenticed as draughtsman to the same office, becoming head draughtsman in due course. Three years ago nearly, a very distant connection of Walsh's, and a still more distant one of Mr. Abbott's, had died in Ceylon. He was a Mr. Carlisle, a tea planter, and had left his fortune, about a quarter of a million, to his next-of-kin for life. Then on to whoever should be the nearest surviving relation, also for life, with remainder to the then nearest surviving kin. If the last of the connections should have any family, the fortune was to be divided equally among them and become theirs to dispose of. There were, of course, provisions in case no relative survived or if the last had no children. But Mr. Carlisle was proved to have three distant connections living. They were in order of consanguinity, Herbert Walsh, Ann Smythe and Mr. Abbott. The rector's two children would probably therefore in due time divide the fortune of the tea planter between them. Before this will and the subsequent inquiries, Mr. Abbott had never heard of the Walsh's. Miss Smythe he knew of as a woman of his own age who lived a very useful philanthropic life in a charming house near Vevey. "She's a very hale and hearty woman, I hear," the rector went on; "uncommonly brisk and young for her years. So there is every reason to think she will enjoy the Carlisle fortune for a long time, and also every reason to think that she will make the best possible use of it."

In vain Gibbs tried to get any light on Walsh's past life, or circle of friends. True, the rector added that Walsh had told him that the money came as a perfect godsend, letting him devote himself entirely to what he loved— that was painting. And, the rector added, what we all knew, that he had heard from very competent authorities that in Herbert Walsh the world of English art was going to see a great power, and a founder of quite a new school of painting.

"Mr. Abbott," Gibbs asked in a tone of despair, "is there nothing shady known to you, or told to you, about Mr. Walsh that you could pass on to us?"

The rector shook his head. "Nothing more than the tittle-tattle of our neighborhood. He struck me as a weak character, but kind-hearted. Physically and morally a coward perhaps, but without any real intention of wronging any one. I spoke to him—well, about some gossip in the village, and he assured me, swore on his word of honor, that there was no foundation for it, that it was only the artist who was infatuated. Or, let us say, chiefly the artist. One thing I do know"—Mr. Abbott spoke vigorously—"that Lily Hillock, between ourselves, under these circumstances it is as well to be explicit, Lily Hillock, I say, was in no danger whatever. She can, and will, always go exactly the path which she has chosen for herself. No man could lead that young woman astray. I wouldn't be so certain of the other way round," he wound up, with unconscious humor.

We talked backwards and forwards, but there seemed nothing to be learned here.

"You yourself, Mr. Abbott, excuse my putting the question to you, but I must, of course: where were you yesterday afternoon from half-past five to around seven?"

"I went to see old Mrs. Bainbridge," the rector said, thinking back. "Yes, that was when I caught sight of Walsh just ahead of me."

"Indeed, sir!" Gibbs was all alertness.

"Yes," the rector went on as though reflecting aloud. "I was taking the short-cut across Thatch End, and through the spinney, and I caught sight of Walsh walking very fast along a path that branches off at right angles from mine."

"Was he carrying anything?" Gibbs promptly asked.

Mr. Abbott was not at all sure, but thought Walsh had his usual painting outfit with him.

"And when was this?"

The rector and Gibbs together made some calculations as to distances and pace, and finally agreed that, given the time when the rector had left the rectory, and Mr. Abbott had noticed the hour as he was rather late, it must have been about five, or ten minutes before five, when he had seen Walsh. This robbed the incident of much of its interest, except that the path Walsh was on was one that would lead him to Latimer's Oak, supposing he had continued along it.

"You didn't hear anything unusual?" I asked, merely by way of putting in an oar however feebly. Like many another chance shot it went home.

Yes, now it was recalled to him, Mr. Abbott had heard something, but it had only sounded like an empty tin can knocking against stones. He gave a half-apologetic smile for mentioning such a trifle, and explained that he would not have referred to it at all, had I not asked him and had the sound not come from a part of the spinney where stood the oak under which his kinsman had met his terrible death.

"An empty can striking against stones?" Gibbs repeated.

The rector said again that it was a ridiculous trifle to mention. Pressed by us to enlarge on the sound, he said that it was not as though some one were walking along with an empty tin dangling and striking it occasionally, but more the sort of sound a dog makes when it roots about in a garbage tin. The homely simile he used was exactly the noise that the constable had made, when getting the lid off the box in the ground. The roots of the tree were hard and firm. And there were plenty of stones in the earth around.

"When had Mr. Abbott heard the sound?" was naturally the next question.

Shortly after he had met Walsh. Had he heard the sound of any implement like a spade? Could what he had heard have been the sound of some one digging a hole in stony ground?

The rector was quite certain that it could not, and repeated that to have caused it, some one must have been jiggling a tin around on the ground.

Had it gone on for a long time? Apparently it had gone on just long enough for it to have been, as Gibbs and I thought, the sound of Walsh wrestling with, and finally lifting off, the tin lid from the box.

Gibbs continued to ask questions. My mind drifted away. This bore out my idea of blackmail. But what had caused Walsh to hurry back to the farm? The rector had seen him and apparently heard him before five. I had seen him leaving his room at half-past.

Suddenly something struck me, which would have struck the wretched Hare long ago, that was that the path along which I had seen Walsh hurrying back to the farm was not the one I should have expected him to take. It neither led directly to the nearest door to his rooms nor, now that I knew he had been in the spinney, and supposing him to have come from there, was it the nearest path from the spinney. It had such deep holly hedges on both sides, that it was a most uncomfortably cold and draughty way except on hot days in summer. Only the fact that I had been on a stile and on rising ground had let me see him. I felt my hair stir as I reflected that from the house or from the neighboring road and fields he would have been quite invisible. That hurrying figure along that dark path with death so close on him seemed rather horrible just now. What had he hurried home for? A weapon? None had been found on him. And I, thinking back, now recalled distinctly his usual painting rig out under his arm, and strapped across one shoulder.

I had an idea. I saw Walsh scuttling along to the oak in answer to some early message from the blackmailer, leaving the sum demanded, and then having a spasm of sense and rushing home with the packet of notes, putting it in safety in his desk, only to find when he saw that brass box outside his door that in some way this would not avail. He *had* to come out. Again. Directly or indirectly I felt sure that the box meant that. I saw again that very deeply disturbed, apprehensive look on his face. But he was still wearing his hat and overcoat. He evidently had been going out again in any case. To a friend? And where had he taken the brass box that no one had found it? The answer to the last question was all but inevitable. Walsh had taken the brass box with him to the oak, and the murderer had taken it from him, before or after death. Did he think it contained the thousand pounds which were not there? Or was I right in my idea that Bena had been making restitution, and had the murderer duly obtained the money in that box, and had the blind girl in some way regained possession of it, and restored the money to its owner, or at least put it where it belonged, since the owner lay dead.

Well, we knew a little more than we knew before. Walsh had been twice to that tree yesterday afternoon. If Lily Hillock was speaking the truth she had seen him standing there just an hour after I had seen him leaving his rooms. Gibbs, I knew, would leave no stone unturned to find where he had spent that hour. But was Lily telling the truth? For some reason I could not state even to myself I doubted this. But even to myself I knew that I had no right to assume it. Lily was no more given to lies than are most women. Men, of course, learn as boys at school that lies do not pay, quite apart from the contempt with which they are met. Women, unfortunately, find even as girls that few things pay better than an adroit lie. When truth is concerned the two sexes are not on an equality.

The rector's words caught my ear again. "Miss Smythe must be told of the murder at once, of course. But I hope you will see your way, Superintendent, to allow my son to be the one to go over to Vevey and break the news to her. I would like him to start at once."

Gibbs said that, speaking provisionally, he thought this might be managed. The solicitors were coming down to the farm today, and, after a talk with them, some such arrangement as the rector suggested might be made. And on that we rose to take our leave.

"By the way, Mr. Abbott," Gibbs said, as the rector shook hands, "I'm looking for a shilling with a deep gash across the face. You must occasionally get coins of that kind in the collection bag—" Gibbs had a similar inquiry, though wrapped in appropriate coverings, for every shop in Much Widham, and intended to use them all today. But here, at his first inquiry, he had one of those pieces of luck of which young detectives dream.

The rector interrupted, with: "A shilling almost cut in two, with such a slash as you describe, was put into the offertory bag only last week. I doubted if it was legal tender, and my son took it off our hands. You'll have to apply to him, but I'm afraid I can't even guess from whom it came."

We passed on out, and neither Gibbs nor I spoke for a full minute after the car started. Then he said:

"Nothing easier than to pass a shilling on when asked for change. Some one at the farm evidently got hold of it in that way. Nothing in the world would ever surprise me again if I found that young Mr. Abbott had had any hand in blackmail, let alone murder."

"But would you say the same of his friend?" I asked. "Quite apart from the chisel episode of last night, would you?"

Gibbs shook his head.

"How could I? I've never seen Mr. Richardson before. The two young gentlemen share rooms in Kensington together, I understand. That means little. Offhand, of, course, knowing he had been staying at the rectory, I passed him over among my 'most likely' lists, but as you say since last night he is in a class with Mr. Smallwood and with; possibly, Verbena Hillock."

CHAPTER SEVEN

BACK at the farm, we opened the front door very quietly, and let ourselves into the square hall. Lily was reading the morning paper, and behind her like a bronze figure, stood her father, staring at her with a lowering, forbidding stare, of which she was, or seemed unconscious.

He came forward exclaiming at my head, Lily shot me one of her green looks and then turned a page of the paper.

"It's strictly confidential," she said from its depths.

"What d'ye mean?" asked Hillock, none too pleasantly.

"Not to be inquired into," she murmured sweetly, and I began to talk about the weather.

Gibbs had gone off meanwhile to the kitchen to ask if a chisel that he had "found" belonged here. It did. Esther told him that the "two young gents, from the rectory" had borrowed a screw driver only a couple of days back, to open a case sent on for Mr. Richardson, and must have taken the chisel as well. They had put the screw-driver back all right. How could they know where it belonged? Gibbs asked. Esther explained that, as she had been busy at the time, she had merely indicated with a nod of her head where the tool-box was kept.

The superintendent slipped away to start an unobtrusive search from room to room for chisel marks. Hillock was discreetly asked about hiding places, locked cupboards and that sort of thing. The farmer professed to know of none. Nor could he lend the superintendent any key that would open the bureau used by Mr. Walsh in the dining-room. If the superintendent had left the dead man's keys by accident behind him at the station, Hillock could only suggest telephone message and a constable courier. Again Lily stared hard at Gibbs with her green eyes when put this last question, but she said nothing throughout.

I went on up to see Scullion and test my theory of blackmail, the oak as the meeting place, the tin as the receptacle, and a thousand pounds as the sum involved.

The door leading into the studio from my passage was shut as usual. I heard the voice of McKirdy inside. Very low. Very quiet. As I put my hand on the door Scullion flung it open and stood there a moment silently eyeing me. I did not wonder that McKirdy was pale. Scullion looked a man it were best to avoid in that moment. Then his face cleared and he threw the door wide open.

"Come in, Maltass. Just as well. Come in and close the door, will you? No need for all the house to hear."

No closing of the door would ever prevent him that had ears to hear, hearing all that Scullion had to say.

"McKirdy is accusing me of the murder of Walsh," Scullion went on at the top of his voice, sinking into an arm-chair, and flinging his great legs over the arm. "Now then, McKirdy—repeat!"

McKirdy bit his narrow lips. He looked to me like a cornered rat, as he stood there, half-shrinking, half-bold.

"I didn't say any such thing!" he said nervously. "I—I spoke to you in strict confidence, Mr. Scullion. I only asked you—what I asked you—in strict confidence."

"Blackmail in strict confidence," roared Scullion. "Ask me again before a witness what you asked me just now—in confidence."

"You have no right to accuse me of blackmail." McKirdy's voice was pained and low. "I asked you what you were doing going along the path that leads to Latimer's Oak yesterday afternoon, and why you said nothing about having done so. That was all." McKirdy was almost whining.

"And damned insolence, too," bellowed Scullion, "I know what that means. We all know what that means."

"It means only what it seems to," protested McKirdy meekly. "You are doing me a great injustice, Mr. Scullion.

I'm very conscious of all that I owe you; but I felt it my duty to—"

"What time was this?" I asked.

"Answer!" roared Scullion.

McKirdy made for the door. "You're taking this the wrong way," he bleated again. "I couldn't endure silence any longer, Mr. Scullion. I had to tell you that I had seen you slipping through the woods towards the oak. I had to speak to you about it. I had to! Because you said you were in the village at that time. When you weren't."

"What time was it?" I repeated.

"About five."

"And Walsh left here alive and well at half-past five. I was here alive and well at half-past five, dancing on that damned wench's piece of soap, or rather on your piece of soap, Maltass. Why the devil should I bother to say where I was before that time?"

The last was no question, it was a contemptuous snap at the flinching McKirdy.

"And where were you yourself, McKirdy, when you saw Scullion?" I asked. McKirdy looked frightened.

"Oh, just crossing the fields that lead to Harrow-under-Birch."

"Were you really walking along then in that particular. woods, Scullion?" I asked.

Scullion nodded. "Why not? You can go!" he threw over his shoulder at McKirdy, his great legs waving in the air preparatory to his feet settling down on the carpet, till he looked like a cuttlefish, for the chair was deep and the springs half broken "Get out!" he repeated finally, rising. "Clear out. Bag and baggage."

"I expected this." McKirdy's voice was that of an early martyr.

"You didn't! You expected a fat sum of money, for God knows what reason," roared Scullion. "But out you go! If you're still in the house within the hour"—he strode towards the other who skipped nimbly back—"I'll break every bone in your carcass. But there wouldn't be any to break. Nothing but gristle." He opened the door and seemed to slam McKirdy out with it. Then he turned to me combing his beard savagely. "There's no fight in the slimy slug." He stood glaring resentfully at the door through which McKirdy had been whirled.

"Still, just as a matter of curiosity, why did you say you were in the village around five? And why did you go along into that particular spinney, or wood, as it's called?" I asked.

Scullion looked as though he had a good mind to send me flying after McKirdy, then he threw back his head, and gave one of his great roars.

"I'll have to come out with it," he bellowed; "my trump card. Where's the superintendent?"

"Certainly hearing every word you're saying," I retorted.

"Well, call him up." He pointed to the bell. I waved my hand at it, too. Scullion has a way of commanding service.

"There's the bell, as you say," I remarked genially.

He gave it a jab that sounded as though the push had stuck fast. Arthur and Esther came at the run. The superintendent brought up the rear with a constable behind him again.

"It's only the superintendent I want," Scullion shouted; "for a confidential word." So saying he waved the others away, drew the willing police officer inside the door and shut it with a bang.

"Not here," Gibbs said at once, with a laugh.

"If it's really confidential, Mr. Scullion, I'd rather listen to you in my car. It's just outside."

"Of course it is," shouted Scullion. "Being a police car. Can I park my car by the day in the main street? Not unless I want a summons. But the police—" However, he flung himself into a garment and followed Gibbs out with the air of one going forth to war "Come along, little Maltass," he called to me, "since you make a point of knowing all that's going on and just where the inquiry has got to."

I took no notice of the wording, and settled myself in a corner. Gibbs would have spoken, but Scullion's voice outgunned his.

"My hand's been forced," the artist was roaring, spreading himself over the back seat as though to dry; "forced by that snivelling—"

I'm not fond of words of the kind that now came, but in this case, I had to admit that there was justification. Finally, he told the superintendent of the interview he had just had with McKirdy.

"And why didn't you say that you were near that particular spot around five?" the superintendent asked stiffly, as I had done.

"Because of wanting to keep something to myself," came the answering bellow.

"Your clue?" I asked, with, I'm afraid, rather a malicious grin.

Scullion nodded, with an angry scowl at my amusement. "Two nights ago, or rather three nights ago tonight, to be precise, Walsh came to my rooms after dinner," he began sulkily. "Around ten, I think it was. Or eleven. He came to show me a letter he had received by the morning's post. Now, let me see"—Scullion ran fingers like bananas through that beard of his which the caricaturists loved so dearly, fingers that could paint the down on a petal—"it ran, as nearly as I can recollect, like this: *'I know all about you and Helen of Troy. And I have proofs of what I know. She didn't destroy your letters for one thing. Unless you put a thousand pounds in notes into an empty biscuit tin that you will find behind a tree called Latimer's Oak, where you have been seen painting lately, I shall communicate what I know to the husband of Helen of Troy. He will flay the skin off your bones and enjoy doing it'.* This was signed, *'A fellow guest on the Meridiana.* Or, *'Your fellow guest on the Meridiana,'* I forget which. Oh, the letter mentioned the hour when the money was to be ready waiting to be collected in the box. It was to be put in at seven o'clock yesterday afternoon.

And there was also the usual sentences that if he communicated with the police, the husband would be told, or if Walsh brought a friend, or didn't play fair, and so on. . . And, I think, there was something to the effect that Walsh couldn't find out who the writer was, no matter how he should try. In fact, the usual jargon. Well, you know Walsh"—Scullion turned to me "he was in a lather of terror. I asked who Helen of Troy was, apart from being mentioned in the Bible. It seems on this voyage on the *Meridiana*, which he took to Morocco and back after an attack of flu, there was a Mrs. Helen Gray. Walsh fell for her. He had just come into his money, so she fell for him. Walsh protested that it was all platonic, but he agreed that the letters they exchanged were pretty hot stuff. As I say, he was in a regular sweat about it all. Gray came down to meet his wife, and seems to've been a huge giant. Mrs. Gray had already told Walsh that he was terribly jealous, and that only a most important business affair had made him let her go alone on this trip. Which was also ordered by her doctor!" Scullion gave one his roars.

"If you believe me, Walsh intended to pay the money! Yes! A thousand pounds. I told him what I thought of him, but you couldn't put any pluck into that poor rabbit. Finally, I thought he seemed ashamed of himself, and promised to do nothing and, if a second letter should come, to let me deal with the matter. I intended to take it, and him, down to the police station, of course. If Gray really did come down, I'd talk to him! It would take an uncommonly enraged husband to horsewhip me!" Scullion blew out his mighty chest. "That was finally agreed on, as I say, and I told him to think no more about the matter. Certainly I thought no more about it. Until yesterday, when Smallwood of all people noticed that McKirdy's painting was so bad. No life in it. That brought it home to me that so was Walsh's. First, I thought it was Lily Hillock leading him the dance she loves so well. Then it occurred to me that yesterday was the very day appointed for that ridiculous payment in the sardine tin at Latimer's Oak. I wondered if by any chance Walsh's knees were wobbling again. I couldn't find him, looked at the clock, was not far off five. The hour set had been seven, but as I didn't run across him in the village, I hurried along to the oak, because he was painting Lily Hillock there. Walsh was there, as it happened, painting a foreground study. He didn't see me, and I hoped he had forgotten the whole affair after all, and crept away without a sound."

A grin appeared and disappeared on the superintendent's face. We both visualized Scullion creeping away without a sound.

"And why didn't you pass this most important information on to us—the police?" Gibbs asked, with no trace of a grin on his face now.

"Why the devil should I have told you?" Scullion roared. "It was confidential, wasn't it! Why shouldn't I catch the criminal just as well as little Maltass, here? If he really is after the criminal. I think it's damned suspicious the way he's shoving himself into the inquiry. What's he doing it for? Walsh had hardly spoken a dozen words to him. Now I suppose I was as near a friend as the poor fish had."

"Have you told us everything—now?" the superintendent asked.

"Think so. No man can be certain he's forgotten nothing. I don't recollect anything else Walsh said to me."

"And that letter—did he keep it?"

Scullion did not know. He himself had handed it back to Walsh, and told him to put it somewhere safe. The letter told him to put it with the thousand pounds in the tin.

The Superintendent's eyes met mine for a fleeting second. Both of us were thinking of the sound that I had heard so clearly last night in the dining-room in that dark corner, the sound of a paper being drawn out of an envelope or wrapping of some kind. And it had come after I had heard the rustle of bank notes.

"Did Mr. Walsh say how he intended getting the money when he first spoke of paying?"

"Always kept a thousand pounds by him. Liked to know he had it day and night in hundred-pound notes. Whenever he broke one he had another sent him by registered post from his bank. I told him that had I only known it I'd have murdered him myself long ago." Scullion gave his great laugh.

"Did any one know he had this money on him or with him?"

"Ah! That's rather the point, isn't it?" Scullion exclaimed. "Well, for what it's worth, I don't mind telling you that when I asked him that, he said only Lily Hillock knew of it. And he believed that in some way she was mixed up with this blackmail business. He thought it was spite on her part. Now all this I had intended keeping to myself, but perhaps it's just as well. It would mean a lot of time to hunt all these things up, and my time's short just now. Yes, Walsh had got it into his head—chiefly because of the sum named, I think—that Lily Hillock was in the affair. Can't say I thought the reason sufficient. But that was why"—Scullion turned to me and puffed his pipe into my face—"that's why Walsh raved as he did about women, when I spoke of Lily Hillock yesterday. I had forgotten all about our chat?"

Gibbs was listening intently. "Do you know where he actually kept the money? Was it on his person usually?"

Scullion said that he fancied Walsh kept it in the bureau down in the dining-room which Hillock let him have. But he only fancied that, because Walsh. Always locked the desk so carefully. The notes might have been on him, Walsh, at the time of his death. "That ought to be easy enough to find out, even for little Maltass," he added. "But, of course, he must have put the packet in that dustbin by the tree yesterday, after all, or why did he go there? Alone too!" Scullion could tell us no more, he said. He did not know who, beside himself, knew of the blackmailing letter, but he hardly thought that Walsh would have only had one confidant.

"What sort of paper was it written on?" Gibbs asked next.

"Ordinary sort of letter paper, from a letter pad of usual size. Cream and rather thick paper. Cut edges. But it had a peculiar water-mark. A circle, with some firm's name in the middle, and a unicorn in the center. Well-drawn unicorn. The writing was over the circle, so that all I could make out was the *d* of *and* followed by *Son*."

"And the writing?"

"Written like printed capitals. No peculiarities at all, as far as I could see. Bar one." Scullion looked very important as he prepared to divulge this too. "The pen, I suppose it was a fountain pen, but I don't know, made a funny full stop. A neat square, regular tiny rectangle instead of the usual dot. I'll tell you another thing. That letter was written in a hurry. Dashed off. How do I know? Any artist could tell you that much."

Neither Gibbs nor I said anything for a moment. The full stop after the Esq. on that envelope now in Gibbs' possession, wasn't it, too, rectangular, in shape? I rather fancied that it was. But having been only one stop, it had escaped my notice. It would not have been missed by Michael Hare, though.

Scullion said that this was all he knew, and unless the superintendent was running off with him, he thought it high time to turn round and let him get to his work again.

"And did he say nothing about the brass box?" I asked.

Scullion looked as though he did not know what box I meant.

"The brass box with the St. Mark's lion on the lid," I prompted.

Scullion looked rather nonplused. "I don't know," he said finally; "I'm bound to say I don't know. He talked a lot of stuff . . . I never half-listened . . . he did often say something about that box. . . ."

"Yes, but did he speak of it in connection with that letter? Didn't the letter itself refer to it?"

Scullion thought not. As to Walsh having spoken of the box in any connection with the payment. Scullion looked a little perplexed. "How could he have? When the letter expressly said the tin box he would find buried in the earth exactly behind Latimer's Oak, the place where he usually pitched his easel. Brass box . . . damned nonsense," Scullion muttered. "How on earth can it have anything to do with this?" But he was none too sure, judging by his tone.

"Nevertheless, it was at it that I saw him staring, that Esther saw him staring, and with an expression that we both noticed. An expression of dread, foreboding, apprehension, call it what one will, that was very closely related to sheer terror."

"Rubbish!" Scullion said rudely. "The look on his face was there because of his going off to that interview, because for some reason he evidently thought Gray was after him. As for the brass box—it merely happened to be on the table."

He spoke with an air of utter certainty. But I knew better. Scullion's back had been turned to Walsh as he opened the door to speak to Esther. She and I had both seen that look, and it was at the little brass box itself, not at anything else that he had been looking. No, mysterious as that lost, suddenly seen, and then lost again, little box was, it could not be merely explained away by denying its significance. What had become of it? Gibbs could not search people's belongings—yet, but it was nowhere to be seen. If in any one's possession at the house it was carefully locked away, or hidden. But everything pointed to the fact that Walsh had himself taken it with him when he set out again. Why? That was the question that all the time haunted me, and haunted the superintendent. I thought Scullion was sincere in his certainty that Walsh had not spoken of it during the talk about blackmail, and I thought him so, too, when he said that in his opinion the box stood for nothing. Then with what other, darker secret was it linked? Who was using that gift of Chapman's to Lily Hillock and in what way to cause Walsh so shortly before he was murdered to stand as though transfixed, without moving, staring down at it with that hint of horror on his face?

I fairly bit my pipe stem and refused to let my thoughts run round and round that center again.

Gibbs was asking Scullion whether any one but himself could have beard Walsh's story of the letter. Scullion thought not.

"You know, or rather little Maltass here does, how Walsh mumbled. Never, opened his mouth properly."

The low speaking voice of Walsh mattered little. As in a telephone conversation, people could probably have guessed what Walsh was saying from Scullion's roared answers, but the artist went on: "He insisted on my talking into his ear."

"Mr. McKirdy's room is next to your bedroom. Could he have heard, do you think?"

"McKirdy? Who cares whether he could or not," came contemptuously, from Scullion. "McKirdy hasn't the guts to steal the baby's rattle, and as to blackmail—" Scullion burst into a great laugh. "McKirdy!" he repeated under his breath, with relish at the absurdity of the notion.

"I told him to make a list of the numbers of the notes on him and send it to his bank," he threw in unexpectedly. "Told him he ought to do it as a precaution in any case since he had had some of the notes over a year."

"Really, Mr. Scullion, you have a way of tossing us important details at the last moment as inconsidered trifles." Gibbs laughed outright. "This makes all the difference."

"Of course it does!" boomed Scullion; "for he told me next morning that he had done so. Put me down at this pub, will you? In any civilized country, really civilized country, drinks would be free to people who really need 'em."

"So now, we know his much prized clue," I said to Gibbs, as we drove, on after watching Scullion's massive form disappear in the doorway of "The Seven Skittles."

"Don't wonder he fancied it," Gibbs agreed. "Very useful bits of information in it, but I think you and I will make better use of them than Mr. Scullion would have. Now can I put you down at the farm, Mr. Maltass? I'm going back there myself at once."

That suited me too.

As we stepped in, Lily Hillock hurried to meet us.

"What has happened to make Mr. McKirdy try to leave the house just now? He was in a fearful rush, and has his easel and suit-case with him. The constable you left below made him wait until you should be back. But he says he must go at once!"

"I think he'd better stay until the inquest tomorrow," Gibbs said easily. "I'll speak to him on the point. Where is he? In here? Thanks." Together we passed into the little room. Gibbs closed the door carefully.

McKirdy was standing by the window, staring out. His narrow face was yellow-white in the light.

"Why did you think it so important that Mr. Scullion shouldn't have told us about having been near that oak yesterday afternoon before the murder was committed?" Gibbs asked at once, in a tone of both human and professional curiosity.

McKirdy looked at him with a cloudy black eye. That kind of eye that tells nothing of the thoughts behind it.

"Now that he himself has spoken to you on the point, that ends the matter." He spoke quietly, but very decidedly. "The only question to discuss between us, Superintendent, is whether I can leave the farm. I confess I had forgotten for the moment that we are all more or less obliged to remain on here."

He had some sketches that must go off at once, and to get them to town in time, he must put them in the train which would pass through Much Widham shortly. The superintendent could not refuse. Even a suspect must earn his living. He looked over McKirdy's sketches, though, under the plea of being interested in art. They were addressed to a well-known magazine. I noticed that Gibbs glanced at the signature and the backs of the sheets more carefully than at the drawings, and had a word with some one in a very low key over the telephone as McKirdy left the house. It did not need Michael Hare's brain to guess that he was speaking to a constable on duty at the station.

As McKirdy hurried off I was standing by the window, and watched his little figure in the big cloak hurry down the walk to the gate. As he bent to open the latch, I suddenly seemed to see a resemblance between his figure and that of last night, supposing him to have pulled some sort of wrap over his head. I had been quite certain up to now that it had been Bena, the blind seeing in the dark, but McKirdy might have known exactly where to find what he wanted.

The next piece of information was that Mr. Hillock was given what virtually amounted to a consecutive alibi from about a quarter-past five to well past ten. His own laborers, passing tradesmen who had seen him and Lily in their car, and his sister's maid put the farmer in a place of safety. Gibbs was unfeignedly glad. So was I. Neither of us liked to think what the failure to substantiate his story might have meant.

Chapman came over to the farm to see the superintendent as the latter was still talking to me. He was a tall, rangy, dark-faced young man with hard eyes and a tightly bitten mouth. Not a face to attract me, though good-looking in its own way. It was a ruthless face. Lily Hillock was of the type to admire that quality, I fancied.

He had been away on business of various kinds connected with his farm since yesterday evening, he explained. We knew as much. Gibbs had been leaving messages for him at half the farmhouses around. As to yesterday afternoon itself, he said that he had spent the time from four on at his own home doing accounts.

"Happy occupation for a farmer just now, eh?" he said bitterly to Gibbs. "They kept me in, those damned books did, from four till half-past six, when I had to see young Edgeware about some silo he's buying from me. We did the deal, had a drink each, and I went on with my books until some time past seven. Then Graylock came in about some calves he wanted me to see and I drove over with him to his farm. He put me up. This morning—" Gibbs listened to the names and addresses with a nod. He knew all this already. The trouble was that we only had Lily's word for it that she had seen Walsh alive and well at half-past six—as alive and as well as he had left the farm at half-past five. If her story were true then Chapman was safe.

Gibbs suddenly looked up at the young man seated facing him. And there was steel in his eyes too.

"Can you explain, Chapman, how it comes that the trousers, coat and waistcoat which you were seen to be wearing early yesterday afternoon, have marks of earth and mud all down them?"

I stared. I had not heard this before.

Chapman looked quite calm.

"My dog, Bliss, got stuck in a rabbit burrow in the afternoon, around three, or a bit later, I think it was I had to help her out. The damned little bitch is always going too far in and getting half-buried."

There was nothing to be said to this. I began to realize a little of the difficulty of proving the truth in a murder case. Michael Hare had been let off far too easily.

CHAPTER EIGHT

IT must have been about an hour later that Superintendent Gibbs showed me a message from the expert on handwriting in whom my brother Laurence had such trust. For once the specialist did not hedge. The printed characters on the envelope which had contained the thousand pounds was in Richardson's writing. Specimens of all people at the farm and in any way connected with the case had been forwarded him. He had no hesitation in saying that any other expert would agree with him.

Richardson! I had had a feeling all along . . . a strong presentiment of his guilt since I had first learned of the crime. Bena knew, it too.

I said something to this effect.

"Deep waters, Mr. Maltass." The superintendent put the paper away in his locked despatch case. We were in his office at the police station. "We've learned already that Mr. Richardson may be in need of money. He has apparently a fair income usually, but every one of his investments that we can trace have passed or halved their dividends this year. Chiefly the former. And he's got entangled with one of the building societies which aren't much more merciful than money-lenders. He's thinking of getting married, is the rumor and has arranged to buy a freehold. He's asked the society to let him put off his next payment, they have refused—altogether he may be financially embarrassed at the moment. Deep waters as I say. . ."

"They seem to run off his back, though," I observed.

The superintendent nodded. "He's of a cheerful disposition, evidently. Besides, the investments are sound in themselves. But for the present he's in a hole. How deep only he himself knows—for the moment."

There was a pause.

"Well, what do you yourself make of it, Mr. Maltass?" I knew that question was coming.

"My theory, Gibbs, is that that envelope we found with the money in it, the one we have now learned was addressed by Richardson, originally contained the summons to Walsh and was folded inside the brass box with the St. Mark's lion on it. I think it was there when I saw Walsh leave his rooms yesterday. Catching sight of the box, which he evidently had been told would contain some very important message, or summons, he snatched it up, and took it away with him to open when alone, in the wood somewhere, I think, opened it, slit the envelope, read the letter inside, threw away the brass box and hurrying back to the farm left the envelope in his desk for future inquiries, taking the notes with him as ordered."

Gibbs nodded, more thoughtfully than in agreement.

"I think Verbena was making restitution last night. She put the notes in what she could feel was an envelope. You said there was no other empty or unused envelope in that part of the desk?"

Gibbs nodded unqualified assent this time.

"And there's one more thing," he said slowly; "we've had the passenger lists of the *Meridiana* looked through at once, of course. A very simple matter that. Well, on the way home with Mr. Walsh is this Mrs. Helen Gray that we've just heard of; and also a Mr. Humphrey Richardson. Now Mr. Richardson's father has three sons. The eldest is out in South America, the second is our Mr. Richardson, the youngest is named Humphrey Richardson."

He looked at me meaningly.

"And, of course, this Richardson would have learned all the facts about Walsh and Helen of Troy from his youngest brother," I finished, "and could have unknowingly got the dented shilling from Abbot in a dozen ways, directly or indirectly, and used it, possibly in a dim light, at any rate without noticing that mark. It's possible even that he noticed it, but never dreamed that it could be traced."

Gibbs looked very grave.

"Nothing but actual proof would ever convince me that Edward Abbott is a blackmailer or a murderer, or in with either crime, but it's most unfortunate that a friend of his is evidently mixed up in this crime."

There again was the local man speaking, not impartial justice.

"Mixed up!" I repeated, with some heat possibly. "Why, man, he's the criminal—as time will prove. As for Abbott, he may only have been hoodwinked by him, into being—for the time—his friend. By the way, Bena wants to tell us something about Richardson too. Don't know, of course, if it concerns this or not. She was just off to catch the up train, but she stopped me and said that when she was back in the afternoon, she'd like to see me about him. I didn't ask her, but I don't think she'd have any objection whatever to your being present too, Gibbs."

He rose with me, locked his safe and made for his car.

"About that marked shilling—I tackled young Mr. Abbott on the point just now," the superintendent said as he did so. "Said we were on the track of some silver that should be sent in to the Mint. Cracked half-crown, damaged or nicked coins of all kinds. Told him that the rector had had a dented shilling in the collection plate which he, Mr. Abbott, had taken off his hand. What had he done with it? He didn't seem to connect the matter with this affair at all, fished up all the change he had on him. It wasn't among it. Said he was always giving change. People at the farm never seemed to have any in the house."

I made no reply. Gibbs went on to say that the solicitors who were sending down a junior partner to go, over Walsh's papers—he ought to arrive this afternoon—

seemed to have no idea of anything that would explain their client's murder.

I nodded, and went on with my thoughts. They centered around Richardson and Abbott. The two young men who seemed all cheeriness and breezy good humor, fond of practical jokes, fond of any lark, always in boisterous high spirits—and yet behind whose enamel paint was a blackmailer and a murderer. It would indeed be well for every one who had ever met him to be saved from continuing to take him at his face value. At the farm we heard that Bena was not back yet.

Gibbs passed on at once to Walsh's rooms where he had some work to do. Richardson stopped me in the hall.

"How's the case shaping?" he asked lightly. "I think Walsh's papers should be gone over very carefully."

"They have been or they are being," I said briefly.

"And have found nothing," he went on sarcastically. "You know, I don't think that's possible. I mean, if they searched properly. Every one knows what the police are. And even a close connection with the Home Office doesn't exclude a blunder." His eyes met mine with a smile of sheer effrontery. "I'd undertake to find a dozen clues within as many minutes if the superintendent and you would accept my help."

"I should be very pleased to see you do it," I agreed truthfully. "I'll put the suggestion to the superintendent." And passing on up the stairs, I did so.

"I believe he knows or suspects that Bena put that money back, and wants to see with his own eyes if it's here," I wound up.

"Like Michael Hare!" laughed the superintendent. "Well, how about taking Mr. Richardson on? I'm willing."

We both were more than willing, we were rather eager, I think, to see just what that young man would do.

When we went down into the hall Abbott was there as well. "Two are better than one," he suggested, "two extra helpers, I mean. We don't expect you to let us read all Walsh's love letters," he went on rather hurriedly, "but I do say that Richardson here has quite a flair for detection. He always guesses the criminal nine times out of ten in any story before the detective in the book does."

"I don't want to touch anything," Richardson put in, also with a ring of real eagerness, almost excitement, in his voice; "I only want to glance them over. Sometimes trifles such as bus tickets—"

"You're talking of the plutocracy, not of beggars like you and me," Abbott cut in. "Walsh would be as likely to have a pawn ticket as a bus ticket."

"Well, any sort of tag or end, bit of string and so on." Richardson gave a nervous laugh. "You know the sort of thing I mean, Superintendent."

"I know. The things that Sherlock Holmes always found that the police had overlooked," Gibbs said. He looked very grim as he stood there facing the two young men. All the cheery humor was gone from his face.

As for the two friends they burst into loud, immoderate laughter of the kind that suggested nerves at high tension to me, and followed us, first to Walsh's rooms upstairs, then to his bureau. In each place the superintendent unlocked everything and allowed the two to watch him as he lightly rifled papers, and lifted article after article.

When the bureau in the dining-room cupboard was closed, which finished the exhibition, I saw a vein beating in Richardson's temple. He was so close to me that even without my glasses I could see it throbbing. I had been watching, not what came to light under the superintendent's careful handling, but the faces of the two friends, or accomplices. They were too utterly absorbed in what was shown them to notice me, standing a little behind them and to one side. Their faces, both of them, showed first of all intense almost painful eagerness, then that changed to a look very suggestive of the one that I had last seen Walsh's face wear, a look of apprehension, of uneasy dread.

Finally, Richardson happened to meet my eye, as the bureau was relocked. Naked panic looked out of his eye in that instant. Meeting my gaze he dropped his own, and his face became blank.

"Don't look so downcast, Ted," he said sharply to his friend, "after all I didn't promise to solve the murder for the police."

Abbott started at the sound of the other's voice, and his face, too, became quite void of expression. Chatting again with the same signs of hectic merriment, they finally left us, after drinks of some very unpleasant concoction which Esther called "Miss Lily's cocktail."

"By the way, Esther," Gibbs said, as she passed through a moment later when we were once more alone, "there's a good deal of unsound silver about. Not false, but under weight and so on. If you get hold of any cracked forms or half-crowns, or dented silver of any kind, bring them to me."

"Miss Bena has a shilling like that, sir," came the prompt answer. "I don't know who gave it her. She likes to put the money out for the weekly bills, does Miss Bena. And she likes to be asked for change. Never makes a mistake in her counting, poor lamb. I told her I thought this was no good. It had a gash right across it. But she said it wouldn't make no difference. It's weight was all right."

"When was this?"

"This morning, sir. She has it lying out on the bread-book for tomorrow morning's payment. In the dining-room. I've just laid tea in there for her. She'll need a good meal when she gets back."

Richardson put his head in to ask whether the superintendent had thought of looking through a couple of Walsh's boxes that were in the room used as a trunk room for the farmhouse guests. Gibbs told him that they were empty. Richardson went off with Abbott, and Esther hurried away after repeating that she was sure she had seen the dented shilling of which she spoke, lying on the baker's book in the dining-room.

Gibbs and I made no pretense of sauntering after it. Richardson might well have overheard what Esther was saying. We hurried down to the dining-room, and there, in a neat pile on a table by the wall there was a stack of household books. One beside the others had some coins on it. Gibbs gave one flip as feet could be heard hurrying along the passage. He had just pocketed a shilling with a deep gash across it that seemed to cut it almost in two, when Abbott came rushing in. At sight of us he pulled up short, and stood a moment as though to recover his breath.

"I wonder if I left my pipe in here?" he said finally in a very casual tone, and stepped to the mantel. Then turning his face away from us, he hurried from the room.

Gibbs and I looked silently at one another.

"Nerves," he said slowly, but he looked very grave.

"One has to make allowances for nerves in cases of this kind. He didn't mind speaking of the shilling at all before—" Gibbs stopped as we heard a murmur of voices coming towards us through the open window. It was but the merest murmur. From where we stood we could see two pairs of very shapely young legs walking side by side. They were in the sunlight. The dining-room faced due north. Both Gibbs and I were in dark tweeds which would be quite indistinguishable from the furnishings of the room seen through an only partly opened window.

Suddenly Bena's voice reached us, low in pitch, but extraordinarily tense and charged with passionate feeling. "If you saw me with that brass box—forget it! Forget it!"

"You've put it somewhere?" Lily's voice came swiftly, accusingly.

"For God's sake, drop it!" Bena spoke almost savagely this time. "Or you'll he sorry! Hush!" There came in silence the sound of their feet coming closer still. In silence the superintendent and I tiptoed into another

room, and drew the door shut behind us. Listening
intently, I could hear the steps pause. One of the sisters
had caught sight, I knew, of the open window. One, I felt
sure, was stooping to peer into the room and was relieved
to find, it empty.

Gibbs and I looked at one another. He flitted out
through the second room, too, to take up his stand in the
hall just as Lily Hillock came in, head thrown back, eyes
level with the rafters. She motioned to us that she had
something she wanted to say, but it seemed to' be of no
importance. I longed, and so I knew did Gibbs, to look at
the date on that gashed coin which he had finally slipped
into the back of his watch, as we stood listening to the
two girls in the garden.

After a minute or two of her chatter, I went on
upstairs where an important letter was waiting to be
considered. But after a very few minutes I was back at
Gibbs's side again. He was now talking of the defective
silver that seemed to be in circulation. Smallwood passed
us just then, lingered a moment to hear what Gibbs was
saying, and then sauntered down the passage leading to
the dining-room at its farther end. We saw him enter and
close the door behind him.

"Miss Bena has a cracked shilling," Gibbs wound up,
after another minute or two; "so Esther tells me. I wonder
from whom she got it?"

It seemed to me that Lily stopped breathing for a
moment, but before she could speak, had she meant to,
there came from the dining room a shout of such horror
that one could almost call it a man's scream.

Gibbs was down the passage on the instant. As he
ran, and Lily and I rushed after him, the door of the
dining-room opened and Smallwood faced us.

"Bena—Bena—my God, Bena!" He almost reeled
against the door behind him. Then he thrust out a hand
"Don't let her go in!"

I am afraid I had only half a thought for Lily behind
me. Nor do I think that Scullion himself could have

stopped her, as she ran past me into the center of the room. There, with a sort of sob, she fell her length as though she had tripped over something and lay quite still. She had fainted.

In a high-backed oaken armchair, before a plate of food, sat Verbena Hillock, staring ahead of her with a horrible red froth on her lips. And straight through her, pinning her to the chair as a butterfly might be pinned to a board, was a large thin carving knife. The knife, we learned a moment later, that had been lying on the table beside a loaf of bread.

A moment later, Gibbs was struggling with Hillock, who had hurried in. The father wanted to get to his dead daughter. The police officer could not allow this.

"You can't help her, Hillock," he said, with real sympathy and shock in voice and face; "all you can do now is to help us get her murderer."

"You were in the house. You let this happen. We were all in the house, even Chapman had just dropped in. And none of us were watching over her!" Hillock's grief was terrible to see. Gibbs let Hillock rave on for another moment without replying. Then the room was cleared, even of me. Lily was carried away, still in a dead faint. When the doctor-hurried in, Gibbs alone helped him. Dr. Brown said at once that death must have occurred about ten minutes before he got to the farm, which meant about a bare minute or so before Gibbs had run down that passage in answer to Smallwood's cry. Death had been absolutely, instantaneous. The mere force of the hand thrusting the knife, striking, as it must have, full on the girl's heart, would have been enough to kill her. The knife had been diverted by a rib, and had pierced the lung as well.

"He knew where to strike," Brown said, drawing out the knife with a jerk. Even the doctor was white and shaken. "The swine who killed her had more than a mere smattering of anatomical knowledge."

The body was covered with a sheet, and the doctor went up to see to Lily. Gibbs went to the door and motioned me in. He showed me the knife that had been used. Its handle was so flooded with blood that it had not been possible to test it for prints. Gibbs, anyway, was certain that the murderer would have had a cloth around his hand. Here again the blow had been struck from in front. Here again, there was no sign of a struggle. Some one known, some one at least accepted, trusted, by the girl, as by Walsh, had struck and killed.

The open window into the garden let in a long shaft of sunlight. What dark and horrid shape had it let in just a few minutes before? I knew. But could I prove it?

From outside came one of the sweetest sounds of spring, the riffle of a young bird's wings as it takes off on one of its first short flights, when the feathers are still stiff and awkward.

I never again shall hear that little rustle without a shudder. We looked the room swiftly but carefully over. By now we knew the position of every trifle in it. Nothing was out of order.

First of all a preliminary roll-call was held. I had already tried to locate all the inmates of the house. The trouble was that Smallwood's cry had brought every one together at a run. Every one, that is, except Scullion. He alone had no words of horror or grief at what had happened.

"Far better so," he said callously to me, as I ran up to the studio where he was demanding why in the devil's name Esther was shrieking like a witch of Endor in the kitchen. "Far better so!" he repeated brutally when I had told him of the awful tragedy below us. "Whoever killed her did her a service. He didn't do it for that reason, I grant you." He did something wonderful to the underside of a leaf with his palette knife.

"Aren't you coming down?" I asked indignantly.

"The superintendent will expect it, I suppose," he grumbled, putting down his brushes with open reluctance. "Though why I should join the gapers, I can't see."

"You're a brute, Scullion," I replied shortly.

"I'm honest, you mean," he snapped. "Half the shock and horror every one will show is only fear lest the same fate comes to them. The blind girl is no loss to any one."

"Her sister fainted when she saw her sitting dead in the chair," was my reply.

"Ah, yes—well, I'm not surprised. Cause and consequence meeting perhaps," was his cryptic reply.

I was glad to find that no one else shared this attitude. Even Chapman, who had dropped in for a talk with Hillock about half an hour previously, was full of horror. As for Smallwood, evidently the sight of that he had found in the dining-room was still before his eyes. His white and horrified face stared almost blankly at me when first I spoke to him. Esther and Arthur talked of it with bated breath in the kitchen, all thought of work, or even food, forgotten.

Every one was asked for their whereabouts. Every one seemed able to furnish an alibi except Scullion and, possibly, Smallwood.

Hillock and Chapman had been talking in the former's den. Each said that he had not left the other for the half-hour of their interview. Abbott and Richardson claimed to have been putting on a side-lawn out of sight of the lower windows. Here too each claimed to have been together every minute of the time about twenty minutes—that they had been testing a new putter.

McKirdy was still up in town as far as any one knew. Gibbs had arranged with the London police to have him watched.

Once again the people in the house were questioned one by one. Smallwood naturally came first. He stated that he had strolled into the dining-room to see if there was anything on the book-shelves there that might do to pass an hour or so out of doors with. He had walked over to the shelves and said a word of excuse to Verbena, whose arm he saw lying along her chair, He thought she was having tea, and talked on for a full minute before her silence struck him as odd. Turning then, to have a good look at her, he saw her face—and the knife. Rushing to her, he saw that though still warm, she must be dead, with her wide-opened, glassy eyes and the red froth on her lips. He did not remember what he had done or said then.

Gibbs made no remark on this story, only asked if he had heard no sound in the garden. Smallwood said that now he could recollect thinking he heard a sound on the gravel as he opened the door, but at the time he had paid no attention It might easily have been some one getting out, some one who had immediately slipped to the side among some bushes, but it was but the merest impression.

Scullion, questioned as to where he had been, stated in fiery language that he had been where he would be now but for this time-wasting inquiry, and that was at work in the studio.

"This second murder can hardly be connected with the idea that blackmail was at the root of the first," Gibbs said finally. Scullion shot him a contemptuous glance.

"Not if that blind girl had got hold of some proof or other?" he asked derisively. "The motive in her case is absolutely clear. Some one shut her mouth. The murderer of Walsh found that she, or he, was suspected, that the blind girl had got hold of some proof, some piece of evidence, and decided that she must be silenced. Really, Superintendent, you ought to get Scotland Yard in to help you. Not little Maltass. Where was he this time, by the way? Strolling in the garden?" And he looked me up and down as a bull might before charging, and with a nod to the two of us he went back to his studio and, as I saw by glanceing at his canvas later on, did some very good work on a foreground.

"Was it the shilling or was it the brass box about which she was going to tell me?" I asked under my breath.

Silently, when the door had closed or rather banged behind Scullion, Gibbs pulled out the shilling from his watch case. He held it out to me. It was of this year.

"We'll compare it at the station with the sealing-wax impression," was all he said, as leaving a man on guard in the house we took his car down. A cast from the coin in question proved to be identical with the mark made on the wax that had sealed the envelope in which we had found the thousand pounds.

Gibbs looked at me.

"Now was it this shilling, or was it the brass box?" he asked this time.

I had had time to think. "The brass box," I said firmly. "The very tone in which Verbena cautioned Lily not to have anything to do with inquiring about it, proves that, to me at least, and it also proves that Lily Hillock is quite innocent of any knowledge of her sister's murder. Besides, her faint shows that."

"You think her dropping, as she did, shows innocence?" Gibbs shook his head. "To me it showed some degree of complicity. Something she had done, or said, was connected with that ghastly murder. But I rather think too that the box is behind this second murder. But what—what—" Gibbs knitted his brows "I can see—your idea about it containing a summons, or standing for a summons—it might mean something to Walsh, but why should it be a danger to Lily—according to Verbena's warning—and why did it mean death to poor little Verbena herself, as I too think it did?"

There was a most unhappy silence. I could suggest nothing. What did that brass box still stand for? In vain I racked my brains, in vain I tried to think of every possible reason from voodoo to ancient family curses, I could produce nothing even momentarily plausible.

"Then Lily Hillock," Gibbs began again, half to himself; "why did she detain me with that chatter of hers in the hall? She hadn't anything to tell me really, and yet she wouldn't let me go—as though she were nervous, or waiting for something, I fancied—dreadful fancy, Mr. Maltass!"

"Her faint was no sham," I said to that.

"Granted. But—well, deep waters? Take Mr. Smallwood, he had ample time to have struck that blow. He had blood on hands and even on his face, you know. Not much, but still some."

"He's absolutely bowled over by the awful sight," I retorted to that. "I know real emotion from false, Superintendent. He took hold of the girl's arm in his first horrified doubt, and so got some blood marks on his hands. Then a hand to his face as he stood for a second paralyzed—he often clutches his jaw like that—did the rest."

"All very possible, Mr. Maltass, but it's not merely possible, but true, that he was out the night Walsh was murdered—last night. And then too that shilling—it may have been the reason for Bena's murder. She might have been able to tell us something very damning about Walsh's end."

"Certainly Abbott was after the shilling," I agreed. "And we know it was used to seal that envelope once. When it contained the summons, I think. But that is a connection which one could understand. It's this brass box with the lion on the top that stands to me as a complete riddle. In Walsh's case, one could read a dozen meanings into it, but what does it hold? What secret from the past, that its possession meant death to the blind girl? And she must have known of her, danger since she warned her sister in that solemn way we heard . . . implored her not to concern herself with it . . . she knew its possession meant danger or death . . ." I repeated, feeling like a blind girl myself as I stumbled among these strange perplexities.

"We must have a talk with Lily Hillock as soon as the doctor will let us," Gibbs said at last, after a prolonged reverie. "I don't like that talk she had with me while her sister was being murdered. I've asked Dr. Brown to call as soon as she can talk coherently."

CHAPTER NINE

AS a matter of fact, it was Lily herself who insisted on
seeing the superintendent and me before the doctor
thought that she ought to do so. It could not have been an
hour later when we were shown into her bedroom. The
doctor had told her that she must lie down, since she
refused to go to bed, but she met us standing. As she
turned and came forward, I thought that I had never seen
such a change in any human being before. Gone was the
arrogant bearing. In her small dark eyes was a look
haunted and haunting, a curiously uncertain flicker. This
woman was no longer sure of herself nor of anything.
Even her voice had lost its imperious ring.

"I want to know what this devilish mystery is—I
mean about that brass box with the St Mark's lion on the
lid. The one Harold Chapman gave me," she began. "It's
because of it that Bena was killed—and that Walsh was
killed." Her hands were twisted together. She now
pressed them against her heart. A gesture which I had
always thought theatrical, but here I felt that it stilled
something that was bleeding internally. "My poor Bena!"
she finished unsteadily.

"What makes you so sure?" Gibbs asked quietly.

"What else could be the reason for her murder?" Lily
almost shrieked, and the terror in her eyes told clearly
that there was something else that she was holding at
bay, a horrible fear lest something quite different,
something in which she herself was connected, might be
the cause. So at least I translated her look, as Gibbs had
done her faint.

"There are many odd points about the two murders,
Miss Lily," Gibbs said thoughtfully, his eyes on her
whitening face. "That box certainly is a most perplexing

mystery as yet. But what makes you connect it directly with Miss Verbena's death?"

"Listen!" Speaking feverishly, desperately, she told us that that morning around eight, she had seen Bena wrapping something up in paper with the greatest care. She was absolutely certain that it was the brass box with, the lion on it that her sister had had in her hands. She had noticed its upraised paw, and the gap where the gospel should have been. Lily herself had been dressing at the moment and could only watch from her window, for Bena had been in a little summerhouse below. Lily could only see her for a moment when Bena had been wrestling with box and brown paper on the table. After, and before, her sister had been out of sight. She had not seen her come in or leave the house, but from the very fact that Bena had used the summer-house she thought that she must have been carrying the box, wrapped up, to the station to take it to town with her, and that the wrapping must have come undone on the way to the gate. When she got down herself, Bena had left some time ago. Lily did not see her again until she had happened on her on her way into the house after her—Bena's—visit to the Braille library in town. Then Lily had asked her how it came that she had the box about which such a fuss was being made in connection with Mr. Walsh. At first, to her amazement, Bena had tried to make her think that it was some other brass box she had been handling that morning, but Lily was too sure of what she had seen to be put off, and finally Bena had turned on her and given her the solemn warning which, as it happened, Gibbs and I had overheard, to have nothing to do with that box, to, make no inquiries about it. Lily had, she said, been silenced by her sister's manner and words.

As to any meaning, any significance, that the box might have held for either Walsh or Verbena, Lily seemed unable to help us. Yet, as Gibbs said, she had detained him in the hall while her sister was being murdered a few yards away. As he had said, it was a terrible thought.

Gibbs and I questioned her very closely. She seemed to be hiding nothing, to be desperately anxious herself to understand, to solve, the amazing, because so apparently insignificant, mystery. Shown a piece of paper folded into the marks that we had found on the envelope, she thought it would fairly accurately fit the drawer inside of the box. But as it was a size that would fit many boxes, this was of no great help. Nothing she seemed able to tell us was of any great help, except that Verbena had had possession of the box this morning. It began to look to me as though the thousand pounds which I believed the blind girl to have put back in Walsh's desk after his murder, had been placed by Richardson in that brass box, and that Bena had taken box and contents, and that only when he knew she had the former did Walsh's murderer know who had frustrated his crime. But how to prove this?

Even so, it was no use pretending that we knew or could guess what that box stood for. A man had been seen looking down on it, and was believed to have taken it away with him—to his death. A girl had been seen wrapping it up, had spoken of it in a very terrible way, and had been killed before the echo of her words had more than died away. The two deaths must be linked. The little lion with his upraised, friendly paw seemed the only link. Yet to read his meaning, unless my idea of vengeance taken for a futile murder was right, seemed hopeless. Certainly, unless that was the truth, its meaning was beyond the superintendent and me. Privately I made up my mind that some such little gadget should be beyond Michael Hare, too, in the play which I was writing.

"We may be all wrong, Miss Lily, that box may not be at the root of your sister's murder," Gibbs said finally, "and for that reason I want you to think over all the evidence you gave about Mr. Walsh's murder. Is there nothing you want to alter? Or add? Now that your sister has been murdered too? It would be very terrible for you if any little apparent trifle you had told us, which was not quite accurate, should set the whole inquiry wrong, and let the double murderer escape."

Lily dropped into a chair, and putting her elbows on a table, buried her face in her hands.

"Let me think!" she murmured in a tone of genuine agony, "oh, yes, let me think!"

There was complete silence for some time. Then Gibbs tried again.

"For instance, you are quite sure that it was Mr. Walsh whom you saw under Latimer's Oak yesterday? And that you saw him there at half-past six?"

Lily sprang up convulsed.

"No!" she cried out the word in a tone of anguish "No! I thought a lie would do no harm, and—oh, I've been all wrong. I did see Mr. Walsh there at half past six"—she turned to Gibbs now and spoke more calmly—"but he wasn't standing under the tree. He was lying dead in amongst the bracken." She stared at us both with distended pupils. "Don't stop me!" she went on most unnecessarily, and with a return of her old imperious manner, "I had had an appointment with Mr. Walsh there. He was painting me, you know. And I had just seen Harold Chapman hiding under some bushes near by. I thought he was trying to get away without being seen. So I stood a moment under the oak looking round, and my powder box—it's a ball that opens—dropped from my bag and rolled down into the ditch where the bracken grows so thick. I poked about after it with my walking stick and—and found Mr. Walsh's dead body. I saw his head— and I felt sure that Harold had struck him down. And that my father who met me shortly afterwards might be mixed up with it in some way. Not in the murder, but in Harold's being there at that hour. I wanted to talk to Harold Chapman when my father came on me and practically kidnapped me. He wouldn't let me say a word to him while he drove me to my aunt, and there they locked me in a room."

Her eyes flashed. "My father thought that I was in danger from that little rabbit, Walsh!" Her lips still curled for an instant as of old.

"And when he came and fetched me home he bundled me into the back of the car and drove himself again, and wouldn't listen!" Her eyes were green candles.

"Why did you say six-thirty?" Gibbs asked.

"Because I knew Harold had an appointment which he wouldn't miss at that hour, and it would be an alibi for him. You see, thanks to my father, I hadn't had the word with him I had counted on."

"You feel sure that he killed Mr. Walsh?"

"I know now positively that he didn't!" she flashed indignantly. "The blow that killed Walsh was the sort an angry man might strike without remembering how strong he was. But Harold wouldn't hurt a hair of Bena's head. No one but a wild beast would have hurt Bena."

"Are you willing to have us write down this altered statement of yours, Miss Lily, and will you sign it at the station?" Gibbs asked.

"Yes," she said resolutely; "it'll be terrible for Harold. He'll never forgive me for dragging him into this. I only did it to save him, but I don't want to save the other man who murdered Bena too."

"And that is really all that you can tell us to help us catch him?" Gibbs asked very gravely indeed. His tone suggested his own belief that there was still more to tell.

Just for a second Lily Hillock hesitated. Then she said firmly:

"Everything. I don't know anything that would explain either murder. Nor anything that would help you. I wish to God I did. All I know is what you know, that in some way that brass box from Venice is mixed up in it, or rather in them. There must be something very valuable inside the box—papers, or jewels. . . ."

"But would Miss Bena keep papers or jewels that didn't belong to her?" Gibbs asked, as though feeling his way.

Lily's face flamed.

"We Hillocks don't steal," she said hotly; "nor keep what doesn't belong to us. If Bena kept anything that didn't belong to her along with that box, inside it I mean, then it didn't belong to the person who had it either, and she took it to put things right."

Lily was getting close to my own opinion. But her tone was uncertain. She heard it herself.

"I can't think why she didn't tell me about it," she went on with apparent frankness, "except that she knew there was a dreadful risk in knowledge. Ever since Walsh's death, Bena had avoided me. I thought"—she hesitated—"Bena was strangely quick at feeling things. I thought she knew that I wasn't telling you the facts when I said I had seen him—alive—under the tree. In fact I was certain that she was certain that that wasn't true. But how—" She broke off and sat with her chin in her hand.

We waited.

"She evidently knew very much more than just that," Lily finished finally.

Gibbs said nothing for a long moment, then he asked:

"Was Walsh's body cold when you found it at half past six, or warm?"

"Cold," Lily said.

"Did you shift the body at all?"

She had not.

Gibbs questioned her, and cross-questioned her, but her story stood his probing. Apparently it was the truth—now.

We left her and sent Esther up to look after her.

In the car outside, driving to the station, we neither of us spoke for a few minutes. Finally Gibbs said quietly:

"So you were right, Mr. Maltass, little Bena knew all about it all the time, and wouldn't tell. And, we think, put back the thousands into Walsh's desk last night, and evidently dispose or did dispose of the box in some way. . . . However, that's only guesswork and may be all wrong.

The point is this, now that Lily Hillock has given us what she swears—is prepared to swear—is the correct time when she found Walsh's body, does it make much difference to the case? I can't see that it does. It sets the time of the murder a little earlier, that's all. You and Esther saw him alive at half-past five. Lily finds him dead and cold at half-past six. Quick work! I mean for the body to have got cold. Still, it was lying in a cold, damp spot. But it's odd. Makes one rather question all her story. But she stuck to it. It rang as though she believed it—to me."

"To me too," I agreed.

At the station I left Gibbs to make entries and write reports and went for a walk. I felt as though entangled in some nightmare where things had lost their properties of real life, and mountains became mole hills and mole hills mountains. When I returned to the station the superintendent was looking at a letter.

"Walsh had taken Scullion's advice," he said now. "He had just sent in the numbers of his notes to his bank on a slip of paper marked, 'to be opened in case of my death.' The list tallies exactly with the numbers of the notes we found in that envelope. So now we know that they really represent the sum he had with him, or on him, as a rule."

The telephone rang. One of the solicitors who had charge of the murdered man's affairs had arrived at the farm. Gibbs hurried off to meet him, while I walked up to the farm and then settled down to write. I found myself tearing up sheet after sheet of my play. It was far too easy. Michael Hare was allowed to strut over difficulties with ridiculous ease. I decided that the clues, instead of leading him nicely on and on to his goal should baffle him completely for a change.

Gibbs came in to ask me would I like a word with Mr. Atkinson, the solicitor. I found him a pleasant enough man, who expressed himself as absolutely bewildered and puzzled by his late client's dreadful end.

He confirmed what we already knew about the terms on which Walsh held his fortune. The man had had no other means, apparently. He, too, spoke of the new inheritor as a lady of the highest respectability, adding that she had at one time intended entering a convent, but had had to give up the idea as she proved unable to stand the hardships of the life. She now lived in almost equal seclusion in her charming villa on the shore of Lake Geneva, spending all her time in philanthropic works. Even the lawyer, determinedly cynical in most matters, said that he really could not suspect Miss Smythe of having had a hand in Walsh's murder.

"Just as soon suspect Mr. Abbott, the rector," he said. A comparison that Gibbs, too, had used before as marking the height of the impossible. "It goes to him after Miss Smythe's death, as you, of course, know. Or rather, it goes to his children more likely, as he and Miss Smythe are the same age."

"Divided equally between son and daughter, I understand," Gibbs said.

Mr. Atkinson nodded. "That's it. Miss Abbott, the rector told me just now, is engaged to a friend of her brother's name of Richards or Richardson, I think." He looked at us inquiringly. Gibbs nodded assent. As for me, the blow had been too unexpected and hit me too hard. Laura Abbott engaged! And to a murderer—a double murderer!

Fortunately Atkinson, quite unaware of the feelings raging in me, went on placidly, "This death of Mr. Walsh, of course, brings the fortune her share will amount to about three thousand a year only, after the subtraction of all death duties—nearer to her than one thought possible a few months ago. Walsh was only between thirty and forty—thirty-seven, I think. Quite probable now that Miss Abbott will get her share while she's still able to enjoy it. Anyway, she could raise a *post obit* easier," he added, by way of professional humor, as he began to go through some papers. Of the blackmailing attempt he knew nothing whatever. Nor could he add anything to our knowledge of Walsh's past life. Gibbs had got the police where Walsh had lived to look this up, and had not been able to learn one suspicious or helpful item. As to the brass box which he described to Mr. Atkinson, though without any hope of getting light on it from the solicitor, too, found it a most perplexing mystery, especially with the second, and, in some way far more terrible murder, apparently linked with it. But he agreed that my idea sounded the one possible solution. The idea that seeing it in the blind girl's possession the murderer knew for certain who had balked him. But Atkinson emphasized what both the superintendent and I felt only too sharply, that this notion of mine did not in the least explain Verbena's words to her sister just before her death— words that still rang in my ears with their urgency and their warning.

We soon left Atkinson to go again over Walsh's correspondence in order to see if he could find a clue which had escaped Gibbs's careful search. The superintendent had already learned that a lady called, or calling herself, Mrs. Gray had been on the ship with Walsh and Hugh Richardson; and that the two former had "carried on," according to the stewards, until they were the talk of the ship. Helen Gray was young and pretty and not hampered by being a lady, so said these same keen-eyed observers. She had been heard to talk more than once to Walsh of her husband as of a frightful drag on lively young spirits like her own, with his mad jealousy. And when a huge gorilla of a man had come to meet his wife at Liverpool, Walsh had promptly faded out of the picture. All efforts, so far, to trace husband or wife had totally failed. They were not criminals known to the boat police, beyond that nothing apparently could be learned about them.

I had kept a very watchful eye on Scullion, so had Gibbs, to see if he might lead us to any useful developments. But beyond writing to inquire as to the existence of a Helen Gray on the ship, or of a husband, the artist had let the matter drop.

"Haven't enough money to go into it. I make you a handsome present of my knowledge," he said now, when I found him in the studio still painting as though nothing had happened. Esther had tied a big crepe bow to Walsh's easel early this morning, and Scullion had disposed of this emblem of grief by dropping easel and bow out of the window.

"You do, when you can't help yourself," I retorted. He grinned.

"Only way any one ever gets a present, laddie. But, besides the money, I haven't the time to waste. Time's not money. It's far more valuable. You can always steal another chap's money, but his time's no good to you."

Smallwood now came into the studio. He had not touched his piano since last night. I thought how strained and pale he looked. He was the kind never to forget that dreadful sight when he had turned with a commonplace remark to the girl sitting knifed to her chair back.

"I believe the motive's connected with Walsh's inheritance," he said suddenly, after apparently scrutinizing Scullion's work.

"Very possible indeed," Scullion replied indifferently. "Just stand a bit farther away, I don't like to be cramped. 'Money's the root of all evil,' saith Holy Writ somewhere. That's why every one of us is after it." Scullion roared at his jest.

"I'm going over to Vevey," Smallwood went on; "going to see the woman who inherits. It's all very well to speak of her as a most respectable saint, an ornament to her sex—"

"Priced far above emeralds," misquoted Scullion unctuously.

"The point is," Smallwood spoke irritably, "that she's sixty."

"The criminal age, you think?" jeered Scullion. "An age when any one would know that they had small chance of inheriting from a man not yet forty."

"Well, do you know, I think there's some sense in that suggestion," Scullion boomed in a tone of rather surprised approval. "Why not go, as you say. Look here, I'm due, as usual, to paint her gardens next month. Walsh was coming along too. It was all arranged. I'll put forward my visit and start at once, as soon as the police will let us out of their sight. You can have Walsh's rooms. It'll be all right."

"But"—Smallwood stared at him, "but—I should be there as a spy in the land, Scullion, not in the least as a guest."

"So much the better," Scullion said casually, "nothing like thrashing one's ideas out."

"But, good God, man"—Smallwood's tones were aghast—"you're going to introduce me into the house, as I understand."

"Why not? Old Smythie never killed Walsh, but it's just as well to settle the point. Besides, the weather's just right for me. And talk of night life in London—wait till you've had a try at night life in Geneva!"

Smallwood eyed him with open distaste. "There are times when I think you ought to've been smothered at birth, Scullion. Luckily, you don't mean the half. And if you can do as you say, get me admitted to this woman's house, I'll come. I think it's a duty to that blind girl. Her murder, and Walsh's, are linked, but why and how beats me."

He looked interrogatively at me. I only shook my head and looked owlish.

"You and McKirdy can exchange moral sentiments," Scullion said contemptuously to the pianist.

"McKirdy?" I asked in surprise.

"He's sure to make for there. He's a sort of adopted son of Smythie's. I don't know why she took such a fancy to the worm. But she has. Yes, McKirdy is sure to turn up there sooner or later. Probably, sooner. He's the sort of whining, ranting dreamer silly women like."

"You don't care for this Miss Smythe?" I hazarded.

"Care for her?" He stared at me in amazement. "Why, she's sixty, my dear lad!"

"Well," I replied, thinking hard, "apparently half of the Upfold Farm inmates will foregather at this lady's house. Edward Abbott is going to break the news of Walsh's murder and help her on her journey home."

"You're going to have a squint at Smythie," Scullion turned to Smallwood; "don't forget to have a good look at Abbott first and last. Or that friend of his, Richardson."

"Richardson?" queried Smallwood.

"Going to marry Abbott's sister and co-heir. That's why little Maltass here always gets his knife into him when he can," Scullion went on at the top of his voice.

"You always sign your pictures R. Scullion. What's the R. for?—rhinoceros?" Smallwood asked.

Scullion only laughed.

"I say what I think," he bellowed cheerfully.

"Trouble is, your thoughts aren't fit to be said," Smallwood retorted. Then he stood a moment fidgeting with some paint tubes. "I've been talking with Lily Hillock," he broke out, "she's desperate. About Verbena, I mean. Small wonder. She's certain that that brass box you and Gibbs are so keen on"—he glanced at me—"was the reason for Bena's murder, and possibly for Walsh's too. Lily believes that desperately important papers—to some one—were in the box, and that Walsh was murdered to get possession of them, or to prevent their contents becoming known, and so was Bena. Bena, in some way Lily can't understand, had got hold of that box."

"Lily's red herring," Scullion said around his big pipe, drawing suddenly on the wall a gigantic herring in red ochre, coming straight towards us, mouth open. As we looked, half spellbound by the amazing skill of the drawing, half by the carelessness of other people's property which had made the artist draw it forty times life-size on the papered wall beside him, Scullion, with a brush he took from the armory in his hand, drew on the herring's back a thing in yellow, which, with a deft touch, was a boxing brass lion, one paw, raised to strike. In its other paw was what, with a touch or two with another brush, he turned into papers tied with loops of red tape.

It was irresistibly comic. Neither Smallwood nor I could keep our faces straight as we looked at it.

Then, with a casual smear of his paint rag, Scullion turned the whole into a blot on the wall, and went on with his picture.

"That's not fair, though," Smallwood protested.

"And it's really a damnable suggestion. Lily is what, in another sort of girl, would be heartbroken over Verbena's horrible murder; as it is, being herself, she's fighting mad. I can assure you if there is any truth in her belief that the brass box is at the root of Bena's murder, she'll get at the truth about it, if not find the box itself."

"I thought the box was found," grunted Scullion. Smallwood ran laboriously over the history of its comings and goings.

"Well," Scullion shouted finally, "if Lily's right, and the thing is the reason for those two murders, and she goes after it bald-headed, we shall soon see if she's right or not. If she is, she'll be the next to be killed."

And poking me below the belt as a hint that he needed more room, he stepped away from the easel, and began doing something at arm's length with half-closed eyes.

"You two chaps never seem to have any work to do," he growled. "Sort of thing that I thought only happened in detective novels, when all the crowd downs tools and spends their time deciphering codes or lying out on their bellies in the grass. Well, I must work. Now more than ever."

I left the studio. Smallwood caught up to me in the passage.

"What do you, as representing the inquiry, think about that brass box?" he asked. I could only say that if Lily Hillock could solve its riddle, the whole investigation would be thankful.

"Look here," he went on, "I'm seriously intending to go to Vevey. Why not come too? Scullion gets on my nerves lately. He's extraordinarily careless as to what he says. Why, a little while ago he spoke to me as though"—he gulped and paled—"I—because I found that poor girl—" Smallwood looked as though he could not finish the sentence. "It's his attitude, as well as the fact that I did find her that makes me feel it my duty at least to try to clear this thing up. That blind face haunts me, Maltass. I have a feeling that it will haunt me until I see her murderer's face instead in the dock."

I said I would think it over, and had a talk with Gibbs. He agreed with me that it would be an excellent idea. True, no one suspected Miss Smythe, but it was possible that something, some loose end might turn up at her house, which would be of use in leading us home. If only because so many from Upfold Farm would be there together. We were off to the station to meet Lily, who had rushed up to town to try to trace her sister's movements. Her face showed that she had had no more success than the London police, who had already reported their inability to trace any parcel which the blind girl might have had with her, and deposited in town.

"He got it, the murderer did!" Lily said, with a look of baffled fury in her white, drawn face. "What's the good of the police? Walsh's murder was his own affair. He did something and got punished. But Bena never harmed any one. Oh, if I only knew what that damned box with that damned lion stood for!" And she broke down.

Gibbs stopped behind for a word with a man who had got out of the same train, the last down-train that night. He brought news that McKirdy had been totally lost sight of all day. He had gone up in the morning to call on an editor, as he had told Gibbs that he would. There was only one door out of the office. When, after some time, the publisher, but not McKirdy, appeared, the sleuth watching went up and made a few inquiries. McKirdy had apparently vanished some hours ago, after leaving his sketches. There was a firm of color printers and etchers on the floor above. Here McKirdy, though well known, had not apparently been seen for some time. The detective, prosecuting his search, found that there was a way on to the roof, and that it showed signs of recent use. The roof was flat, and joined two other flat ones in a level promenade divided off only by foot-high copings. The farther house had a trap-door that opened easily. So easily that here again the sleuth was certain it had been used today. Stairs from it led down into a little back courtyard, whence through an arched open doorway a back street could be reached.

Gibbs's face darkened. He said a few curt words to the London man and then went on to the farm, where he found me.

"McKirdy could easily have come down here today," he said briefly. "If Mr. Scullion wants to go to Vevey, I shan't stop him. I shan't even subpoena him for the inquest tomorrow."

CHAPTER TEN

McKIRDY turned up at the inquest, which was held at the next morning. A double inquest, purely formal in character but to which all the papers in England, so it seemed to me, sent down their star reporters. Thanks to Gibbs, Esther was questioned about the brass box, and within half an hour the streets of London echoed to the call of *Brass Box Mystery. Missing Box Mystery. St. Mark's Lion Box Mystery.* This seemed to the police, and I agreed with them, in the present static condition of the inquiry, to be the best chance of stirring up events.

As for McKirdy, he seemed surprised at the superintendent's interest in his doings of yesterday. He had met an artist friend on the stairs on coming out from his interview with his publisher. The friend—he gave the name—worked for the art firm on the floor above. They wanted him to do a view of London, and the artist was on his way to the roof when McKirdy ran into him. Together they went up, decided that the view from the farther roof was the best, and McKirdy waited while his friend sketched it. An open trap-door caught their eye too, they went down by it, emerging in a little courtyard from which they gained a back street. At lunch they had parted. McKirdy had spent the afternoon, the all-important afternoon, at the Persian Exhibition, he said. As this was thronged, his statement could not be checked. As for the open trap-door, Gibbs found that the house in question was partly used by a firm which made a very special point of fire drill by its staff, and that only that morning the roof had been used for the purpose.

As for his immediate plans, McKirdy said that he was going to Vevey. The news of Walsh's murder would be a great shock to Miss Smythe, who had been very good

indeed to him when he had stayed at her house with
Scullion last spring. As for the account of Verbena
Hillock's murder, he only hoped she would not see it until
she was in England. At any rate he himself was going to
her as soon as possible.

"You think she's in danger?" Gibbs asked with
calculated bluntness.

McKirdy did not answer.

"Just as well you're going," Gibbs said to me after the
talk, "there's something queer about McKirdy to my
mind. I'm wondering if he's quite normal—quite right in
his mind—I don't mean mad in the usual sense of the
word, but there's something—" Gibbs tapped his head.

"In what way did it show itself," I pressed.

"Random answers," was the reply. "I'd ask things and
get replies that didn't seem to fit."

"Do you think he was acting vagueness?" I questioned.
Gibbs had asked himself that too, and was not able to
give a satisfactory reply.

"In any case you'll be there to act as extra guard to
the old Miss Smythe," he said uneasily. "I'm anything but
easy about her. Anything!" And we went into details as to
what could best and most unobtrusively be done to
safeguard her on the home journey. In her own house, of
course, I could do but little.

"Richardson is going instead of young Mr. Abbott,"
Gibbs said finally; "the chief doesn't think Abbott should
leave England yet awhile, and Richardson asked to be
allowed to go in his stead."

I stared, unable to speak, but Gibbs would say no
more, so we five met duly at the railway station in town
and crossed together, Scullion, Smallwood, McKirdy,
Richardson and I. McKirdy alone was sick. He looked the
type to be, as Scullion pointed out to him in the train
afterwards.

It will always remain in my mind as the most horrible
journey I have ever undertaken. To have to be with a
murderer, and the murderer of poor little Bena at that—

and not dare to let him see that I knew him in spite of all his efforts to seem like other, men, was an ordeal which tried me enormously. But I did not need the superintendent's one word of warning as to the danger of letting a suspect know that he came under that heading to be careful.

Even the others seemed to feel the strain. All of us were thankful when the blue sheet of the lake came into view early in the morning. Scullion had flatly refused to proceed direct without one good night's sleep at Geneva. And unwillingly we had agreed to stop over too.

I like the lake. I like its shores. I even like the Dent du Midi in spite of postcards and *Greetings from Friends*.

Certainly Bois Riant, the house of Miss Smythe, looked a picture as our taxi stopped at it about noon. The gardens, though small in extent, struck me as being quite unusually beautiful. I could well understand Scullion's love of them. A little stream ran through them, widening out at one place to form a tiny lake. The ground sloped down to it from the house, and rose on the other side again in a lovely sweep of green turf dotted with magnificent trees to a line of trees which formed the hedge and gave an impression of vast size.

There were water lilies and wild fowl, and to one side of the house were a few formal beds and terraces. The house was rather dilapidated inside, I thought. It looked the home of some one who lived outside—not inside it. We were all shown into a dreary drawing-room, and Scullion went off to find the lady of the house, for we had been unable to tell the exact time of our arrival.

She came in with him a few minutes later. Miss Smythe was a slender, vivacious woman, who might be sixty in years but not in spirit. She must have been an enchantingly lovely girl, was one's first thought, and much of an ageless charm she retained. Scullion flung us collectively at her as it were, and then retired to the table, where some bottles of light Swiss wine had been opened for us. It was McKirdy who really introduced us one by one. He did so with an air of being thoroughly at home. I looked at Miss Smythe closer. Yes, it was a weak chin, and a rather silly little mouth. She was timid, too, I found, and easily dominated by anything in trousers. To talk to her was to feel oneself charmingly placed on a pedestal where the god spoke and his servant heard and obeyed.

Richardson kept himself absolutely in the background; as for Scullion, he simply trampled on her. With hardly any pretense of seeing in her the hostess, he was occupied solely with arrangements for his studio, and for the new pictures that he was planning He abused the gardener for some fancied or real mistake in setting out some backgrounds.

"I don't suppose it matters to you much longer now," he went on, turning at last to Miss Smythe. "You're leaving at once, aren't you? I shall be quite comfortable here. Malchen understands my ways, so does Pierre, and after all, if Vervier won't make himself useful in the garden, there are other and better men to be had." He helped himself to a round dozen of tomato sandwiches.

"Oh, yes, yes!" fluttered Miss Smythe, her color coming and going, a pretty color still. "Of course you'll stay on here—as long as you want to. And in England you must help me choose the right sort of garden again."

"Lord, no!" Scullion said at once, "I don't paint English gardens. Not the right light; no warmth. This light here just suits me."

"I had thought of selling the house," she said timidly.

"This house? Bois Riant?" He stared at her. "You mustn't do that! I shall often want to come and paint here."

It was really comic. Catching my eye, he had the grace to add very belatedly and grudgingly, "Very kind of you, Miss Smythe, to let me come here. But, of course, I counted on painting here when I made up my plans for the year. Walsh and I were coming here together."

After that he turned his back on her and refused to be drawn into the very labored talk that we tried to spin.

Miss Smythe announced that she would be ready to leave next day. That meant that I had only one day and night in the house to discover what had brought Richardson to the place. A discovery, the possibility of which in Gibbs's mind as in my own, outweighed the risk of letting the guilty man leave England. I had watched him every moment of the journey and discovered nothing. I felt fairly certain by now that it was in order to have a word with McKirdy. A word that must be all-important, or perhaps even to hand over something to him. That brass box? His luggage had been very carefully searched indeed by the Customs, to whom a word had been sent by the police, but though no sign of it had been found, it might be in his possession all the same. Though why? what? In other words, I still could propose nothing. If it was some message that was to be given, a dozen might have been exchanged without my knowledge once the two were under the same roof. There was that walk the two took together almost immediately after our arrival. I would have gone too but by some perversity of chance, Smallwood had spoken to Miss Smythe of my acquaintance with a certain Paris Abbé who was an object of special veneration to her, and it was precisely for the half-hour during which McKirdy and Richardson drifted off together that she chose to talk about the priest in question. As for Miss Smythe herself, I agreed with Smallwood, who said that anything less like a murderess, or a criminal of any kind, than this rosycheeked, bright-eyed, slender woman, it was impossible to imagine. And though in my plays I have, of course, to dress my woman criminal in every noble appearance, as I had said to Gibbs, in reality villainy and goodness carry their own atmospheres with and around them.

I had no reason to suspect McKirdy beyond the fact that Richardson was here, had come here at grave risk of attracting attention to himself. And even so, McKirdy might be, as I felt sure Abbott was, but an innocent catspaw of the other. But there was the fact that McKirdy had hated Walsh—secretly. He was evidently deeply attached to Miss Smythe, quite genuinely so, I thought. So deeply indeed, that I wondered whether it were possible that the heart of a Eurasian, an Anglo-Indian, is a strange mixture—his mother was a daughter of a Kali priest, Gibbs had learned. Kali, goddess of death, destruction, and murder. There was something distinctly fanatical in McKirdy's long narrow face. Walsh's murder had benefited this woman for whom he seemed to feel so great a regard and at the same time had removed a rival for Scullion's favor, artistic interest. It was a dark tangle.

I bore a letter from my brother in the Home Office which made the Swiss police anxious to help me in every way. I explained to them that there was no question whatever of suspecting Miss Smythe, but that, as she had just fallen heir to a fortune owing to a murder, we must have all possible details concerning her.

They produced what, together with what we knew already, amounted apparently to a consecutive life story of the lady.

She was the only child of a Doctor Smythe of Dublin, a well-known and much respected physician. Her life had run along the lines one would expect. A convent girl, she had been for a year a novice in a convent of Poor Clares, but the hardships of that stern order had been too much for her, and, broken down in health, she had left to live here in the sunny climate of Vevey, where her charitable works and character had made her a host of friends, Swiss and English-speaking. She used the house which her father had bought for her as a sort of holiday home for convalescent nuns and missionaries and a host of slum workers in all lands. Her father, in his will, had left her only an annuity, stating that otherwise she would beggar herself within the year. As it was, she had Bois Riant and a comfortable six hundred a year, which let her live in comforts, for the vegetable gardens made the house almost self-supporting to her, a vegetarian.

Altogether, a more creditable story could never have been studied. I took charge of a copy of the facts which I earmarked for Gibbs and finally returned to the house to show it to Smallwood. It contained nothing which could be of use even to the criminal. He smiled a little wryly as he handed the sheets back to me.

"Just what one would expect. And she says she's never heard of a brass box with a damaged or whole St. Mark's lion on it. Which I thoroughly believe." He snapped his long powerful-looking fingers in impatient vexation.

"Lily Hillock'll be disappointed. She wanted to come, too, and see Miss Smythe for herself. Only I think the superintendent gave her a hint that she wouldn't be allowed to leave England. Matter of mere form, of course. She's working night and day to find out where that brass box could have been before and after it was seen by you and Esther on the table outside Walsh's door, and by herself in Bena's hands. That silly, meaningless, and therefore most important brass box!"

I had an impulse to ask him if that box was connected with his strange excursion from the house the night of Walsh's murder. But a sleuth must not give way to impulses.

We had arranged to start early next morning. Scullion came to my bedroom late that night in a vile temper.

"I've got my tickets," he bawled as though in fury. "Damn it all, what does the woman want to go to England for? To weep on Walsh's grave? She never knew him."

"Get your tickets?" I asked sleepily.

He pulled at his beard till it looked as though combed with a hay rake.

"I know! I know! But, after all, that blind brat was killed, wasn't she! And with very much the same gang around her."

"Gang?" It is hard to speak with hauteur when repressing a yawn, but I tried it.

"Just so," he went on in the same angry voice, "there's Richardson, there's Smallwood—"

"Who was heard playing steadily away at his piano from five till dinner the day Walsh was murdered," I threw in contemptuously.

"May be. Who can swear that he didn't stop long enough to rush to that oak and back? He stopped in that dining-room by himself quite long enough to have silenced that blind wench. Then there's yourself, Maltass. No offense; but you did go for that ramble, you know. And you were off 'somewhere' when that girl died."

"And you?" I asked coldly.

"Oh, quite so. This last time. But not both times, Maltass. It's the two times one has to look at."

"Well," I conceded grudgingly, "I suppose we are the same set, barring McKirdy—"

"Why bar him," snapped Scullion "Personally I bar nobody neither from blackmail nor from murder. And after all, poor old Smythie has a claim on me. I should have got to the top in any case, but she did hold the ladder for me. Oh, sentiment be damned! It's damnable that I should be dragged back just now, but I find I can't let the woman go without seeing her safely into the lawyer's hands. Besides," he went on in the same indignant voice that made me grin, "I can't paint, I find, until I know she's all right. Mind you, no stopping down at the rectory as Richardson has twice suggested to her. That's not in the program." He glared at me. I glared back. His meaning was obvious.

"What about your ticket?" I asked. "You said you'd one."

"I've taken McKirdy's."

"But I thought he particularly wanted to be back about some work he's been offered?"

"Better ask him. He's probably outside."

And, whether by chance or not, McKirdy was not far off when Scullion on the instant flung the door open.

"Maltass here wants to know why the devil you're not going back to England, as you said," Scullion roared at him in a voice better suited for mid-day in an auction room than midnight in a lady's house. McKirdy came in quietly, and closed the door without a sound.

"Mr. Scullion thinks he would be uneasy about Miss Smythe if he stayed behind," he said meekly, "and Miss Smythe told me she would be glad if I could stay on here and, as it were, take charge while she is away, until she can make other arrangements."

"So now you know," Scullion said to me, and without wasting any good nights on either of us banged the door behind him.

"But I thought you had to be in town—about your work?" I said, wondering, as Gibbs had wondered before at something odd in the man's manner or a lack of something in it.

"I've given up painting—or at least illustrating," he said in a curiously indifferent tone, when one reflected that his painting was his livelihood.

"Been left a fortune?" I asked, trying to make my jocular tone pass off the impertinence.

"Rather I've recently discovered where my fortune lies buried," he replied with downcast eyes and an evanescent smile playing around his lips.

"Scullion has just pointed out that Miss Smythe will have the same people around her who were in the house when poor Verbena Hillock was murdered," I went on, trying to probe the man's mind.

His eyes still evaded me. "I don't see any danger, in any case, but as it will make Mr. Scullion feel more comfortable about her, I let him have my tickets. I owe a great deal to Mr. Scullion." And wishing me a gentle good night, he softly passed out again into the corridor.

So we left, very much the same party as we had come, with the addition of Miss Smythe. Naturally none of us mentioned the tragedies at the farm, however much they were in our thoughts. On Miss Smythe they seemed to have made singularly little impression. I decided that she lived already more in an eternal than a temporal world, one where death has no meaning and where the manner of leaving the body behind is of small account.

We were crossing by the Ostend night-boat. Smallwood had arranged for cars to meet us at the train and take us on the boat. They were to be sent from the garage of an ex-regular officer, an old acquaintance of his, to whom he wanted to do a good turn. We had to wait rather a long time for them. The excuse given when they finally arrived was that the driver of the second car had been taken ill on the way and a substitute obtained.

The car was roomy enough, but Smallwood took the seat beside the driver in front. He said he wanted the air, though it was a wild and blustering commodity that night. So inside we four bestowed ourselves, Miss Smythe with Richardson beside her, Scullion and I opposite.

The tragedy that followed is common knowledge. How our car, blinded by the dazzle of lights on the water at a ferry across the Scheldt, plunged down off a six-foot bank into the water instead of on to the ferry boards.

As for myself, I hit the roof with a violent crash and remembered nothing except mud closing in on me. Luckily for us, the ferry had two other cars on it and their occupants came to the rescue. Smallwood too had been flung clear, and led them with desperate energy. He was the first of those outside to get to Miss Smythe. Eventually what looked like five lifeless bodies were got out of the mud and rushed to the nearest hospital. Two were really dead. The driver had been crushed against his wheel, and Miss Smythe's heart had stopped from shock.

I was the first to come round, as I had been the first to be knocked senseless. I could give no account of what had happened, but Smallwood gave a clear enough description of the accident to the authorities, amplified as it was by those of the other rescuers.

He and they alike had nothing but praise for the conduct of Richardson and Scullion. The latter especially had shown an absolute disregard of his own life in getting Miss Smythe out of the window and holding her up, while drowning himself by inches. He could not know that it was a dead body he had saved at the apparent cost of his own life.

Richardson was the second to come round. His words were: "Accident. Dreadful—accident," and he relapsed into unconsciousness again.

I was up and tottering around when Scullion for a second came out of his unconsciousness. His eyes suddenly opened and fixed themselves urgently on the doctor, who was making camphor injections.

"I'm dying. Fetch Maltass!" came a ghost of a whisper as the medical man bent down. I was rushed to the bedside in a trice. For a moment I thought I had come too late. Then Scullion's big, bold eyes opened for an instant with nothing of their old glare in them.

"I'm going," he whispered into my ear. "Want first— say—he was holding her down—not helping. She was murdered. Good-by." His eye began to film.

I tried, and the doctor tried to revive him, to get one more explanatory word, but Scullion could not be brought back to consciousness. The doctors did not give up hope of ultimately saving him. He had tremendously overtaxed his heart and lungs during his immersion in the icy water, by his efforts to save the woman who had given him his chance in life, however much in some moods he might deny it, the kindly old maid, for whom, after all, he had a feeling that often stands a strain better than warmer emotions.

I had been able to give Gibbs's cable address on first coming round, and the superintendent was with us only an hour or so after Scullion's terrible words.

"Let's hope to God he pulls through!" Gibbs said fervently, turning away from the room where Scullion lay looking already as though he had half slipped away from this world. "Certainly, his evidence should be a final nail in Richardson's coffin."

I disliked the sound of that phrase intensely.

"Even if he doesn't pull through," I said finally, "there's what he already has said. It only applies to Richardson."

"Richardson could say it was meant for Mr. Smallwood," Gibbs said to that. "Also there's McKirdy."

"I suppose there's our Royal family too," was my retort. "How can McKirdy be brought in?"

"He has just telephoned me from Vevey that he is ill with influenza, alone in the house. That the cook went off an hour after Miss Smythe left, and that the other two servants went shortly after that. There's been a conference arranged at Vevey itself just this month, it seems, and the hotels are giving any wages the servants choose to ask. That much the police confirm. But it means that McKirdy hasn't been seen by any one since Miss Smythe left. And could have got back there had he caught the Ostend express for Geneva just after your accident, if it was an accident. I suppose you have no idea or recollection of anything before you lost consciousness yourself?"

I had not. It was all confusion and darkness and oblivion coming almost at once. Vaguely I could seem to remember cries and, the noise of water and splintering wood.

"Did you hear Miss Smythe cry out?"

I had not. The sounds I seemed to recall were the shouts of men.

It was maddening. Here again was moral, but not legal, proof. I said as much.

Gibbs nodded with a very gloomy face.

"I feel like that too, Mr. Maltass. For unless we can bring it home to Richardson—alone—young Mr. Abbott will stand in the dock alongside of him."

I stared.

"You mean he might be supposed to share the motive—the eventual handling of the Carlisle-Walsh-Smythe fortune?"

"There's more than that. There's that double alibi he and Richardson gave each other during both murders. Now, as regards the first—well—" Gibbs looked at me gravely. "You see, I believe in the innocence of Edward Abbott, and yet—the facts are pretty damning. He and Richardson were seen hiding near Latimer's Oak around six or just past it, by old Morley. He used to be the rector's houseman until he married a widow with a little money. They keep the little grocer's shop now. He didn't want to speak, and wouldn't have, but for the murder of Verbena Hillock. That has haunted him, and he finally came forward —to the station that means—and made a statement. He, came forward very unwillingly, for he loves the rector, which, of course, makes his evidence doubly valuable, or doubly damning. I cautioned young Mr. Abbott, and asked him for an explanation. He denied having been at the oak, denied that Richardson was there. Well, of course Morley's evidence knocks out the first alibi, and by doing so automatically knocks out the second one too."

"I knew Richardson's was faked!"—I spoke with pardonable exultation—"but it certainly is an appalling situation for Abbott. He's been had, cheated in some way. In strict confidence, Gibbs, I wanted to marry Miss Abbott—" Something in his faint smile made me realize that this was no news to him.

"And I still hope to do so," I went on. "Her infatuation for Richardson will vanish as soon as she knows his real nature. But for her sake, apart from my sharing your own belief in his innocence, I want most desperately to clear Abbott too."

He looked at me rather a long moment, as though undecided whether to say something that was in his mind or not. After a brief pause he went on a trifle doggedly:

"There's one more thing. As you know, Lily Hillock's very insistence that that brass box has something to do with her sister's murder makes me know there is something else which Lily won't acknowledge even to herself, which may very well be the real reason. That's why she fainted, as we both agree. That's why she's up in town day after day trying to find what Bena could have done with that box, supposing her murderer didn't take it. Lily feels sure that her sister was taking it to the station and on up to town, you know. But nothing we can do will find out where that box got to. She must have gone somewhere between the time that her train got in and the time she arrived at the Braille library. But where? We have a porter who says he saw her walking off with another young lady. Some one in a pulled-down little felt bonnet such as our grandmothers used to wear, barring the strings, but which might mean a child of fifteen nowadays. He didn't see the face. All he saw was the bonnet, a cloak, and a high fur collar, and fairy short skirts. None an indication of age. He saw the two turn out of the station, the blind girl's arm tucked confidingly into the other's. After that, we can find no trace of Verbena until she appears at the library. The trouble is," the superintendent went on slowly, "that between the time Bena's train got in town and the time she herself got back home, another train left for Much Widham. Any one—this other man or girl, for instance—could easily have run down by train and been hiding in the garden by the time Verbena got there. If so, she was, of course, some one who knew the farm garden well. Knew that path with the thick hedge on both sides"—he meant the path along which I had seen Walsh hurrying—"and must have been some one whose presence in the house, even coming in by way of the windows, perhaps, would not make Bena exclaim. Or rise from the table, but continue placidly with her meal."

A cold sweat was on my forehead. It was nonsense, monstrous, ludicrous, but Gibbs was carefully not looking at me.

McKirdy arrived at the hospital that evening. He had flown from Geneva. He seemed changed again. Not only I, but Gibbs thought so. In some inner and remote way happier and more at peace. McKirdy had always hitherto, since Walsh's murder, given me a strong sensation of uneasiness if not of something deeper. But not now. It was as if for him something had been accomplished, finished. Remembering his mother's race, it was with a strange feeling that I heard him murmur, "An act of God. A clear act of God," as he came out of the room where Miss Smythe lay white and very still. Looking at his face, I was more than ever certain that for him in some region of spirit or mind, the death of this woman closed some chapter.

Neither he nor any one beyond Gibbs and I knew the words that Scullion had whispered to me. The doctors had been out of earshot, like the nurses. Waiting till the dying man, as he seemed to be, should have finished his few words to his friend.

He had asked at once to see Richardson, but was told, truthfully, that Richardson could see no one.

The refusal did not seem to disturb McKirdy. If he was in this threefold murder, he seemed very certain of his own safety, and of having got something that he wanted. Got it in a very secure grip. I rather wondered whether it would not have been better to allow him to see the other man, and have had their conversation overheard, their meeting watched, but Gibbs was unwilling to assume so much responsibility.

The inquest was held that day. It brought out nothing fresh except repetitions of what were described as the heroic efforts of the two men inside the car with her to save the woman fastened in with them. They seemed, both of them, to have done all that brave men could, with an absolute disregard of their own lives. Scullion, being the bigger man physically, had taken the major part, and, if there was any difference in bravery, the more selflessly heroic part, in what would have been a rescue had Miss Smythe not suffered from 'a dangerously weak heart.'

Smallwood's friend, the garage owner, Captain Green, gave what seemed a perfectly straightforward account of the ordering of the car. No blame attached to any one, in short, was the verdict, except to the authorities for not lighting the ferry better. Sympathy with the victims and admiration for the conduct of the two men in the car with the unfortunate lady were duly expressed and recorded.

When it was over, McKirdy announced his intention of going back at once to Bois Riant in accordance with Miss Smythe's last request to him. He and Smallwood were both subpoenaed to attend the adjourned inquest and Gibbs made no objection.

"Switzerland's a capital place for the police to get hold of people in," he remarked a trifle oracularly.

I asked Smallwood to stay on at Ostend in case Scullion should be able to say a few more words, or even but one more word, the all-important name. It was a dreadful thought that it might be lost or misunderstood by being whispered into foreign ears. He at once agreed.

"I would look in on Richardson now and then, too," he added, "only Gibbs tells me the poor chap's still too ill to see any one."

Gibbs told me, on my repeating this, that an extradition order had been already applied for, and would be used should Richardson, supposing, as the doctors did, that he would shortly be able to travel, not return to England of his own accord.

"Oh, he will!" I retorted bitterly, "he'll go harking back to Much Widham before a fortnight's over."

"That's what we want," the superintendent said hospitably, "and then we'll nab him. But as to whether his arrest will clear young Mr. Abbott—" He left the sentence unfinished.

It was a gloomy return flight we two made together back to Croydon aerodrome. I had hardly reached my rooms in town, and changed, when my man announced him again. Superintendent Gibbs hardly waited for the formality.

"Mr. Maltass, something is all wrong. All wrong!" He spoke very low but with despair in his tone. "I never could quite see Richardson in the light you did. I mean, that something sinister you so often spoke about—"

A ridiculous exaggeration that. But I let it pass.

"I ought to've realized that of course you'd be prejudiced." Here I did interrupt. If ever there was a calm, impartial weighing of facts by an absolutely unbiased legal mind—

"Do you mind telling me what all this tirade is about, Gibbs," I asked quietly.

He did not seem to feel the rebuke. "It's this," he went on rapidly. "If you're right, if Richardson is guilty, then so is young Mr. Abbott. Whatever it is, they're in it together. Listen"—as I would have spoken—"this morning Edward Abbott tried to get off on the Dover-Calais boat, wearing some ridiculous sort of disguise that nearly dropped off when he tried to bluster it out. He acknowledged to me that he was trying to get to Richardson when I taxed him with it. Oh, yes, he was stopped and sent back under escort to Much Wihham police station—"

"Arrested!" I said in blank horror, as I thought of a dear, pale face, with its air of happy content in life.

"Not yet—officially. He's being detained only as yet, but his arrest is only a question of hours, of course."

"But however foolish his attempt was to get to the man who has hoodwinked him so completely," I put in, "still it was only some idiotic idea of the duty of friendship about which I happen to know he holds very strong views. I still don't see what you mean by saying that he's in the same boat with Richardson." I spoke calmly, trying to make the excited man before me look at things more sanely. For, though he did not show it, obviously the superintendent was excited, or he would not have said the quite unbelievably idiotic things that he had.

"He says it himself, Mr. Maltass. Refuses to say what he and Richardson were doing together, sticks to his denial that they were near Latimer's Oak but won't swear to that denial. Refuses to make any statement except the unofficial one that he and Richardson are on exactly the same footing. It seems one of the papers has a hint that Richardson is to be arrested, or is already under arrest pending extradition proceedings, and will be charged with the double murders down at Much Widham. The paper gives no names, of course, but refers to the man in words that would leave no doubt in any mind that knew the facts. It's that application for extradition that's torn it. It generally does. But to come back to young Mr. Abbott, as I say, he swore to me that if we arrest Richardson we must arrest him. That they stood on exactly the same footing in everything, as he can, and will, prove."

"But, good God, it's lunacy," I gasped. "It's chivalrous suicide, for the sake of a scoundrel who—"

"It's the truth, Mr. Maltass," Gibbs interrupted me bluntly. "Listening to young Mr. Abbott convinced me that he was speaking the sober truth. Whatever the two were up to, they're both in it equally. And in my belief it's something that's closely intertwined with the murders. So closely that young Mr. Abbott daren't speak. Or can't take the responsibility. If Richardson is really guilty, then I see no way but for young Mr. Abbott to be guilty too— which is impossible. Yet Mr. Richardson'll be arrested as soon as he's well enough to travel. Either by the continental police or over here—by me. That's what we've got to face. That's where we stand."

"Abbott's been hoodwinked," I repeated, my heart sinking. "Richardson has used him as his tool, made him swallow some clever tale—"

Gibbs again interrupted.

"Impossible, Mr. Maltass. After the way he spoke to me. Besides—it always has stuck in my crop that if misled before the murder, young Mr. Abbott should have remained so after that crime. No one but a fool would stay deceived by any tale after that. And not only did he not speak out, but he and Richardson were thicker than ever after Walsh's death. And the same is true of Lily Hillock—until her sister was knifed. Since then, she's avoided the two, and they her. Oh, there's some dark tangle here, Mr. Maltass, and—well—it's deceived us. That's my opinion. I've just come from a talk with the Deputy Chief Constable. I've told him he must call in the Yard or accept my resignation from the case."

Gibbs's eyes were glowing. "This job is too big for me, and, excuse my frankness, too involved for you, Mr. Maltass, too. I won't arrest a man I feel about as I do about young Mr. Abbott. And on the evidence, as the police officer in charge of the case, I can't refuse. So there's nothing for it but to hope that the Yard will help me out. And help out young Mr. Abbott," he added under his breath. "For he needs it —desperately."

"And the deputy said?" I asked rather coldly. The affair had not at all been too involved for me. I had seen through it from the beginning. It was only this outer tangle, this Abbott-Richardson tangle, and the oddity of the brass box that still baffled me.

"He's called in the Yard. I'm to see the assistant commissioner in an hour. I understand that you're to be present, too, Mr. Maltass?"

So that was the meaning of a cryptic notice I had had over the telephone from my brother.

"But I'd like to run down in the car and see Edward Abbott first," I said. "I can just do it. Any objections?"

"None whatever. I only wish you could persuade him to speak out."

"So do I! He's shielding the real villain," I replied, as I rushed a few things together.

CHAPTER ELEVEN

AT the Much Widham police station I was asked to wait a moment as young Mr. Abbott's sister was with him. To my surprise, Lily Hillock was in the waiting-room as I passed through. She looked like a hunted thing, I thought, as I stopped and shook hands.

"How's Mr. Richardson," she asked, hardly listening to my greeting. "You were with him, weren't you? They say—the papers are full of some stuff about his having had long talks with you and the police superintendent, and that it may lead to important developments in the investigations over here. It's nonsense, of course, but Mr. Abbott has been arrested! How could you let them do it!— young Mr. Abbott! To think of Mr. Gibbs pretending to be such a friend and then to do this! Mr. Abbott had nothing to do with that dreadful Walsh. How I wish I could speak to him a moment! What on earth has his sister to talk to him so long about?"

I said nothing, and after a sudden pace to the window and back she burst out: "And no sign of that brass box that's at the bottom of this trouble. It's my belief that Laura Abbott has it. I can't think what her object is, but she won't say yes or no when I tax her with it."

"I think it's very forbearing of her not to say a good deal more than 'yes' or 'no' to you, in reply to such a statement," I said coldly.

Lily only gave a sort of exasperated toss of her head. "Of course you would say that! You're like Bena. She never could see any faults in her adored Miss Abbott. But listen to this, Mr. Maltass, that description of the woman, or girl, who met Bena at the station in town and with whom she went away, fits Laura Abbott."

"It fits any girl or woman nearly."

She shook her head. "Not as it fits her. And she was Bena's only friend outside the librarian of the Braille Club, who's short and wears a cloak and a little bonnet. There's absolutely no one else but Laura Abbott with whom Bena would have gone like that. And so I told her—Miss Abbott, I mean. She only looked at me and said how sorry she was about Bena. Mind you, I know she is sorry"—Lily's lips quivered—"but she won't say that she wasn't that girl. And I feel sure she was, and that Bena gave her that dreadful box."

"Be careful, Lily!" I said earnestly. "You shouldn't say such things, for many reasons. Your sister, just before she was murdered, told you what practically amounted to the information that to be concerned with that box was to be in danger. You mustn't go about saying that Miss Abbott has it. Apart from many reasons, you're drawing down on her the same danger that your sister told you would menace you."

Lily paled. "I see," she said in a whisper. "You think she knows that, and is keeping the box in order not to pass on the danger—whatever it is?"

"I don't think anything of the kind," I replied. "But I do say that you mustn't say that she has that devilish box."

Lily nodded. "I never thought of that reason," she said gently. "It would be like her to keep it, if she thought it would be dangerous to any one else to let them have it. But—but—I must have it all the same. I must know what it means—why Bena was killed because of it." Here she became incoherent and half hysterical.

I was not surprised. But it was not merely the box that was wearing Lily Hillock down. That something she was keeping back, that something she was afraid Richardson had spoken of . . . that something she wanted to see Edward Abbott so desperately for. . .

But I felt that my brain had been too long on a stretch, it refused to work. It merely lay and watched.

Lily Hillock finally went off without seeing either Edward or his sister. She had some engagement with young Chapman which she seemed unwilling to break. Apparently he was helping in the brass box hunt too.

She had hardly gone when Laura came out. I was prepared to find her calm and outwardly undismayed, but there was about her a quiet confidence and serenity which, I confess, puzzled me. She looked at me rather pleadingly as we shook hands.

"You don't think—you're not suspecting Ted," she began. "My father says there isn't enough evidence to send him to trial. Apart from our own certainty—"

"No," I said, "not for a moment. But Laura"—I had come determined to be frank; she was not to openly link her name with that of Richardson if I could help it—"it's not against Edward that I think evidence will accumulate, but another person."

"Hugh," her lips trembled, "Hugh Richardson, you mean?"

I nodded. Just then the inspector entered. Mr. Abbott wanted to speak to me. I followed him into a pleasant enough room where Edward Abbott sat smoking and reading a newspaper, or at least playing with it. He did not hold out his hand until I did. Then he grasped mine with the unconscious fervor of a man clutching at something valued.

I wrung his fingers without speaking. Looking into his eyes I felt as certain as was Gibbs that this was no criminal. But he was intensely disturbed, and, I fancied, intensely frightened. Yet I got nothing out of him.

Finally I left him and hurried away. Laura stopped me as I was jumping into my car. She only said a word or two, but again I marveled at her air of deep serenity, as though whatever happened was only passing cloud, and, that time would make everything right.

She little knew that time would probably bring brother and lover, if one could call Richardson that, to the scaffold instead.

I rushed up to town and on to New Scotland Yard, where my brother was waiting for me. He took me on to the assistant commissioner's office. There I was introduced to Lawson, the Acting Chief-Constable of West Surrey, who, together with Gibbs, was evidently having a talk with the man of power. I thought Major Pelham, whom I know rather well, was looking distinctly suave and gentle, which always means irritation with him. And both Mr. Lawson and Gibbs were a bit red in the face. Pelham can put things sweetly and yet with more sting to them than most men.

My brother hurried away, and we four plunged into the middle of things.

"What did young Mr. Abbott say?" Gibbs asked me almost tensely.

"Nothing," I replied. "I wasted my time. He won't say anything, except that he's innocent, and that Richardson is as innocent as himself."

Gibbs turned with a gesture to Mr. Lawson, who in his turn faced Major Pelham.

"But you don't refuse to lend us Scotland Yard's help, do you?" he asked, as evidently the end of rather a warm debate.

"It depends," Pelham said coldly. "You didn't call us in at first, when the scent was warm. Now it's cold. Now that all clues have been swept away, except such as you yourself can't find. You want me to send a good man down to take over, in fact, though not in name. I don't see it. I'm tired of these belated requests for help when it's no longer possible to help. They do no good, and only bring us into discredit."

There was rather an awkward silence. I felt that the two men had exhausted their arguments and had nothing more to say. On Gibbs's face was a look of dour resolution.

"It's a question of an innocent man, we think," I said finally, "the proofs we've found seem to point to his being guilty, and we, all of us who know him, feel sure that he's

not. That's a dreadful position. The police must bring a
charge on the evidence they have, and yet believe it's
pointing to the wrong man, or rather, that one of the men
to which it points isn't guilty of anything more than of
being hoodwinked by a clever murderer."

Pelham looked thoughtfully at me. "You put it
strongly," he said finally. "Of course—" There was a
pause. "I'll tell you what, you shall lay the case before one
of our men, and if he sees a way, any way, to alter the
reading of the evidence, he can take it on, provided it
won't be a long case. I'm due in the commissioner's room
for a meeting in a moment, so I can't stop. Let me see,"
he flipped over a loose-leaf ledger, "the only man suitable
for such a decision whom we have free for the moment is
Chief Inspector Pointer. I'll have you taken to his room,
and if he can see his way to help you under those
conditions—a quick case and some new reading of the
evidence that you haven't seen yourselves—I'll spare him
for a week at the outside. Not an hour longer. He'll be
wanted then in a very intricate case on which he's
working with Superintendent Goodson."

This was not quite all that we had hoped for, but it
was better than nothing—much better. Pelham shook
hands and hustled away with a last word to me of "Don't
be peeved, Maltass, if Pointer turns you down. He can't
work the impossible, and he knows his limitations."

"I've worked with him once on a case," Gibbs said as
the door closed. I noticed that he looked eager and
pleased. "He's awfully good on a trail. But"—his face
clouded again—"this way that we've got to just sit here
and tell him the story, and then have him decide whether
anything can be done—" Gibbs shook an impatient dark
head. "Sounds all wrong to me. He ought to come down
and go over the ground. And question the people. How
can he tell from a distance what's what? I never did
believe in those armchair prophets who twiddle a bit of
string and tell you how things really were done. It's like
old ladies who look in their teacups and read it all there."

Gibbs was getting more and more despondent. "It's not fair to the chief, not fair to young Mr. Abbott, not fair to us, and, in a way, though that doesn't matter, not fair to Chief Inspector Pointer either. This way the assistant commissioner has tied us all up."

He stopped his fervent grumbling as the door opened, and a tall, slender, bronzed-faced, youngish man came forward with a very pleasant smile on his face that I judged was usually rather grave. A detective is supposed to look like anything but what he is, an idea which I followed in my Michael Hare, who looks like a famous musician with his long hair and slender fingers.

This man looked his calling, I thought. Something in the swift glance of his gray eyes made me feel, though they rested on me but for a fleeting second, that he could have told you afterwards the color of every article I wore, its probable maker, and the lamentable fact that one of my socks wrinkled, owing to a loose suspender, a trifling defect of toilet which I had fondly thought would not be noticed, until I met his eye for that one moment. And there was another quality about him, a quality hard to define but easy to feel, that of a man used to danger, and who by nature and by training never heeded its presence. The men of my own age, the men who fought in front lines during the Great War have it.

Pointer let first the Deputy Chief-Constable, then Gibbs, tell the story, I coming in finally with my account of life at the farm from the inside.

Pointer made no notes. When he had finished the deputy showed unexpected good sense by rising and saying, "I'm a solicitor by profession, you know. Police work is new to me. I don't think I can be of any further help, and there's a firm near here that I ought to see this morning, if possible. So I will leave you three to thoroughly thresh the matter out. I need hardly say"—he held out his hand to Pointer—"how very glad I shall be if you see your way to coming to our assistance."

Pointer responded equally courteously but very non-committally, and closed the door after him. Then Gibbs drew a deep breath and fairly waded in. He gave a remarkably concise and yet detailed account of the whoe case, I thought. When he had finished, the chief inspector asked me to tell the story from my point of view, from inside the farm, as it were. I did my best, though I found to my great surprise how much longer it took me than it had taken Gibbs.

Pointer listened with an attention that was stimulating in itself. Now and then he would ask a question which showed that his mind was traveling along, and just a little ahead of one's own. Finally I, too, stopped. I had told everything that I knew, saw, suspected, felt.

The chief inspector sat sideways at his table, his hands thrust into his pockets, his head bent, his eyes fastened on his shoe tips, which he occasionally bent up and then down. It was a very long silence, or seemed so to me. Gibbs looked at him with the eyes of a dog whose master has his hand on the bone cupboard. Perhaps I, too, had the same yearning intensity in my eyes, for they positively smarted afterwards.

Still the silence went on. I noticed that Pointer's pipe had gone out. Still he only stared at his shoes, but now with a slight frown between his well-marked, level brows.

Then he asked a question or two about the brass box, listening, I thought, as though for some answer that would fit some idea of his own. If it did, he gave no sign. Again silence fell.

"I don't think it can be done!" Gibbs burst out finally. "I mean, just telling you a long story and not being able to take you over the place or let you question the witnesses for yourself, sir—"

"I don't think that would be of any use," Pointer said quietly. "You and I worked together once, Gibbs, and I don't think that if I hunted the place over for a week, or questioned the people down there for a month, I should learn more than you've found out and told me so clearly."

Gibbs flushed with gratification. "It's very good of you to say so, Mr. Pointer," he murmured. Then, emboldened, he went on, "Do you see anything that can suggest a fresh line?"

"Above all, do you see how to explain that devilish little brass box?" I burst out, "other than the idea that it contains incriminating papers, of course; that's obvious. But have you any clue to its appearance and disappearance, the fact that it was seen for a moment in the blind girl's possession and never afterwards?"

"Yes," Pointer said unexpectedly to that. "Yes, I have a theory which is possible—only possible, mind—"

"And which would explain that box?" I asked incredulously.

"Yes."

"Was the fact that she had it in her possession the cause of Bena Hillock's death?" I asked tensely.

"If my theory is right, it was."

"Then what does it contain?" I pressed; "that box has haunted me. What does it hide?"

"The blind girl may have put something into it," Pointer said slowly. "I wouldn't be surprised if she had, though I don't feel sure of that. But if my theory is right, the box did not necessarily contain anything at all when she had it."

"But its meaning to Walsh?" I protested.

"If my theory is right," he said, with a faintly deprecating smile, "which isn't proved yet, it stood for nothing to Walsh either."

"You mean there isn't anything valuable in it, sir? Neither papers nor money nor valuables of any kind?" puzzled Gibbs.

"Not in my theory. As I see it," Pointer rose, "it held nothing, stood for nothing—"

"But was in itself of value!" I said, jumping up too. Vague ideas of some old Cellini masterpiece masquerading undetected through the years as a plain brass box floating through my mind.

But he shook his head. "Nor, as I see it, is it of any intrinsic value whatever."

"A warning!" I muttered. "That was my idea, too. A warning."

"It's not my idea," he said to that. "I see in it neither a warning nor a portent."

"And yet you say that, like us, you think that because she had it in her possession, Verbena Hillock was murdered."

"Because she was known, or seen to have it in her possession," he amended. "I do. I can't be more explicit until I've tested my theory."

"Then you are going to take the case on?" Gibbs's eyes shone. He looked as though a weight were slipping from his shoulders.

"I am," Pointer said promptly. "I certainly want to."

"But about that box," I harked back, "what about its being in the possession of any one at the moment? Would that person be in danger too?"

"If I'm right, the, box can do no more harm to any one unless it now contains a message from the blind girl. That, of course, is possible. But it wouldn't be the box that would be the danger."

"But Verbena's words of warning to her sister," I protested; "does your theory explain them?"

"It wouldn't be much of a theory if it didn't fit all the facts as so far told me, which I believe to be, as so far known," he said genially.

"Do you think that Abbott is innocent, and is only shielding Richardson?" I felt I must clear a little way into the impenetrability of the detective officer.

"I wouldn't venture yet to say who is innocent, who guilty," Pointer said gravely. "It all depends on whether my theory proves to be possible or not. And whether, even then, it is provable. Frankly, that's my difficulty as I see it. How to prove my idea."

"Something we overlooked?" Gibbs asked.

"I wouldn't say that. A better way to put it would be that as I see it, unless those two young men are guilty, the only alternative is my theory, which is why I hold to it. Otherwise, I can be of no use. But I'll work along it for the week during which Major Pelham will give me leave of absence from the case on which I'm helping. If my theory is right, it ought to be proved by then."

"Proof," I said to that; "do you agree with me that there's no proof except what we see for ourselves?"

"To a policeman the proof must be one he can put before a jury," the chief inspector said evasively. He evidently was not to be drawn.

"And now," he said, rising, "I must have a word with the assistant commissioner as soon as he can see—"

Just then, that important person walked into the room.

"Well?" he asked, "see any light, Pointer?"

I think he was surprised when the officer nodded. "I see the possibility of a theory, sir."

"Theory! There's such a long way generally between theory and criminals," Pelham spoke with, feeling. "We can only spare you for a week, you know. Even supposing your theory proves right, how long will it take to find the criminal? You're not likely to have solved the whole of this crime at one sweep. The how, and the who, and the why."

Pointer said nothing. Major Pelham wheeled on him.

"You have? By Jove! you think you have?"

"I think it may be so," Pointer said to that, "and if so, I ought to be back within the week."

"Come into my room," Pelham said promptly, and after telling Gibbs and me that he would be down at Much Widham in a little over an hour, Pointer shook hands and followed his superior into the passage.

Gibbs drew a deep breath in our car.

"Saved! Young Abbott is saved!" he said optimistically, "and to think that just sitting in his chair, there at the Yard, he could solve what you and I have been knocking our heads against all these days."

I considered that a very silly way of putting the case, and said so. "I saw Richardson's guilt from the first. It's just because we have been working night and day that he could get a theory together so quickly," I replied tartly. "Whatever this theory of his is, it rests entirely on what we have found, also it remains to be proved," I reminded him. "And we mustn't assume that it's right, because it's not ours."

"No, but because it fits those funny things we can't get any explanation for," he said slowly. "Now, what was there in the facts we told him that we hadn't thought of . . ." And the rest of the drive was given over by both of us, who ought to've known better, to the futile task of debating what the chief inspector's theory was and what it was not.

Inspector Pointer met us to the moment, and we took him over to the farm. He had a few words with Mr. Hillock—a still more silent, still grimmer man than the Hillock I had met only a couple of months ago. Next came Lily Hillock, still insistent on the key to the tragedy lying in the brass box which could not be found in spite of all her efforts. From neither of these did the chief inspector ask any questions. Then he looked over the house. First of all, he had me show him where each of us stood when I had had that glimpse of the brass box, though I had not noticed it at the time. He gave the scene but the briefest of glances. Then he repeated the same thing with Esther. Next he asked me to take him to the dining-room where I had found what I still thought was Bena opening Walsh's bureau in the darkness. But it was here where I had been when the attack was made on me that his interest seemed to lie. He turned his back on the room and looked at the door, moving it to and fro, as though testing it. Then he called for Esther.

"Anything missing from this room since the night after Mr. Walsh was found dead?" he asked.

She said there was not.

"Nothing found broken next morning?"

Again he got a negative.

"What about that plant in that pot? It seems to be dying?" he was speaking while roaming the room, apparently at random, turning over the leaves of a volume on British Butterflies which some collector had left behind him at the farm, presumably on account of its bulk.

"That plant," Esther said in a tone of awe, "has drooped like that since the day Mr. Walsh was murdered. It never gave no trouble before. Lovely plant it was, but since that day—" She went over to it and shook a mournful head.

"I'll have a gardener give it a look," Pointer said in the tone of a man doing his one good turn a day and conscious of his benevolence. "Pity to see a plant suffer," and with that he turned away. An hour later I heard the gentle tapping on a flower-pot with which a gardener coaxes a plant out of its home. There, in the dining-room I found the chief inspector and a red-nosed, raw cheek-boned man bending over the plant, now out of its pot. "Been done roughly, too. Crammed into a smaller pot and just rammed home. Stamped in, one might call it," the stranger was saying.

"Done about when?" Pointer asked.

"Only about two weeks ago. Not more." The man examined with the eye of knowledge the tiny wormlike roots, white and twisted into a tight ball.

Pointer turned to me after the man, who, it seemed, was a gardener, had left.

"Care for a run in my car to the station?" he asked.

Seated beside him, he said slowly, "Would you be surprised to hear that there was no attack on you that night of the first murder, Mr. Maltass? I mean, that what seemed to leap at you as you opened the dining-room door and struck you down, was a rather too heavily constructed booby trap."

I stiffened. "Impossible!" was on my lips. But was it impossible?

"That plant?" I queried.

"Was probably perched on top of two big books, one a directory, one a work on butterflies. Both show the dents one would expect, and specks of earth. The butterfly work has come loose from its binding. Altogether the pile might have killed you."

"Was meant to, perhaps," I suggested with some heat.

"I think more probably it was the result of ignorance. Some one who knew of the idea but had not had much practice."

"Then it wouldn't be Abbott or Richardson." I knew the skill of the two in all kinds of practical jokes too well to underrate their talents.

"Unless some other person thought they had not provided sufficient weight to stop any intruder, and added another half ton of plant, forgetting the height from which the whole would fall."

"You really do think it was a booby trap?" I challenged.

"It looks that way, yes," he said slowly; "I do. The flower-pot probably broke on your head. The plant was already pot-bound or you would have been smothered in earth. As it was, you only found a couple of crumbs on the floor. All the rest had evidently been very well swept up before you came."

"That couldn't have been the work of the blind girl," I said.

"Ah, the blind girl restoring the stolen money." he murmured. Something in his tone made me look at him.

"You don't think she was?" I asked.

"It's not proven, is it?"

"Of course, there are always two ways of looking at every fact," I agreed, rather at a loss.

"And sometimes more ways still," he replied with a quiet smile.

"You don't think it was she at all?"

"That much seems very probable," he conceded. "She and her sister, and young Mr. Abbott and his friend Richardson, make a very complete group which would explain a great deal. I've talked to Miss Lily Hillock, and I want to talk to Mr. Richardson. For that reason I think we shall let young Mr. Abbott come to Ostend too, so that all three can talk matters over with us before I go on to Bois Riant and have a word with Mr. McKirdy there."

"Lily Hillock, Abbott, and Richardson," I murmured. "Both Richardson's tools, so Smallwood said. But will you get them to speak when they're together? I should have thought separately. . . ."

"That's where I can take short cuts, Mr. Maltass, You and Mr. Gibbs have tried them separately, without any result. If I'm to get the truth out of them I must try them together."

I nodded.

"Mr. Smallwood is still at Ostend, isn't he?" Pointer went on, casually.

I said that in a letter only this morning he had written as though he would stay on as long as Richardson was detained in hospital.

"He's the best of fellows," I finished up warmly, "just staying on in a place he loathes from kindness to a mere acquaintance, in whom, I fancy, you're more interested in than you choose to say."

I glanced at him, but his face gave me no sign of his thoughts. It struck me afresh that you could never guess from it what was in Pointer's mind for all his apparent look of frankness. Yet I liked him with his good features and steady eyes, very fine, eyes they were, too.

"I wonder if it would surprise you to learn that Mr. Smallwood's piano has an electric player attachment?" he said quite unexpectedly.

"Eh?" I felt that my jaw dropped. "You mean—?"

"Just that, Mr. Maltass. In Mr. Smallwood's piano, I've examined it, is a plug socket well out of sight. He only had to plug in a connection with that lamp beside him on

the wall, and his piano would play, though he himself
were miles away. Mind you, I don't say it did, but it could
have done so the afternoon that Walsh was murdered."

"But—good Heavens!" I hastily thought over the quite
staggering words.

"Was that what he went out to fling away that
night?" I wondered finally.

"It may have been. Quite likely, I think, for it's
nowhere to be found and the plug shows signs of a violent
wrench. I fancy the plug fitted very tightly. They usually
do in these pianos. And some one was too impatient to
work it off carefully. Seeing that Mr. Smallwood has
given no hint to any one of his pianos being capable of
being played by electricity as well as of being worked by a
treadle, I think it's quite likely that he was very anxious
indeed to conceal the former fact. So anxious that I see no
reason to doubt but that he took the first chance he got of
throwing away what would certainly have revealed the
fact next morning. That was the flex with its two-point
plug at one end and lamp plug at the other."

I sat really stupefied. Smallwood! Not possible!

"Then he hasn't an alibi at all—for the time that
Walsh was murdered," I finally muttered.

"He has not," Pointer agreed. "As I say, that piano in
his room might have been playing—"

"Playing over, and over, and over," I filled in
automatically.

"Yes. There is a little lever which can be set to
'Repeat' and the piece would be played, with short
intervals for the roll to wind up and unwind, until the
lever was reversed."

"Smallwood!" I murmured. "But of course this proves
nothing. I mean, he lost his head when we all assumed
that he must have been playing because the piano was
going on, I think he didn't want to lose such a wonderful
alibi. I mean, I don't doubt his word for a moment that he
was in the room all the time. He might let us go on
assuming that the piano was the ordinary player kind

you pedal away at, but he wouldn't tell an out and out lie. You see, I know Smallwood."

"And young Mr. Abbott says he knows Mr. Richardson," Pointer said with a rather puzzling smile as we drew up at the police station.

CHAPTER TWELVE

WE flew over that night in a fast police plane, Abbott and Lily Hillock sitting silent and constrained beside me, while the two officers had a front seat and talked in low tones together. I thought that both my companions were something more than uneasy, but they carefully avoided even the appearance of mutual interests.

At Ostend Gibbs took charge of them, taking them off to a quiet little hotel for a rest and breakfast, while Pointer was busy interviewing the various police heads of that gay little seaport and gambling center.

I do not know Ostend at all, so I decided to make for Smallwood's hotel. It would be sure to be quiet, unpretentious, and good. But I had not counted on running into him in the lounge before I had more than given my keys to the valet on my floor.

We, or rather he, sat down promptly and started a talk about the one affair that concerned us all. He told me that Scullion refused to speak, but that the doctors hoped he would, in time, pull through. I answered haltingly. Do what I would, I could not get the accustomed ease into tone or manner.

"Is anything wrong, Maltass?" he said finally, looking at me earnestly. "Has anything fresh happened? I thought you were accompanying this Scotland Yard man and Gibbs over here more for form's sake than anything?"

He looked at me very closely indeed, very searchingly. I felt myself redden. What was I to say?

The chief inspector's card arrived just then. On the back were a few lines. Would Mr. Smallwood mind sparing him and Superintendent Gibbs a moment? They would like a word with him, and unless he had any objection, they saw no reason why Mr. Maltass should not come too.

Smallwood again looked at me. I tried to assume an air of cheerful ignorance, but something betrayed me, for this time it was he who flushed scarlet.

"So you know?"

I managed a look of inquiry.

"About the piano," he said.

"Oh, that—yes."

"And they know too?"

"It was the officer from Scotland Yard who found out. Why on earth, Smallwood—"

He stopped me. "Of course I ought to've explained about it to Gibbs at once. But there are some things which, if not said at the right moment, can't be said at all. I was in my room during the time I said I was—"

"I'm certain you were," I said warmly. "I've told both of them that I'd take your word for that in spite of all the electric devices ever invented."

He gave me a warmly grateful look. "Thanks. I—I lost my head a bit, and when an alibi seemed found for me, I drifted."

He said as much to the two men waiting for us in the private room into which we were shown.

"But what about being out that night, Mr. Smallwood?" Gibbs inquired very gravely. "It's not only the fact of that piano being playable when you were absent, but your climbing out of your window and in by it that night that must be explained."

"I know." Smallwood flushed again deeply. "I was a perfect fool. It was the electric attachment that I dropped into the duck-pond. It was rather a bulky thing, and I saw no way to prevent its being found, if any one looked through my room next morning—as in fact was done. I trusted to the difficulty of seeing the holes for the plug inside the piano works. But if that attachment with its very thick flex was found—" He did not need to finish.

Again he assured them both on his word of honor that he had spent the time exactly as he had stated—trying to learn a very difficult piece of music by heart. Playing it over and over, and listening intently, which was his only way of memorizing music, as he could only play by ear, not by eye.

We left him very much flustered and very sorry for himself, and stepped into a car placed by the Ostend police at the disposal of the chief inspector. Gibbs gave the address of the nursing home where Richardson was staying. We stopped for a moment to pick up Lily Hillock and Abbott, both looking very nervous; both quite silent.

Evidently the hospital authorities had been given some sufficiently plausible explanation, for we were all shown without a word into the room where Richardson sat with his leg in plaster. He gave a startled look at the chief inspector's tall figure, and after a word of introduction from Gibbs, shot another very keenly inquiring look at the two silent figures.

"It's just this," Pointer began at once cheerfully. "I think that a general talk of the family council type might clear the air best and quickest. You've got yourselves, as I see it, into a very nasty position—extremely so—it may be worse than that. But short of complicity in the actual murders, I think that frankness is by far your best policy, Mr. Abbott, and yours, too, Mr. Richardson. Very grave facts are in our possession. Superintendent Gibbs agrees with me in thinking that you should be told them." And with that Mr. Pointer ran over all the points in question. The evidence was very appalling as piece by piece of it piled up before us as it were.

The blackmailing letter on rectory notepaper; the envelope to match found after the murder, addressed to the murdered man in Richardson's writing, the envelope which the prosecution would contend had held the letter in question. The sealing with the shilling traced so immediately to Edward Abbott, and known to have been in the possession of the blind girl before she was murdered, before she could tell the superintendent by whom it had been given to her. The absence of any satisfactory alibi for both during the two murders. The evidence that the two young men were seen hiding near the oak around the time of the first murder, and could have had access to the dining-room together, or singly, at the time of the second. The weights taken from the farmhouse kitchen. The biscuit-tin which it seemed—this was new to me—had been traced to Lily Hillock. The method of tying the weights together which was familiar to both or rather all three. The advantage to the two young men of removing the man in temporary possession of the large fortune left by Carlisle. The immediate death—to put it at that—of the next person to whom that fortune passed so that now it had come to the father of the one and the expected father-in-law of the other. In Lily Hillock's case the removal of Walsh, against whom she had a grudge owing to his having let her see that he had no intention of marrying her after she had quarreled because of him with a young man who, at one time, would have gladly made her his wife.

It was a most formidable tale. The two young men were very pale. And when Pointer went on in the same concise way to detail their own financial difficulties, a sickly green spread over the faces of both. Only Lily Hillock sat erect and almost indifferent, her burning eyes fixed on the speaker.

When he had finished there was complete silence for a moment, then Lily Hillock sprang up.

"Where's the brass box in all this talk?"

"Unimportant. Outside the crime," Pointer said indifferently.

She spun round on him. "You think so! Much you know! Listen! Oh, you've found out a lot of things that don't matter. Nothing about the one thing that does. Now I'll tell the whole truth. I don't care whether you want me to or not"—she flung over her shoulder at the two young men—"in a way I ought to be the one to speak first, for I got them both into this." She sat down again now and spoke in a hard, firm, composed voice.

"I wanted to get even with Walsh—and rightly. You've put it very bluntly but quite truthfully as to his intentions and that he had come between Harold Chapman and me. When I found that Walsh thought he could amuse himself with me I turned on him. Also I raved a bit to young Mr. Abbott and Mr. Richardson here. I was red-hot, and I suppose I stoked them up. Anyway, Mr. Richardson knew something about Walsh and a woman on the boat he had been on, and we all decided to teach him a lesson. We concocted a ridiculous letter telling him that he must put a thousand pounds in a biscuit-tin behind Latimer's Oak, or have the skin flayed off his bones by the husband of the lady he'd flirted with on the ship. I happened to know from him that he always had that amount with him, or on him, or getatable anyhow. We—the letter—set the hour for six for the money to be paid. We were quite sure he would do it. Walsh was a most frightful coward. I wanted to be there early so as not to miss anything, but as it happened it was past six. I caught sight of Harold Chapman going away from the direction of the oak, and wondered if he had come to watch a supposed interview between me and Walsh. That startled me. I didn't—we didn't—want any one else to be there. When I got to the place and saw nothing of Walsh, I thought Harold must have frightened him away. I stood there wondering what we had better do, and when the two boys were coming, when my powder puff and box rolled out of my hand into the ditch close by. I fished for it with my walking stick and found Walsh's dead body. His head was all battered in. He was quite cold, but not stiff yet. I rushed away after Harold, and met my father, who simply carried me off, in his car and wouldn't let me speak to him. These boys came later to the oak—they got held up by some thing or other, but they found the money all right in the tin, took it, sealed it up in an envelope they had ready, and taking it back to the farm, placed it in Walsh's bureau which could only be unlocked by his own key and one I had, a key belonging to my mother's workbox. That envelope wasn't the one containing the 'blackmailing' letter as you call it." She flashed a glance of scorn at Pointer. "In with the note these two boys put a letter we had drafted all together. It ran like this: *'This was to teach you a lesson. Next time you try your games, you may not get off so easily,—The Jokers.'* I had written it finally out on paper and—well, when we heard of Walsh's murder we didn't know what to do. Of course we should have taken proper precautions had we meant real blackmail, let alone murder. As it was, Mr. Richardson had written the address on the envelope in printed characters, and I had written the slip with no pretense of disguising my writing. You see, I wanted Walsh to know who was at the bottom of the joke. I wanted him to know that I knew all about him and what a little coward he was!

"But his murder! For a time I hadn't thought about our part in what might happen to us, how it might look. But when I got home it all began to come back. At first I only thought of Harold and that his life was to be ruined. We three had a talk and decided that we must get hold of that letter that was put in with the notes. Mr. Richardson thought that his writing was quite disguised, so didn't trouble about the envelope, but some one must get that letter. We knew Superintendent Gibbs was in the house, and—well—while we were talking it over there came a fearful crash. It was Mr. Maltass on the dining-room floor with the big pot on top of-him. Bena, plucky, unselfish, little Bena, had done it all, while we were talking. She had been in the room with us and stolen out, arranged a booby trap as she had heard could be done, with a big cudgel, a couple of books and a plant, and got out the letter I had written from among the notes. She didn't need light, you see, but could tell the notes by their feel. Unfortunately, she made the trap much too heavy. However, Mr. Richardson was sure Mr. Maltass would come round in a little while and be none the worse for it, so we tidied and swept up the room again, and then made for our own rooms. Each moment we thought that you, Mr. Gibbs, would come in, and that we should have to think up some explanation."

"It didn't occur to you at the time or later to tell the truth?" Gibbs asked in a very police-official manner.

"I'm nominated for the Stock Exchange," young Abbott struck in nervously, "it would have meant ruin. Richardson here's at Lloyds—got a jolly good berth. What chance of keeping it if we got mixed up in a blackmail and murder charge? We've had the most ghastly time—" He pulled himself up and only set his mouth as he looked at Lily Hillock. She barely glanced at either of her two tools.

"And what did you seal the envelope with in which you put the notes?" Gibbs asked them.

"Red sealing wax, I think Lily produced that, and I sealed it with a shilling, the first coin I fished from my pocket," Abbott replied, "without glancing at what it was. But I remembered afterwards it was a shilling. And Lily put two and two together when you started talking about marked shillings, or rather cracked one's, as you called them—she was quicker than I—and we wondered whether by bad luck I had used the one that I had taken from my father—we couldn't tell, but it seemed possible."

Lily had listened with scant patience. "Oh, all that doesn't matter. I don't suppose you'll believe a word of it just because it's the truth. But we none of us know anything that really matters—who murdered Bena after murdering Walsh. Why, she was killed because of that damned brass box Chapman gave me, a box of no value and no interest to any one. No one could have kept anything important in it for it didn't lock, and it stood on the hall table until it got lost—as we thought. I believe Miss Abbott has the box—"

Edward Abbott flushed with anger and half started to speak, but she did not pause.

"Oh. I'm not bringing any accusation against Miss Abbott. But I believe Bena gave it into her care. If so, she's in danger, too. And perhaps if you had that box you could understand what it all means, but she won't confess to having it. She refuses to say anything one way or the other. Can't you make her give it you? Can't you make her speak?"

"I don't think it will be necessary," Pointer said quietly. "Well, is this all you have to say, all three of you?"

Receiving only assurances that it was, he asked a few rather catchy questions without tripping any of them, then Gibbs said finally:

"Why did you detain me when you seemed to have nothing to say, just after I had—before we discovered—" Gibbs hesitated.

Her pallor showed that she knew the time to which he referred. But—she made an impatient gesture with her fingers.

"Oh, that! Harold had just come to the house, and my father wanted to have it out with me before him! I knew father wouldn't have me fetched if you were talking to me. . . ."

She was watching Pointer, who glanced at his watch.

"Thank you for coming over here. I fancied that I might get something out of you together since you refused to speak singly."

"How could any one of us speak?" Lily Hillock asked, "behind each other's back? We're all in it together, but we're not in murder, and we're not in blackmail. We're only in a silly joke I started."

Chief Inspector Pointer spoke first.

"You, Mr. Smallwood, can please yourself. Mr. Richardson, you will stay on until you are able to leave, when we will communicate again with you. As for you, Miss Hillock and Mr. Abbott, be good enough to return to England and Much Widham with an officer of my own, who has instructions to give no trouble if none is given him."

With which plain statement Pointer and Gibbs rose. The interview was over. I followed them out of the hospital deep in thought. Was this all? Was what we had just heard the whole story? Did Lily Hillock believe it to be complete? I did not. I felt sure that one of the two men had, for his own purposes, played a lone and terrible hand where she thought all were playing a round game.

What an opportunity Richardson had had. But still the brass box would not fit. Nothing that I could see would explain its importance either to Walsh or to his murderer. Yet Bena Hillock had rated it aright.

"We may know soon," was all the Chief Inspector would say, as we drove swiftly along to the aerodrome where we took off for Geneva in a waiting 'plane, for Mr. Scullion was too ill to be questioned yet. We got there that evening.

Pointer and Gibbs were the guests of the Prefect of Police. I went to a hotel where I always stay, but not even its comfort could bring sleep.

How was it possible for the Scotland Yard officer to have evolved a theory that would fit all these loose odds and ends? I doubted its possibility. I got up, dressed, and went for a long walk in the beautiful moonlight. Twice I passed Bois Riant. The second time I stood a long while watching it with almost unseeing eyes. Was the brass box with the little lion on its lid here? Or did Laura Abbott really have it? Why had it been fatal to poor Verbena, and yet, according to the Scotland Yard man, was no longer to be feared? This mysterious box, which, according to his theory, was of no value, held nothing of value, and stood for nothing, and yet which, when seen had been followed by two murders.

My eyes were resting on the gardens. Suddenly I grew alert. Something like a bat stirred under a tree. I had my glasses out in a trice, my night glasses which I had taken with me, for at no time are the mountains as beautiful as on a moonlit night. Yes, something like a bat was among the shrubbery, reminding me of Bena's hooded figure when I had seen it in the library. It was a man, I could see that much, carrying something in one hand, creeping towards the garden gate. I hurried stealthily forward to cut him off. He all but got past me before I caught him. It was McKirdy. He hit at me with something he held in his hand, an ineffectual blow like a clown's with a bladder, then throwing it aside, he wrenched himself free and started to run. I ran after—I think I must say I ran better—but McKirdy knew the road evidently, and I did not. He doubled and twisted and dodged into this lane and up that, I always on his heels until he sprang through some big gates, flung them shut, and by the time I had them open was lost among the dark trees beyond.

I wasted some time in trying to catch him, but at last decided to return to the villa. Outside the gardens I stooped to pick up whatever it was he had flung away, my torch showed it to be a large empty petrol tin. Even as I picked it up, the first pillar of fire shot up from the roof of the villa, spreading as though a gorgeous firework exhibition had been staged. I heard shouts. The gardens were full of people. Evidently from the other side the fire had been visible for some minutes. Vervier was there directing home salvage operations until the fire brigade should arrive. But I had eyes only for the big north room which was Scullion's. In it a figure, made monstrous by the fire and the smoke, was flitting about in the sharp glare. I saw that he was intent only on saving the pictures. What was Smallwood doing here?—for it could only be he. He must have come on here too and accidentally seen the fire. The room was paneled with Scullion's work. Three on each wall and each wall representing one season—a noble calendar. Watching the figure working desperately behind that swaying, curtain of orange and red and gold and black, I shouted to him to leave the paintings and jump, we would catch him. A fire-engine rushed up.

Ladders were stretched, but not high enough. The madman, for Smallwood was nothing else in that moment, was flinging down something wrapped in a towel, or a torn sheet.

"Plucky chap! That's the right breed. That's the bulldog!" came ecstatically from some English tripper beside me.

"He's trapped!" breathed another voice in horror. "He's cut off, and the ladder's not long enough!"

"Smallwood!" I roared in a voice almost equalling in volume his own, "Smallwood!" The firemen were shouting too. But undisturbed, though working desperately in his race with death, the man flung something else out of the window. Then another, and another packet. They were caught by the men on the ladders and passed on down. Finally a police officer swarmed up. From his face it looked as though Smallwood was to be ordered to jump, or be arrested for loitering. But a great bale of canvases was neatly dropped into his outstretched arms, before something like a huge spider swung out of the window and began to twist in descent. The firemen shouted, again, cheered him, yelled to him to fling his weight this side. Like human ants they clambered on top of each others' shoulders and so at length the man was caught and swallowed up in the helmets.

I tried to get near him.

"Smallwood, you madman," I began, then stopped. It was the chief inspector from Scotland Yard.

"Come along with me and hear the story. It'll be worth listening to." Gibbs took me into a room where the Chief Inspector sat in what looked like a Turkish bath cabinet, only he was sitting in cold water up to his neck.

His face a mask of cooling ointment and flour, he gave a wry smile.

"How did you get on to him at once, sir?" Gibbs fairly panted out.

"It was easy to strike the right vein, because you had worked all the others. If you were right, there was no other. But was there no possibility of your being wrong? I could find no flaw in your building up of the facts. That meant that if a flaw existed it must be underneath them—under what you two had built on, which was the fact that you, Mr. Maltass, and Esther, had seen Walsh alive and well at half-past five leaving his room at the farm. If that hour were altered Scullion's and Smallwood's alibis fell to the ground. That was my first general thought. You had sifted all possible suspects, but what about those that seemed impossible. I found that Smallwood's was cardboard. But I could learn nothing against him. How could you be mistaken, you and Esther? Had you really seen Walsh himself? It could be no question of impersonation, for the face had been seen clearly, though you wear spectacles and Esther is of an age when eyesight is not so keen without their aid. Walsh was an only child. There could not be a twin brother or near kinsman in question. Leaving chance resemblance on one side, it was either Walsh or—" He paused. "You've guessed it, of course." He looked at me inquiringly.

Strange though it may seem, bitterly humiliating though it is to confess it, I did not. So deep were the ruts made in my mind by my own theories, and by my constant digging of them in, that still I did not see it.

"Look here!" Pointer threw open the door of a fitted-in cupboard facing me. I jumped to my feet. So did Gibbs.

We were looking down the corridor of Upfold Farm that ran on past the studio. With the door knob in his hand Walsh faced us, hat on head, cloak around him. His head was a little bent, on his face a curious expression of apprehension or dawning terror. Where his eyes rested on the table beside his door gleamed a brass box, on the lid of which stood a winged St. Mark's lion, one paw drawn up as though to have it shaken.

"A picture!" I almost shouted, advancing towards it, "and by Heavens, what a magnificent one!"

Pointer nodded appreciatively. He, too, was staring at the canvas.

"Best thing Scullion ever did, I fancy. That's why he couldn't bear to destroy it, or its companions, though he knew the danger of keeping them."

"A painting!" I said again, still trying to get my bearings, "a portrait of Walsh! And Scullion's the murderer!"

"Yes," Pointer had resumed his seat, "it occurred to me that you might have been looking at a picture of a man, supposing it to have been painted by a great painter, for the plans you showed me of the studio and your rooms, yours and Mr. Walsh's, showed me that a canvas might well have been stood, or temporarily fastened, into the doorway leading on into the corridor where Walsh's room was. It would, of course, have had to be prepared beforehand to exactly fit the doorway. But suppose the passage behind was painted in just the right light, and suppose that Walsh had been painted, knob in hand, looking down at—" Pointer paused again.

"The brass box," I said. "*Why* that brass box?"

"Simply because it stood there when Scullion had made the sketch, or finished the painting. He did several to fit the right kind of weather. It would not have done to have painted brilliant sunshine and had to put up the canvas on a rainy day, or had it been evening outside yet with morning light on Walsh's face. On the back of the canvases I flung down are a good choice of Walshes in varying lights, but all showing the passage in every detail. Among the details is always a brass box with a little winged brass lion on the lid whose gospel is gone, and who seems to be holding up a paw as a dog does when told to shake hands."

"But Bena had the box!" I could not understand it.

"Just so," Pointer said slowly. "Just so. I think that when Lily Hillock let the gift that Chapman had brought her from Venice be stood anywhere in the house, where it got damaged, Verbena finally took the box for herself, and said nothing about it. That would evidently be after Scullion had painted it in its place on the table. Gibbs's idea that she loved Chapman is true, I think. So when she heard you all talking of seeing Walsh staring down at the little lion, and knew she had the box all the time safe and sound locked away among her things, she guessed the truth. That you had seen a painting. Which was why, of course, Esther found no box on the table when you all went to look. It had not been there for nearly a fortnight, as she said. Apart from the box, however, Verbena must have known, or guessed, the truth, for she must have recognized Scullion's step as he hurried back dressed in Walsh's cloak and hat with a muffler hiding his own big beard. You told me she could tell you all apart by your steps. You see, *you*, Mr. Maltass could be deceived by the familiar get up, but the blind girl's ears must have heard Scullion come in and yet smelled Walsh's painting coat. Since she also recognized the smells of your garments."

"Yet she shielded him!" I muttered, aghast. "I think she loved him, not Chapman."

Pointer shook his head decidedly.

"She hated Walsh, I fancy, for coming between the two beings she cared for so dearly: Chapman and her sister. She wanted Walsh's eliminator to escape."

"She hated Walsh so much, in other words, that you think she wanted the murderer to get off," Gibbs nodded to himself.

"When she heard the brass box talked about so much," Pointer went on, "she realized its importance and decided to put it away in town. But she had nothing there that was her own. And a blind girl has many difficulties in hiding things from seeing eyes. So she handed it, done up in brown paper, to some one whom she could trust. Not, I think, telling her what the packet was, but—I also think—making her promise solemnly not to undo it unless she, Verbena, were ill, or dead, or incapacitated in some way, and unless any one were accused of the murder of Walsh, and had been found guilty. That, at least, is how I explain Miss Abbott's silence."

So Lily had been right!

I recalled Laura's serenity when her brother had been detained. This idea of the chief inspector's might account for it.

"I wonder, then, if there's something in that box— some statement of Bena's since she took the trouble to get that promise. It wouldn't help otherwise," I said hurriedly.

"I wonder, too," Pointer agreed, "though that would be almost too much to hope for. But even without it, valueless in itself, containing nothing, it meant to Scullion the upsetting of all his clever plan if any one learned that, at the time when it was supposed to have been seen standing in the passage outside Walsh's door, the box was in reality hidden away among Verbena Hillock's things. Scullion must have overheard those words of the blind girl to her sister, realized that she knew the truth, and that, given sufficient strain, she would crack, or that Lily might wheedle it out of her, so he killed her, instantly. Her words to her sister were a warning, true, but not in the sense they were taken to mean. 'Let sleeping dogs lie' was what they really meant in an intense form."

"But that look of dread—or terror—on Walsh's face!" I was seeing it again. "Why that?"

"That was a touch of gloating cruelty in Scullion," Pointer said, with a grim look over at us. "He wanted to paint his victim afraid."

"But Scullion had no motive to murder Walsh!" I protested, coming to myself as out of a dream. "He couldn't inherit his fortune!"

"But Miss Smythe could, and did. Scullion, I have learned, is illegitimate; brought up by a working man's wife, and none too kindly. Some ten years ago inquiries were made by a Miss Jones of this woman's husband— she herself was dead—with the object of getting on the track of the child—Scullion—left in her charge. We have worked back, and found that a young woman, calling herself Miss Jones, gave birth to an illegitimate child forty years ago in a nurse's house, and handed him over to the nurse as she had no way of looking after him herself. Now, we also know that Miss Smythe, for six months previous to that birth, was 'traveling abroad' for her health, and that two months after the child was born she entered a convent of Poor Clares as a novice, but could not endure the rigors, or was not permitted to—this is all nebulous—but hers is the writing on Miss Jones' touching letters of inquiry, the letters in which Miss Jones states that now she can provide after all these years for that child, as she could not at the time of its birth. The foster-parent, I think we shall find, got into touch with Scullion, who next spring appears at Bois Riant, and paints the gardens there."

"In other words Scullion was Miss Smythe's son!" I muttered. "Well, well! Was that why he hated her? For having forsaken him?"

"He made her pay for it, I fancy," Pointer said to that. "From what you told me, he had her completely under his thumb, and her bank book shows heavy—comparatively to her income—drawings to 'self' since he appeared on the scene. Let Miss Smythe come into a fortune of six thousand a year, and Scullion could confidently count on the spending of five thousand odd himself as long as she lived."

"Then at least he didn't murder her too!" I said thankfully.

"Murder her!" The chief inspector's white mask gave a faint grin. "Her existence was his only hold on the fortune for whose sake he had committed two murders! He would have killed her without the least compunction, I fancy, had it been to his advantage to do so, but as things were, he treasured her life, and all but lost his own in trying to save it. Without her his existence was—to him—worthless, or a sort of bitter jest. She was well out of it, poor woman. She paid dearly for her one slip, even as it was."

"Think of the blow to him!" put in Gibbs, with an unpleasant chuckle, "two murders, one literally a work of art, and no good result to come to the murderer. Financially, all he had done was to help the rector of Much Widham to a fortune." Gibbs smote his knee in pleasure.

"Which was why doubtless he was keen on having the son suspected and the friend too," Pointer went on. "When he thought he was dying, he made what, as a dying man's confession, would have enormous weigh; that formless, baseless, unprovable accusation. But he knew that he might recover, and so he kept it vague."

"Of course, that so called blackmail plot of those two silly fools, or three silly fools—though, I don't reckon Lily Hillock a fool—was the chance of a lifetime to an intending murderer," mused Gibbs.

"What made you suspect that might be a would-be joke?" I asked Pointer. "I think you did suspect as much."

"I thought it might be something of the kind from the way the thousand pounds was found in Walsh's desk, and from the apple pie beds you spoke of," Pointer said easily. "It seemed an idea to fit the characters of the three as drawn by you both."

"When did Scullion first intend to murder Walsh, do you think?" I asked.

"When he first met him, I suppose. I can see no reason for his choosing Much Widham as their painting center except a plan to get the rectory suspected of the crime as the next but one heir. And I think he encouraged Walsh to make love to Lily Hillock, knowing that her father or lover might prove useful suspects, second strings to his bow, if need be. But, as Gibbs says when he heard about the blackmail letter, Scullion decided that the opportunity of such a false red herring was too good to lose. It was he—whether we ever prove it or not—who sent a message to Chapman which would bring him to Latimer's Oak after the murder had been committed, so as to very likely implicate him."

"I thought at first that the use of the farm's own weights and clothes line by the murderer looked as though he were outside the circle in the house," Gibbs murmured.

"Either that or the murderer considered himself so safe that he didn't need to care. Well, the only really safe man was Scullion. With Smallwood a far off second—" Pointer's head looked like some magic illusion as it rested apparently on the lid of the bath cabinet, and spoke words that lifted veil after veil from our eyes.

"As it turned out," he went on, "that blackmail red herring wasn't at all what he expected it would be. I'm as certain as I can be of anything that he hoped one of them, if not all, would keep the thousand pounds He must have had quite a shock when he found he had come across only fools, not knaves."

"Those poor wretches!" Gibbs said, with a half laugh, "we didn't tell 'em we had found that thousand. They were on tenterhooks to know why nothing was said about it. Had we got it, or had we not? That was partly why none of them dared speak out. If the thousand pounds couldn't be found they were indeed in a nice mess! Well, there's nothing like earning a lesson early in life."

"When was Walsh actually killed?" I asked.

"At five, as nearly as we can make out. Scullion killed him with those weights knotted in a way which he hoped would throw some suspicion on the rectory inmates, rolled his body into the ditch, rushed home in Walsh's cloak and hat – they're among his things here—fastened up his painting, opened the door when you opened yours, Mr. Maltass, and when Esther, too, was outside in the passage just the right distance away—"

"But his slip on the soap. It really was a badly swollen ankle!" I protested.

"It probably was. Strained, I think, while pretending to be Walsh, who is taller than Scullion. I think Scullion wore lifts in his heels and found the walk back to the farm agony. Especially as he did not dare limp. Possibly that was why he was rushing up the path between the hedges at that pace you described."

The telephone bell rang. It was a telephone call from England. Gibbs went to answer it.

"But McKirdy—and the fire," I murmured.

Pointer looked doubtfully at his shoes.

"Difficult nature McKirdy's, I fancy. I think he, too, guessed the truth. Because he knew that Scullion was the last man to praise any man's painting, as he did when it was—as McKirdy knew Walsh's was—mediocre. That praise of Scullion's threw dust in the eyes of the world and alone explained his constant companionship with Walsh, but some of the critics, like Mr. Preston of the *Sunday Events*, never ceased to protest against Walsh being considered an artist. McKirdy, when Walsh was murdered, guessed something of the truth. Just as I think he had guessed the relationship between Scullion and Miss Smythe. He refuses to say anything. I doubt if a charge of arson will be proved. Even if it is, I don't think he will mind prison. McKirdy is a bit of an Eastern."

"Half," I said.

"Larger half," Pointer thought, with a smile. "I've had a word, almost literally just one, with him—he was arrested on Vervier's insistence during the fire—I think the man has got religion as it used to be called. Only in his case it's Eastern religion. It came to him by chance the day Walsh was murdered, he says. The knowledge that he must return to India and enter the faith of his mother's people. He intends to make straight for Benares and a begging bowl when he's let go. But speaking of his suspicions of Scullion, we may be sure he guessed where Scullion intended the money to go when Walsh was murdered. So when Miss Smythe died, and he realized that Scullion would not benefit from his crimes, I think McKirdy felt that that affair was closed."

"By an act of God!" I quoted.

"But I think he also feels that no crimes of Scullion could wipe out the fact that he did give him a helping hand out in India, did teach him all that he, McKirdy, knows of really good painting. Knowing that Scullion was being kept in hospital, when he heard we were coming here, he guess for what reason, and determined to fire the villa and burn down the pictures and the proofs on their backs. He had no opportunity of taking them away, thanks to Vervier and to the fact that Scullion did not trust him. It's a thousand pities Scullion was a criminal. There's no doubt about his genius."

"Of which he's well aware," I could not resist adding.

"That's why I felt more than a hope that I should find the pictures in existence somewhere."

"Why here at Bois Riant?"

"As far as I could learn, he only took his painting things here. Those canvases are large ones—life-size each of them. I doubted if he would have risked sending them off alone. Here in his big studio up on the top of the house, he unscrewed the panels that he had painted some time ago, and fastened these into the backs. I went by the screws that had been most recently touched. The police down below had word to look at the backs of each as I flung them over, and if any represented the picture described to them, to place Scullion under arrest at once."

Gibbs had come into the room again, his face shining. He grew grave again as he caught the last words. "Unfortunate man!" he said simply, looking with real regret at the painting still facing the room.

"Yes, he considered himself one, too, when Miss Smythe died, Well, Gibbs?"

"Mr. Maltass was right, sir. Verbena did leave a message in that brass box. A long detailed statement which she solemnly swears is the truth. It's exactly what you've been saying, sir. She did hear Scullion come in, and knew by the smell of Walsh's tobacco that it was Walsh's coat Scullion was wearing. She also gives the dates during which the box was in her possession. It's not necessary, but it's a nice little bit of corroboration for the jury."

I rose. "Well, Gibbs," I asked, "what did I tell you about murderers being disliked? Nobody cared for Scullion, and he cared for nobody."

"His paintings, when they're not portraits, show that," Pointer said unexpectedly, "they're the compositions of a man who hates humanity. Every human being in them, child or not, is always degraded or deformed."

"His apparent suspicion of me was clever," I said magnanimously, "it looked like the groping in the fog of bewildered innocence."

I left the two discussing questions of extradition, and walked back to my hotel. That the chief inspector, merely from our account of what had happened, had been able to correctly read the—to me—inexplicable mystery of the happenings of Upfold Farm, was rather a jar. It took me some time to get my ideas correctly assorted again. Just before I turned in finally, a cable was handed me. It was from my manager, and ran:

"Play just received impossible. Makes Michael Hare out a perfect fool."

I grabbed the waiter's pencil, and wrote on answer form:

"Not impossible. Agreeable change."

THE END

Other Resurrected Press Books in *The Chief Inspector Pointer Mystery* Series

Murder at Bridge

When an afternoon bridge party attended by some of Hamilton's leading citizens ends with the hostess being murdered in her boudoir, Special Investigator Dundee of the District Attorney's office is called in. But one of the attendees is guilty? There are plenty of suspects: the victim's former lover, her current suitor, the retired judge who is being blackmailed, the victim's maid who had been horribly disfigured accidentally by the murdered woman, or any of the women who's husbands had flirted with the victim. Or was she murdered by an outsider whose motive had nothing to do with the town of Hamilton. Find the answer in... **Murder at Bridge**

One Drop of Blood

When Dr. Koenig, head of Mayfield Sanitarium is murdered, the District Attorney's Special Investigator, "Bonnie" Dundee must go undercover to find the killer. Were any of the inmates of the asylum insane enough to have committed the crime? Or, was it one of the staff, motivated by jealousy? And what was is the secret in the murdered man's past. Find the answer in... **One Drop of Blood**

- The Problem of Cell 13 by Jacques Futrelle
- The Conundrum of the Golf Links by Percy James Brebner
- The Silkworms of Florence by Clifford Ashdown
- The Gateway of the Monster by William Hope Hodgson
- The Affair at the Semiramis Hotel by A. E. W. Mason
- The Affair of the Avalanche Bicycle & Tyre Co., LTD by Arthur Morrison

RESURRECTED PRESS CLASSIC MYSTERY CATALOGUE

Journeys into Mystery
Travel and Mystery in a More Elegant Time

The Edwardian Detectives
Literary Sleuths of the Edwardian Era

Gems of Mystery
Lost Jewels from a More Elegant Age

E. C. Bentley
Trent's Last Case: The Woman in Black

Ernest Bramah
Max Carrados Resurrected:
The Detective Stories of Max Carrados

Agatha Christie
The Secret Adversary
The Mysterious Affair at Styles

Octavus Roy Cohen
Midnight

Freeman Wills Croft
The Ponson Case
The Pit Prop Syndicate

J. S. Fletcher
The Herapath Property
The Rayner-Slade Amalgamation
The Chestermarke Instinct
The Paradise Mystery
Dead Men's Money

The Middle of Things
Ravensdene Court
Scarhaven Keep
The Orange-Yellow Diamond
The Middle Temple Murder
The Tallyrand Maxim
The Borough Treasurer
In the Mayor's Parlour
The Saftey Pin

R. Austin Freeman
*The Mystery of 31 New Inn from the Dr. Thorndyke
Series*
*John Thorndyke's Cases from the Dr. Thorndyke
Series*
The Red Thumb Mark from The Dr. Thorndyke Series
The Eye of Osiris from The Dr. Thorndyke Series
A Silent Witness from the Dr. John Thorndyke Series
The Cat's Eye from the Dr. John Thorndyke Series
*Helen Vardon's Confession: A Dr. John Thorndyke
Story*
As a Thief in the Night: A Dr. John Thorndyke Story
*Mr. Pottermack's Oversight: A Dr. John Thorndyke
Story*
*Dr. Thorndyke Intervenes: A Dr. John Thorndyke
Story*
The Singing Bone: The Adventures of Dr. Thorndyke
The Stoneware Monkey: A Dr. John Thorndyke Story
*The Great Portrait Mystery, and Other Stories: A
Collection of Dr. John Thorndyke and Other Stories*
The Penrose Mystery: A Dr. John Thorndyke Story
The Uttermost Farthing: A Savant's Vendetta

Arthur Griffiths
The Passenger From Calais
The Rome Express

Louis Tracy
The Strange Case of Mortimer Fenley
The Albert Gate Mystery
The Bartlett Mystery
The Postmaster's Daughter
The House of Peril
The Sandling Case: What Would You Have Done?
Charles Edmonds Walk
The Paternoster Ruby

John R. Watson
The Mystery of the Downs
The Hampstead Mystery

Edgar Wallace
The Daffodil Mystery
The Crimson Circle

Carolyn Wells
Vicky Van
The Man Who Fell Through the Earth
In the Onyx Lobby
Raspberry Jam
The Clue
The Room with the Tassels
The Vanishing of Betty Varian
The Mystery Girl
The White Alley
The Curved Blades
Anybody but Anne
The Bride of a Moment
Faulkner's Folly
The Diamond Pin
The Gold Bag
The Mystery of the Sycamore
The Come Backy

Raoul Whitfield
Death in a Bowl

And much more!
Visit ResurrectedPress.com
for our complete catalogue

About Resurrected Press

A division of Intrepid Ink, LLC, Resurrected Press is dedicated to bringing high quality, vintage books back into publication. See our entire catalogue and find out more at www.ResurrectedPress.com.

About Intrepid Ink, LLC

Intrepid Ink, LLC provides full publishing services to authors of fiction and non-fiction books, eBooks and websites. From editing to formatting, from publishing to marketing, Intrepid Ink gets your creative works into the hands of the people who want to read them. Find out more at www.IntrepidInk.com.

Lightning Source UK Ltd.
Milton Keynes UK
UKHW021908070221
378382UK00013B/177

9 781943 403011